Micah the Prophet

Micah the Prophet

HANS WALTER WOLFF

Translated by Ralph D. Gehrke

FORTRESS PRESS   Philadelphia

Library of Congress Cataloging in Publication Data

Wolff, Hans Walter.
  Micah the prophet.

  Translation of Mit Micha reden.
  Includes bibliographical references and index.
    1. Bible. O. T. Micah—Criticism, interpretation,
etc. I. Title.
  BS1615.2.W6413   224'.9306   80-2380
  ISBN 0-8006-0652-3

8266J80   Printed in the United States of America   1-652

Contents

Foreword   vii

Abbreviations   xi

INTRODUCTION: ORIENTATION   1

Micah of Moresheth: The Profile of a Prophet   3

Micah's Cultural and Intellectual Background   17

EXPOSITION   27

The Approaching Blow from the Lord: Micah 1   29

Thou Shalt Not Covet! Micah 2:1–11   45

The Gathering and the Breakout: Micah 2:12–13   59

Against the Prophets Who Lead My People Astray:
  Micah 3   63

Zion's Future: Micah 3:9–5:14   81

Clear Principles: Micah 6   99

Confusion and Forgiveness: Micah 7   115

UPDATINGS   133

"Certainty of Faith" and Public Responsibility:
  Micah 2–3   135

What Will Become of the Church? Micah 3–5   159

"Neither Shall They Learn War Any More": Micah 4:1–5   171

Contents

During the Weeks of Terror: Three Evenings of
Bible Study

Woe to Wishful Dreams (The Roots of Terrorism):
Micah 2   177

What Is Good for a Human Being? (Living with
Terror): Micah 6   187

The Path Out of Isolation (Victory over Terror):
Micah 7   199

NOTES   211

INDEX   219

Foreword

This book documents a full year of traveling with Micah. It was preceded by the least traditional academic arrangement of my career as a teacher of higher learning: a six-hour research seminar, in which twenty students gathered twice each week at an early hour for a three-hour session devoted to common study of the prophet Micah, an inspiring partnership of studies. The seminar was designed to prepare the way for a forthcoming detailed commentary on Micah.

But before that task could be completed a year had first to be spent in field testing all the passages in Micah at the various places where I was asked by different groups to present addresses, Bible studies, or sermons. The Old Testament expert dares to leave his field of specialization and ask what the significance of the prophets' words might be in the same sort of harsh contemporary reality to which they originally belonged. Perhaps we too often dig ourselves down too deeply into the investigations of historical questions instead of seeking out those confrontations with the world in which we live that correspond to their prophetic counterparts. As an interpreter I recognize the necessity of preparing to write a scientific commentary by engaging in practical exposition. Similarly the person now engaged in practical exposition will, it is hoped, be able in the future, with the help of the scientific commentary, to seek and find his or her audience.

The Chr. Kaiser Verlag, which asked me for this collection of presentations, now offers them to the German-reading public under the title, *Mit Micha reden* [Conversing with Micah]. This is an appropriate title since only the first two presentations, in the Introduction, are *about* Micah, the second dealing basically with literary matters.

All the other presentations are intended to facilitate a conversation between the prophetic voices that speak from the Book of Micah and today's hearers.

The first main part, Exposition, offers a serial exposition of all the chapters in the Book of Micah. Here attention is directed to the ancient Scripture, in order that nothing of what it says may be missed by us today.

The second main part, Updatings, gives parallel explanations of the same passages dealt with in the Exposition section. These explanations differ from the serial exposition mainly in that they take current problems as the point of departure and ask what Micah might have to say about them. Thus a dialogue with Micah develops as we listen to him and ask him questions. (Can a Christian, as a matter of principle, live with the biblical books in any other way?)

In this connection I must ask the reader's indulgence in appreciating the fact that certain repetitions were unavoidable, if the varied contexts in which the various presentations were given were not to be destroyed. The same expositions and the same contemporary applications of the passages had to be presented in similar fashion at different places. The resultant doublets invite perceptive homiletical examination, as one sees how the interpretation relates the path-breaking word of the prophet to the questions of each respective audience.

The collection is designed to be a book used by alert contemporaries of all backgrounds as well as by learned theologians. It is hoped that, in the midst of our busy day-to-day life, this book will prompt us to give attention to one of Jesus' precursors. In the midst of today's upheavals it invites us to a quiet conversation with the man from Moresheth. Such a prophet can provide us with direction and goal, pointing out specific resting places and suitable segments for traveling. Thus Micah is able to get us out of our byways and dead ends and help us travel on the highway that has promise.

The reader will experience what the author experienced: we must work at these selections from the prophets until they finally work within us.

Foreword

For much valuable aid in the planning and preparation of this book I herewith thank my colleagues, Dr. Frank Crüsemann and Dr. Jürgen Kegler, students of theology Hans-Jürgen Abromeit and Ulrich Ahrens, and, last but not least, Mrs. Erika Leister as well as the directorship and staff of the Chr. Kaiser-Verlag.

HANS WALTER WOLFF

Abbreviations

AOAT	Alter Orient und Altes Testament
FRLANT	Forschungen zur Religion und Literatur des Alten und Neuen Testaments
KAT	Kommentar zum A.T.
KB	Köhler and Baumgartner, *Lexicon in Veteris Testament libros*
PJB	Palästinajahrbuch des deutschen evangelischen Instituts
WMANT	Wissenschaftliche Monographien zum Alten und Neuen Testament
ZAW	*Zeitschrift für die alttestamentliche Wissenschaft*

INTRODUCTION:
ORIENTATION

Micah of Moresheth:
The Profile of a Prophet[1]

"I besieged and took Samaria, led away as booty 27,290 inhabitants thereof, together with their chariotry. . . . The terror-inspiring glamor of Ashur my lord overwhelmed them. At the very mention of my name their hearts pounded in fright; their arms lost their vigor." Thus Sargon II boasts of his conquest of Samaria in 722 B.C. Twenty years later his successor on the Assyrian throne, Sennacherib, reports, "As for Hezekiah of Judah, I besieged forty-six of his strong fortified cities. I drove out as booty 200,150 persons, young and old, male and female, horses, mules, asses, camels, cattle and flocks beyond counting. Himself I shut up as a prisoner in his royal city Jerusalem like a bird in a cage. . . . The brilliant terror of my lordship overwhelmed Hezekiah." The entire second half of the eighth century B.C. (after the appearance of Tiglath-pileser III) quakes with paroxysms of sheer terror in the face of Assyria's imperial strength, its military might, its practice of enslaving the vanquished, and its policy of calculated cruelty which included such atrocities as ripping up pregnant women to destroy the recalcitrants' unborn next generation. Terror and unprecedented fear grips the entire ancient world.

This is the heyday of Israel's classic prophets, including Micah of Moresheth. The superscription of his book (1:1) dates him to the days of the kings of Judah: Jotham, Ahaz, and Hezekiah. According to this information (and we realize that the chronological data at our disposal are a bit uncertain), Micah appeared on the scene at the very latest in the year 734. He was active until at least 728, but perhaps much longer because his words are filled with the sense of imminent horror. Even if he did not experience the events themselves, he foresaw the inexorable incursions of Assyrian might in the destruction of Samaria in 722 and of Jerusalem in 701 (1:6f.; 3:12). He proclaims as the word of his God:

3

I am making Samaria a heap . . . ;
I am pouring her rubble down into the valley;
Her foundations I am laying bare.

(1:6)

Later he must speak similarly of Jerusalem.

Micah was, however, not living at his nation's political center.
His native town Moresheth lay some twenty miles southwest of
the royal capital in the beautiful hill country of Judah, command-
ing a broad view across the coastal plain to the Mediterranean.
But he was not a backcountry hermit either. Lively contact with
Jerusalem was assured by the fact that the Judean kings main-
tained five fortress cities within a radius of less than six miles
round about Moresheth. They were to protect the Judean homeland from encroachments by the Philistine cities or attacks
launched by the superpowers from the favorable staging area of
the coastal plain. The administrative officials and officers of the
fortress cities must have ensured lively communications between
the capital and Micah's hometown. Beyond that, I see a number
of indications that Micah was an elder in Moresheth, one who
belonged to the collegium of the elders of Judah. As such he
must also have had official connections with Jerusalem. One
thing, however, is indisputable: he appeared as a prophet in
Jerusalem (3:9f., 12). For, according to 3:10 (RSV), he addresses
the leaders as those "who build Zion with blood and Jerusalem
with wrong." He threatens them, "Because of you . . . Jerusalem
shall become a heap of ruins" (3:12 RSV). We know no more
about the external details of Micah's life than these sparse references to the time and place of his activity. What holds true for
all the prophets holds true for Micah: his life has disappeared
behind the word which he was sent to proclaim.

A PROFILE OF HIS PERSONALITY

From those sayings of his which have survived we can draw a
few conclusions about Micah's self-understanding and his relation to his fellow countrymen. The outline of his profile is the
sharpest where he confronts his opponents (3:8),

But as for me, I am filled with authority, justice, and courage
to declare to Jacob his transgression
and to Israel his sin.

4

What a testimony to fearless self-assurance! Nothing in the other prophets comes close to it! One might, of course, suspect that this statement expresses the strained self-glorification of a person obsessed with power (something which would not be very pious!). But we are warned against such a misinterpretation by the commentary-like gloss which states that he possesses these gifts only along with "the Spirit of the Lord," i.e., by virtue of the special divine authority which completely fills him. At the center of his gifts (between the gifts of "authority" and "courage") stands, according to his own statement, justice (that is, his sense of justice). He does not have to say explicitly that here he is referring to the will of God. He underlines "justice" because he really is *not* dominated by the desires and whims of personal ambition, nor by pressures from members of his own party, nor by threats of his opponents. His full authority, his courage and sense of self-assurance in taking a stand despite opposition, is derived from nothing else than the fact that he leaves no room within himself for anything except that sense of justice which completely fills him. This justice empowers him to reveal to Israel the unvarnished fact of its own injustice and lawlessness. Are we able to say, "That is Micah, the way he was each time he appeared on the scene"? Or must we not say more carefully, "That is Micah on one of his better days," or are we to say, "This is what he once said at the climax of his prophetic activity"? We don't know. Perhaps, like Jeremiah, he first had to tread a path through anxieties and disappointments. We also don't know whether, like Elijah, he later longed for death because it seemed to him that the word "futility" was written in capital letters over the enterprise he had undertaken. That is the way Mendelssohn puts things toward the conclusion of his oratorio *Elijah*,[2] even though that prophet's own perception of the futility of his mission is contradicted by the final testimony to his work that is given in the oratorio's final chorus, sung by a mighty choir of later witnesses,

> The prophet Elijah burst forth like a fire;
> his word blazed abroad like a torch;
> he brought proud kings down to their fall.
>   (Cf. Sir. 48:1–6)

As for Micah, we know that he did have his hour of blazing

forth like a torch. Sayings have been transmitted from him which
are still blazing abroad. Israel, yes, God's people throughout the
world, live by the fact that individuals have been enabled and
still are enabled to stake their all for justice with complete self-
assurance.

Micah opposes two groups. First, he opposes other prophets
(3:5), and that means people who are his colleagues. They aim
their word, Micah says, not in accordance with justice but with
their own advantage.

> They cry "Peace" when they have something to eat,
>   but declare a holy war on the person who does not give
>   them what they demand.[3]
>
> (3:5)

Hence they also turn on Micah, trying to prevent him from speaking (2:6). His accusations, they say, dare not be the topics for
prophetic pronouncements. A prophet like Micah cannot remain
unopposed among colleagues who share the same vocation.

Whoever raises his voice as a prophet on behalf of justice will
find, in a world of injustice, public opponents. The second group
against which Micah speaks, therefore, are the responsible officials in Jerusalem, persons whom he addresses (3:1, 9) as "leaders" and "rulers."

"Are you not supposed to be concerned with justice?" he asks
them (3:1). And in 3:9 he accuses them of "abhoring justice."
In this way the stormy champion of justice focuses on nothing
else but the duty which he sees being neglected by that group
of leaders.

Why does Micah attack these spiritual and secular authorities?
Certainly not out of some abstract sort of fanaticism for justice.
Why then? He addresses: (1) the prophets "because they lead
my people astray" (3:5); (2) the political leaders in Jerusalem
"because they eat the flesh of my people" (3:3 [2]); and (3) the
officials at Moresheth because they "drive the women of my people out of the homes they love" (2:9). He addresses them all in
general, "because they rise against my people like an enemy"
(2:8). In all these passages it is clear that what motivates Micah
is concern for his oppressed kinsmen. Love for those who ex-

perience bodily suffering is what drives him to expend himself on behalf of the justice that God has established as help for the helpless. It is a peculiarity of Micah's preachment that he clearly distinguishes "his people" (his needy fellow countrymen) from both the prophets and from those who wield power in the vicinity of Moresheth and in Jerusalem. Hence we see Micah and his wholehearted devotion to justice more clearly profiled at the juncture where two lines cross: the line of the oppressed and the line of the oppressors. That is the arena where prophets take their stand: between those who instigate the reigns of terror and those who are terrified by them. What does Micah's prophetic behavior on behalf of others at this crossroads look like?

If, in seeking the answer, we consult chapter 1, what strikes us first of all is a feature which is very personal. After Micah has announced Samaria's destruction (1:6f.) and before he proclaims terror to the towns in the Judean countryside (1:10–16), he introduces himself thus:

> ⁸Because of this I am going to lament and wail;
>   I am going to walk about barefoot and naked.
>   I am going to howl like a jackal
>   and shriek like an ostrich.
> ⁹Indeed, the blow from the Lord cannot be escaped.
>   Yes, it is coming even to Judah,
>   it is reaching the gate of my people,
>   even Jerusalem itself.

A broken figure bends down low. From the top of his head to the soles of his bare feet he resembles a prisoner of war who, stripped of his clothing, is on his way to captivity. We gradually perceive the outlines of his face. No, we discern only the quivering of his lips as they break out again and again into shrill screeching. This also is a profile of the man from Moresheth.

This prophet is not striking the pose of "the educator of his people." Nor is he wearing the robes of a judge. He certainly is not resorting to the poison or spite of court flatterers. Now is the time for no other activity but lamentation, repeated again and again; and what characterizes Micah's lamentation is his sharing thereby in the suffering that is approaching as the Lord's judgment "smites Jerusalem, the gate of my people" (1:9). Why does he call Jerusalem "the gate of my people"? At a city gate victory or defeat was decided, once a siege had begun. "Can the entrance into the city be defended or will it be captured?" At the capital city's gate the decision is made for the entire country. At the gate decisions are also made about justice and injustice. Hence it is at the gate that we must look for a Micah who is entering the lists on behalf of his oppressed compatriots.

Now the decision is being made for all at the gate, which is really the heart of the people. A blow struck against the gate is a fatal one for the nation. Micah is experiencing that deathblow in his own body. He is also carrying, along with the suffering, the people's guilt and punishment. He stands first in line to take upon himself the misery of a dishonored captive—he is "barefoot and naked." This is the other side of his extraordinarily courageous stand for justice. Genuinely prophetic activity results solely from two ingredients: powerful accusations raised in the name of justice and wholehearted sharing in the suffering of others to the point of accepting the judgment that is striking them. Only when both these ingredients are combined can the outlines of the profile of Jesus Christ be recognized as it casts its shadow, long ahead of its time, on this Old Testament prophet's proclamation of God's royal reign (in the accusations he raises) and his taking upon himself the judgment of God (in this grievous lamenting). Enough has now been said about Micah's person and personality. In fact, as we sketched its features, we were already leaving our description of his personality far behind.

A PROFILE OF HIS MESSAGE

Now we shall consider the content of his sayings. What are the specific injustices which he indicts? And what are the specific threats of judgment that he announces?

A. *The Accusations Micah Makes*

First of all, let us take up his accusations. Injustice shows itself, according to Micah, primarily in three activities: in coveting what belongs to others, in perverting justice, and in hypocritical religiosity.

Selfish coveting is for Micah the source of all sorts of evil. (Similarly, theology from Augustine through Luther to the present has recognized *concupiscentia* as a basic human sin.) Micah takes the word "covet" from the ninth and tenth commandments (Exod. 20:17) and says (2:2),

> They covet fields and seize them,
> and houses, and take them;
> they oppress a man and his family,
> a man and his inheritance.

One thinks immediately of officers and administrative officials from Jerusalem who are assigned to the fortress cities around Moresheth. They seek beautiful fields and houses in the pleasant countryside. Micah describes their psychology (2:1) as they keep themselves awake in bed at night, devising their plans. The next morning they carry out the plans "because it is in their power to do so." As a result of their imaginative planning their basic covetousness quickly matures into brutal acts of violence against property and people: property they "seize"; people they "oppress" (2:2). Both measures are strictly forbidden by God's law, "Thou shalt not oppress thy neighbor or rob him" (Lev. 19:13). The weaker the owners, the easier they are overcome: "The women of my people you are driving from their cherished homes" (2:9a). The fact that children also possess dignity in God's sight is none of their concern (2:9b).

The topic of arbitrary expropriation of another's inheritance by those who wield power and can impose coercive measures is a topic that concerned prophets since the days of Elijah. Unfortunately Mendelssohn did not include in his oratorio the story of Naboth's vineyard (1 Kings 21).[4] It shows clearly how coveting property leads in some mysteriously sinister way to violence against people. The story, in fact, tells how such coveting begins on the bed of one who is never satisfied with what he has. "He threw himself on his bed, turned away his face, and would eat no food" (1 Kings 21:4). This hunger striker is asked, however, by his wife Jezebel, "Are you not king of Israel?" She then contrives the "legal" murder of Naboth.

Features of covetousness are continual plottings for increased profit and for "the good life." When his opponents attempt to escape his accusations, Micah sketches the features of the celebrity preacher whom they really prefer (2:11),

If a man were to go about uttering wind and lies, saying,
"I preach to you of wine and whiskey,"
he would be a proper preacher for this people.

Micah must accuse Jerusalem's leading officials in every field of one crime above all others: the hankering for money (3:11).

This city's leaders give judgment for a bribe;
its priests interpret the law for pay;
its prophets give their revelations for money.

"Pay" in this passage is no longer the proper recompense which each worker earns. Instead of rendering just payment (a recompense corresponding to the achievement) those men practice the very opposite in their public service: they arrange their official activity according to the increments they gain. The income they receive determines the outcome of their activities.

Thus justice is distorted by covetousness. Such distortion is what Micah attacks with special vigor (3:9b), "They abhor justice and distort all equity." Goethe sees through the basic characteristic of such people when he says, "Cleverness abandons gifted men least of all when they are wrong." Small wonder then that those who have been murdered are considered murderers; that what is really murder becomes "a just execution"; and that a murder for which a criminal is definitely guilty becomes a crime of which other persons are guilty. In 3:2 Micah says, "They hate what is good and love what is evil." One of the foremost tasks of a prophet is to expose distortions of justice. A prophet is to unmask the robbers—those who rob but pose as if they were being robbed. A prophet is to expose those who are guilty, so that those who are innocent will be considered innocent. A prophet is to put back on its feet what has been turned upside down. The story of Naboth's vineyard shows how closely covetousness is allied with deceit. Queen Jezebel gets rid of Naboth by means of the false witnesses she sends into the court and thus sees to it that the king gets the property he covets. Her false witnesses say, "Naboth spoke blasphemy against God and the king" (1 Kings 21: 10, 13). God is dragged into what are nothing but monstrous machinations to satisfy greed when the allegation is made that Naboth cursed "God and the king."

Hypocritical religiosity is also pilloried by Micah. It is particularly those who are greedy for money, those who turn justice upside down (3:11b) who, in the midst of such endeavors, appeal to the Lord to justify what they are doing. They say, "Is not the Lord in our midst?" "No evil shall come upon us." They use such pious religious affirmations in order to reject Micah's threats; similarly in 2:7 they asked, "Do you imagine that the Lord has lost his patience?" Here they are quoting the Psalms (a neat exercise in specious religiosity). Micah responds in the name of God, "Yes, God's words do good for those who walk uprightly, but you rise against my people as an enemy" (2:7b–8a). Thereby he states unambiguously that they cannot claim God's goodness for themselves when they take it away from their defenseless fellowmen. In their pseudo-orthodoxy they claim that grace will triumph while at the very same time they are keeping it from having any worth in their own lives. But when they reject the weak members of society, they are really rejecting God. To be sure, Micah's opponents appeal to God's goodness, to God's presence, and to God's blessing—they have the name of God on their lips more frequently than the prophet! In actual fact, however, they are thereby merely serving themselves. Self-serving distortion of justice and hypocritical religiosity are inextricably intertwined. And Micah's accusations expose both of them sharply and vigorously. But covetousness remains the real driving force behind the other two. That is why the mightier, the richer, or the cleverer a person is, the more endangered he is.

B. The Doom Micah Announces

Upon those who have been thus accused Micah pronounces doom most unambiguously. The very first word of chapter 2 strikes the basic note with its *hôy* (woe):

> "Woe to those who lie awake and plan evil upon their beds,
>   so that when morning comes they may perform it!"

Woe! *Hôy!* That is the cry of lamentation which was customarily heard throughout ancient Israel's clans whenever death struck home. According to Micah's adaptation of this woe, the selfish schemers are actually rotting corpses. Whoever pushes people

11

aside in a selfish quest for things is pushing life aside and seeking death. The prophet is not, however, proclaiming a general abstract proposition. His "Woe!" is an announcement, made ahead of time, of the evil-planners' doom. Their doom itself he describes in 2:3 ff.: "Therefore thus says the Lord, 'Behold, I am planning disaster!'" Man's evil planning has already been encircled by God's superior plan. Micah becomes more precise: "You will not remove your necks from disaster; you will no longer be able to walk uprightly (erect)." Micah even puts a dirge into their mouth:

"We are utterly ruined. Our captors divide our fields."

Expropriation and expulsion threaten the expropriators and expellers. They fall into the pit they have dug for others. Elijah says to Ahab, according to 1 Kings 21:19, "In the place where dogs licked the blood of Naboth shall dogs lick your own blood."

The punishment fits the crime. The false prophets are similarly threatened in 3:5ff. Those who twist God's word to fit their own fancies will themselves receive no response from God (v. 7); those who aim at nothing but their hearers' applause will find that God's voice no longer speaks to them (vv. 6–7),

⁶The sun shall go down upon the prophets
and the day shall be black over them;
⁷the seers shall be disgraced,
and the diviners put to shame;
they shall all cover their lips,
for there is no answer from God.

Those who do not want to be directed by God's instructions will themselves soon no longer be able to hear any instruction from God. So neatly will the punishment fit the crime.

The worst threat is reserved for the responsible persons in Jerusalem (3:10) who "build Zion with blood and Jerusalem with wrong." Blood-guilt and injustice are not foundations capable of bearing the weight that must be borne; they are, in fact, fatal traps (3:12),

Therefore because of you
Zion shall be plowed as a field;
Jerusalem shall become a heap of ruins,
and the temple mount will be given over to the
beasts of the forest.⁵

This saying of Micah's made a very deep impression. In fact, even after a century the elders of Judah are still able to cite it at Jeremiah's trial. They warn against executing Jeremiah who had threatened Jerusalem with a similar fate and refer to the precedent set at the time of Micah; then, they say, the king did not kill Micah, but found a way to fear (obey) God (Jer. 26:17–19). Micah's saying must therefore have made a deep impression. "Because of you"—thus he hurls doom into their consciences! Despite the confession of their lips ("God is in our midst!"), the temple mount (Micah no longer says "the Lord's house") will become a field scattered with ruins, a hunting ground for jackals and foxes. In Lam. 5:18 we later hear, "Mt. Zion lies desolate; jackals prowl over it." That is the climax of Micah's threats of doom: those who trample justice under foot in God's city will experience God's doom in the city which they first plundered for themselves.

Two general observations about Micah's threats of doom and judgment are in order. First, Micah addresses the guilty wielders of power directly:

> You will not remove your necks from disaster and
>   escape (2:3)
> It shall be night for you, without vision,
>   and darkness to you, without divination.
>
> (3:6)

"Because of you" Jerusalem will be destroyed (3:12). Likewise in his criticism of social ills Micah does not, as some might expect, convene the oppressed classes of the population in order to rouse them to revolt; we never find that sort of thing in Old Testament prophecy. Instead, the prophet turns to the oppressors themselves to tell them most sharply the whole truth about injustice and its consequences.

Second, Micah's threats tremble with paroxysms of terror and dread of what is coming: deportation for the upper classes, occupation for the country, and destruction for the capital of its country towns and villages. All of this reminds us of the military might of Assyria described at the beginning of this chapter in the words taken from the Assyrian annals themselves. Micah, however, makes no mention of either Assyria or of any of its rulers. Rather, we hear unambiguously, "Evil comes from Yahweh to the gate of Jerusalem" (1:12). Terror comes to Israel from the Lord (who was either forgotten in all the planning and prognosticating or was shunted aside as irrelevant). "Yahweh's blow is inescapable" (1:9); it is the Lord's plan which is being brought to pass by his own word through the prophet Micah. What is involved in all these horrors is God's judgment upon their despising his word, a word that is intended to lead to justice (3:7f.).

HIS LANGUAGE

The prophet's profile would remain imprecise if we did not consider examples of his linguistic artistry and power. The implement Micah employs, the word of the Lord, is sharply honed. That is evident in the way he uses wordplays. They are difficult to translate; but an attempt will be made to illustrate this by means of a few examples in 1:10–16:

> ¹⁰In Dustville (Beth-le-Aphrah) roll yourselves in the dust!
> ¹¹They are blowing the alarm for you on a ram's horn,
>   you inhabitants of Hornvillage.
> ¹⁴Deceittown's (Achzib's) fortifications are a deception for
> Israel's kings.

Beyond that, Micah likes alliterations, as in v. 16 when he summons the community to funeral rites:

> No *h*air on your *h*eads as you *h*owl in mourning for the children
>   you loved.
> Bare yourself *b*ald like the *b*eaked *b*ird (the eagle),
>   for your children are leaving you and going into exile.

In this way the prophet impresses his word upon his hearer's memory. But he is also able, by the coarseness of his rough metaphors, to rip open his hearers' ears, as when in 3:2f. he addresses the heads of Jerusalem as those

> who eat the flesh of my people,
>   who flay the skin from off their flesh
> and break their bones in pieces,
>   who chop them up like meat for the cooking pot,
>   like steaks for the frying pan.

Such language is both drastic and clear, screamed forth as it was with a burning sympathy for his exploited fellow countrymen and aimed at those who "build Zion with blood" (3:10), i.e., it seems, with the blood of those who were beaten by taskmasters until the blood flowed or who perished in industrial accidents. The prophet's choice of metaphors reflects his keen sympathy for those who were being moved by various coercive measures from their home villages toward the capital. Like pieces of steak, they were being cut up for the frying pans of the privileged classes. Micah's drastic language here makes it impossible for anyone to escape his message: humans are being treated like cattle. The high and mighty live by acts of brutality against the commoners. In order to satisfy their taste for pleasure they hate what is good and love what is evil (3:2). Micah not only has something to say; he sees to it that no one can fail to hear what he is saying.

No wonder that Micah's message kindled new fire long after his own times. That is attested not only in Jeremiah 26.[6] Further attestation comes from those chapters in the Book of Micah which follow the bitter threat of doom for Jerusalem (3:12). Chapters 4 and 5 collect the most varied types of later prophetic sayings, all of them concerned with the burning questions that were elicited by the announcement of Jerusalem's destruction (3:12): What will become of Zion? When will the doom strike? How can we survive the judgment? Is that message of doom God's ultimate message, or is it only penultimate? In that connection we hear, to select one of the responses, that Jerusalem's end does not mean the end of God's history with his people; rather, he will cause the ultimate Prince of Peace to arise from the insignificant rural town of Bethlehem (5:1ff.). In another response to 3:12 we hear that in the last days Zion will project its peak above all the mountains and will draw all peoples to itself, so that, as a result of the Lord of Zion's instruction, all peoples will finally disarm themselves and enter perfect peace, each person enjoying rest and prosperity under his own fig tree and vine bower (4:1–4).

In chapters 6 and 7 we find even a further echo of Micah's message. Here voices are again heard which lament the fact that all institutions of ordered community life, external and internal, are breaking down and that life in community (even in the family) is unbearable (6:9ff.; 7:1ff.). But these laments and accusations are encompassed by still another type of question, What shall we do now as we live in God's presence (6:6; cf. also 7:7)? The answer had been learned from Micah by a later disciple who recalls his master's teaching. He says, "He has showed you, O man, what is good; and what the Lord requires of you, namely to do what is commanded, to love a sense of community solidarity, and to walk attentively with the God who is preparing for you the path on which you are to travel" (6:8).

Throughout subsequent ages down into our own times (when Mic. 6:8 was heard at Jimmy Carter's inauguration as President in January, 1977[7]) this passage has assisted in the renewal of public and private life.

The conclusion of the book of Micah bears witness (in almost New Testament terms) to the fact that all people are in the end dependent on the boundless and unconditional mercy of God, who tramples our debts under foot and casts them into the depths of the sea (7:18-20). That divine activity is described with utmost astonishment, "Who is a God like thee, pardoning iniquity?" (7:18). In this awestruck question at the end of the book—coming after all that had previously been spoken about crime and judgment—we are able to puzzle out the name of our prophet (disguised though it is) as the name which in fuller form is also a statement of awestruck adoration: *Mi-ka-el*, "Who is like God!"

Micah's Cultural and Intellectual Background

The interpretation of the Book of Micah is still beset with numerous unsolved problems. Key among them is the question of the cultural context in which Micah learned to observe, think, and speak. This is a difficult problem because the extent of secondary material in the Book of Micah is also still much disputed. But precisely because we must deal with that uncertainty it is important that we gain clarity about the origin of the forms and topics which Micah uses as he speaks. Methodologically, therefore, it is necessary to proceed from a few of his sayings that are critically assured. Using that undisputed material as our point of departure, we can establish criteria for identifying what else in the rest of the material could have come from the same prophet and what is better explained as of different origin.

Contemporary scholarship unanimously assigns to Micah three passages: 1:8–16; 2:1–11 and 3:1–12. Only a few brief fragments within these sections are problematic as possible supplements added during the gradual compilation of what has come to be known as the prophet Micah's book (e.g., 1:13b; particularly 2:3–4. See below pp. 23–25). Moreover, in my opinion, we can with good reason ask whether authentic Micah material is not also present in 1:6f.; also, albeit in a precarious state of preservation, at the lowest stratum of 4:9–5:4[3], and within 6:9–16. The criteria for making decisions about these latter three passages are, however, not uniform. Hence it seems advisable to cite only 1:8–16; 2:1–11; and 3:1–12 when making decisions on the question of Micah's intellectual and cultural home.

Beyond these passages there is only one other which is indispensable for our task: that is the reference in the title of the book (1:1) to the fact that Micah came from Moresheth. This information is corroborated in Jer. 26:17–18 when certain of "the elders of the land" cite "Micah the Moreshethite." Then, in a tradition apparently independent of the literary tradition in Micah 3:12, the prophet's threat against Jerusalem is cited. According to Jeremiah 26 it had been proclaimed "to all the people of Judah"; here in Micah, however, it is directed "to the heads of the house of Jacob and rulers of the house of Israel" (Mic. 3:9). In the book of Jeremiah it was introduced by the messenger formula ("Thus says the Lord"); here in the book of Micah that formula is missing. In the Jeremiah passage reference is missing to a feature that is included in Micah's version, namely, that Zion's demise will occur because of the iniquity of the ruling classes ("therefore because of you" in 3:12). The narrator in Jeremiah 26 seems to reflect the true state of affairs when he has "the elders of the land" still preserving the saying that Micah had spoken a century before, preserving it in their memory until it should at this occasion be brought to the attention of the priests and prophets of the Jerusalem temple as well as of the court officials.

The mention of Micah in Jeremiah 26 makes three facts certain. First of all, a person acquires an epithet like "the Moreshethite" ("the man from Moresheth") only outside his place of birth. In precisely the same manner Amos is called "the man from Tekoa" (Amos 1:1) when he appears in the northern kingdom far from his home. It is probable that Micah was called the Moreshethite in Jerusalem after his appearance on the scene there.[8] Within the group called "the elders of the land," which convened from the various different towns of Judah, he came to be known specifically as "Micah of Moresheth."

Second, Jer. 26:17f. invites the conjecture that Micah's sayings were first transmitted among "the elders of the land." In that case the primary transmitters of Micah's sayings would be circles similar to those comprising the so-called "old school of Amos."[9]

Third, Jer. 26:17f. makes it possible that Micah himself may have originally belonged to the group called "the elders of the land." In that case the appearance of a "man from Moresheth" in Jerusalem was an official appearance, made while he was there on official business. The fact that Micah preached as a prophet in Jerusalem is presupposed by 3:9–12 as well as by Jer. 26:17f. "The elders of the land" spoken of in connection with Micah are identical then with the well-known "elders of Judah" (1 Sam. 30:26); they convene in Jerusalem on the occasion of the great festivals and at the special directive of the king (1 Kings 8:1; 2 Kings 23:1). The possibility that they visit the capital on their own initiative is, however, not to be excluded, particularly not if they came for the performance of a prophetic task; each of them represents his own town and the clan which had settled in it (cf. Ruth 4:1ff.; Deut. 19:12; 21:2f., 6, 19f.).

Working from this basis we arrive at the working hypothesis that the prophet Micah is to be looked upon from the outset as one of the elders of Moresheth. This hypothesis explains many a unique feature of his language and of his appearance on the scene.

1. The titles with which the responsible persons in Jerusalem are referred to, "heads of Jacob and rulers of the house of Israel" (3:1, 9), occur as word pairs ("heads" and "rulers") only in one other instance in the Old Testament. That is as the designation of Jephthah's function in Judg. 11:11, where the words "head" and "ruler" have synonymous meaning, as is indicated in Judg. 11:6, 8. Jephthah had been installed as "ruler" by the elders of Gilead, in point of fact as a military ruler (cf. Josh. 10:24). Micah addresses neither the king nor the royal officials by the title with which they are referred to, for instance, in Jer. 26:10, "the governors of Judah." Also, the area where they worked is not designated as "Judah" or "Jerusalem," in accordance with customary political usage; rather, the areas where they function are referred to as "Jacob" and "Israel," in accordance with ancient Israelite thinking. Micah cannot be referring at this point to anyone else than those officials who were endowed with judicial functions, who were responsible for justice not only in Jerusalem but also in the Judean country towns, especially the fortified ones.[10] These judicial authorities easily came into conflict with the ancient, historic, local administrators of justice at the gates of the clan settlements,[11] especially since the king could install family elders as royal officials.[12] Accordingly, in addressing the Jerusalem admin-

istrators, Micah is addressing those leading groups in Jerusalem which are in competition with the office of an elder from Moresheth.

2. The situation becomes even clearer when one considers the fact that Micah describes his task with precisely the same word ("justice") which is used to describe what the Jerusalem judicial authorities should have been fostering in their official capacities (3:1). They, however, "abhor justice and pervert what is just" ("all equity" 3:9). Both the officials of Jerusalem and the clan elder from Moresheth are, all of them, duty bound to the same system of justice. The elder of Moresheth, however, proves to be Yahweh's prophet by going far beyond the boundaries of his clan "to declare to Jacob his transgression and to Israel his sin" (3:8b) and by being endowed for this task with "special authority" (i.e., with full authority as the Lord's plenipotentiary), with "the sense of justice," and with "courage" (3:8a). According to 2 Chron. 19:6 "speaking justice" was a function entrusted by the king to the judges whom he appointed. And according to 2 Chron. 19:8 "Yahweh's justice" was entrusted to the heads of the families in Jerusalem (together with the Levites and priests; cf. Micah 3:11a). Micah becomes the accuser of those who betray and pervert this justice. In the person of Micah "Yahweh's justice" confronts the distorters of justice; it confronts them in the form of accusations and the pronouncement of judgment. The accusations deal with the mistreatment of workers (3:2f., 10; cf. Jer. 22:13f.) and bribery (3:11; cf. Amos 5:12; Isa. 1:23; 5:23). As for the judgment, Micah announces the fall of Jerusalem (3:12). The prophet Micah transcends the office of a judge in Israel not only in the daring of his accusation but also in the totality of Jerusalem's threatened fall. The fact that Yahweh is himself the judge Micah states with noteworthy infrequency (2:3; 3:5).[13] Almost like a champion who boasts of his prowess (cf. 1 Sam. 17:43ff.), Micah puts himself into the midst of the fray as the representative of justice (3:8).

3. At the same time Micah views himself as the representative of his fellow-countrymen. He speaks of "my people" no less than four times (1:9; 2:9; 3:3, 5).[14] What does he mean by "my people"? It is not entirely easy to explain what is meant in the lament

of 1:9, which speaks of the inescapable blow (inflicted by an advancing hostile army) that "is reaching Judah, yes, even the gate of my people, Jerusalem." Why is Jerusalem here called "the gate of my people"? Does it refer to Jerusalem as the seat of government where the decisions are made for Micah's people, just as decisions in litigations are sought at the gates of small towns?[15] Or does "the gate of my people" refer to the route of access, the entranceway by which the enemy (from the north) may enter the land of Judah (whose cities are named in the verses that follow, Micah's home [Moresheth-gath] being expressly mentioned in v. 14)?[16] Either way, "my people" seems to refer to the country's population, not to the inhabitants of the royal city of Jerusalem. Perhaps the term refers only to Micah's kinfolk in the immediate vicinity of Moresheth.

The matter becomes clearer in 2:9. Here Micah accuses those "who drive the women of my people out of their cherished homes." The context of 2:6–11 is the altercation with those whom the prophet has scolded and threatened in 2:1–5. In 2:2 (RSV) it had been said,

> They covet fields, and seize them;
> and houses, and take them away;
> they oppress a man and his house,
> a man and his inheritance.

In the ensuing discussion in 2:9a he mentions particular hardship cases, e.g., defenseless women (widows) who are driven from their homes. Nothing indicates that the sayings of chapter 2 were proclaimed in Jerusalem. Rather, one must think of them as having been pronounced in Micah's immediate home territory. The place Moresheth (which has been mentioned, alongside Lachish, already in the Amarna correspondence),[17] present-day *ed-ǧudede*,[18] lies in the west Judean hill country about twenty miles southwest of Jerusalem, nine miles east of Gath (*'arak el Menshye*) and a good eighteen miles west of Tekoa, Amos' home. It is 1200 ft. above sea level and situated on the edge of the Shephelah (the Lower Hills). Noteworthy is the fact that no less than five of the fortified cities founded by Rehoboam (2 Chron. 11:7–9) lie within a radius of less than six miles from Moresheth, namely

Azekah to the north, Sochoh to the northeast, Adullam to the east, Mareshah to the south, and Lachish to the southwest. They secure the access to Jerusalem from the coastal road and from the Philistine plain. That means, however, that in the immediate vicinity of Moresheth Jerusalem officials were constantly coming and going (cf. 2 Chron. 19:5). These people are, however, not called "my people" by Micah, but rather "that people over there" (2:11). One can imagine how they were attempting to commandeer by official coercive measures the most beautiful fields and houses in and around Moresheth for their private or "official" purposes.

In Jerusalem the rulers' lashes strike the conscripts directly. In 3:3, therefore, Micah says of those responsible in Jerusalem, "they are eating the flesh of my people." From the country towns construction workers (cf. 3:10) and other conscripts are not infrequently brought to the capital, there to suffer terribly under their taskmasters. "My people" is what Micah calls these kinsmen of his (his people in the strictest sense) in 3:3 as well as in 2:9. These are the people to whom he is devoted in the first place as an elder of the land but now also as a prophet endowed with special authority while they are being exploited by the officials and also by the Jerusalem prophets (cf. 3:5, 11). Thus Micah's official function as an elder of the land can make comprehensible both his appearance in Jerusalem and his referring to his compatriots as "my people" in contrast to the groups of officers and officials in the royal capital and in the fortified towns near Moresheth.

It is striking that Micah never once calls his afflicted fellow countrymen "poor" or "helpless" or "oppressed," as is very frequently done by Amos (2:6f.; 4:1; 5:11f.; 8:4, 6) and not infrequently by Isaiah (3:14f.; 10:2; 14:32), although Micah also sees, as well as do those other prophets, that they are being brutalized and afflicted to the point of blood (2:2, 8f.; 3:2f., 10). From his perspective, Micah sees them more as free men (2:2) in Yahweh's community (2:5) who must suffer at the hands of Jerusalem's officials. His use of language is entirely comprehensible as the language of one of the elders of the land who is very closely attached to his fellow citizens.

4. The bluntness and coarseness of Micah's figurative language has often been noted. Especially drastic is his reference in 3:2f. to the Jerusalem officials who tear his people's skin and flesh from their bones, breaking their bones and chopping their flesh to pieces for the cooking pots and frying pans. Such drastic word pictures are traces of a life lived in close proximity to peasants. To be sure, he is "a man from the country";[19] but the deduction that he himself is to be classified as "a poor peasant" or "a rural laborer,"[20] is no more warranted than the other deduction that he was a cult prophet.[21]

5. Micah's cultural home comes into sharper focus when we see how he adopts for his message typical forms of the ritual mourning that was practiced within the clans and rural communities on the occasion of a death.

The cry of woe in 2:1 ought to be considered first. It is followed by characterizations of those against whom the woe is raised. Scholarship still vacillates between two form critical attempts to trace the origin of such a cry of woe. Was Amos (5:18; 6:1) the first person to take up the dirge for the dead (1 Kings 13:30; Jer. 22:18; 34:5) and apply it metaphorically to the officials as being as good as dead?[22] If so, Isaiah (especially Isa. 5:8ff.) and Micah would perhaps be dependent on Amos by way of his Judean disciples. Or do the prophets' cries of woe relate to sapiental forms which, in sharp antithesis to the cries of "blessed," teach the difference between the way to life and the way to death to the clans in rural communities—especially as such forms were used by the elders at the gate?[23] If this is the case, its application to persons still living would be readily understandable, as well as Isaiah's special closeness to sapiental traditions and the simultaneous appearance of cries of woe in the prophecy of Amos, Isaiah, and Micah. However, what are missing are precedents attested in the wisdom tradition's collections of proverbs.[24] In any case, the cry of woe originally belongs to the ritual mourning that occurred in rural communities.[25]

A similar setting is even more clearly indicated for the dirge or mourning lament which the prophet intones. In 1:8 he uses it as his own lament; and in 2:4 he invents such a lament for his opponents' use at their time of future disaster. In 1:8 he begins such a "lament on the occasion of destruction,"[26] in this instance the destruction of the villages in the land of Judah:

> I will lament and wail;
> I will walk around barefoot and naked.
> I will make lamentation like the jackals
> and mourning like the ostriches.

Neither this introduction nor what follows is reminiscent of a cultic lament. No invocation of Yahweh follows, as would be obligatory in any lament on the occasion of destruction that was performed in a sanctuary. Hence the voice of a priest is not feasible for this cry of woe (cf., e.g., Joel 2:17); rather, what is proper for it are the voices of those in the rural community who are experts in lamentation.[27] The proper locale for such a mourning lament is the street or the square of a town, not its sanctuary.[28] Likewise, the mourning lament cited in 2:4 (*nᵉhî*, which can also be called a *māšāl*) is a profane poetic song about destruction which perhaps originally consisted of two double cola, in a 2 + 2 meter.[29]

> We are utterly ruined,
> our fields are divided.

Both form and content fit the profaneness of the rural community in which Micah is at home. Note that in Jer. 9:17 those who are experts in lamentation are also considered "the wise." In the lore of such wise persons the lamenting prophet Micah also shares.

6. Much else in Micah's sayings may well remind us of the wisdom lore of the elders in rural communities. I mention only the disputation style that occurs in 2:6ff. (cf. Amos 3:3–8) and the antithetical explication of injustice in 3:2a ("hate what is good and love what is evil"), which reminds us of the antithetical explication of injustice in Amos 5:14f.[30]

It has been rightly pointed out that such individual observations are not yet conclusive proof of an element in "ancient Israelite clan wisdom."[31] Nevertheless I have sought to point, with specific reference to Micah, to a type of wisdom that was cultivated by the elders at the gates of country towns and which is to be found in a related form in Amos and his earliest disciples.[32] To judge from what has been preserved of his material,

Micah stands less close to the cultic world of sanctuary worship than Amos who can on occasion adopt the speech forms of priests in order to parody them.

The discussion of Micah's cultural home may be enriched (in keeping with the observations just made about his language, his perspective on the world, and his manner of thinking) if we seek his intellectual and cultural home in the sphere of the elders of Judah. He is familiar with what an elder in a Judean country town has to do both in making decisions at the gate and in instructing the youth. Above all else, he knows what "justice" is; he also knows the forms of the local ritual mourning lament. In addition to being associated with Amos and Isaiah by means of the form of woe lament and occasional-disputation style, he is associated with them by means of three themes which are also well-known in the wisdom tradition expressed by Israel's proverbs: the suppression of free citizens,[33] the corruption of adjudication,[34] and undisciplined drinking.[35] His prophetic authority enables him to pillory injustice with special force, to announce its unsalutary consequences with utmost sharpness, and to extend his accusations and his threats beyond the boundaries of his immediate home to the capital Jerusalem.

For evaluating those passages in the book of Micah of which the authenticity is disputed, the following question can serve, then, as a useful criterion: Can the material be explained as having come from the sphere of speech of an elder in a Judean country town in the last third of the eighth century B.C.?[36]

EXPOSITION

Exposition

The Approaching Blow from the Lord:[37]
Micah 1

[1]The word of the Lord that came to Micah of Moresheth in the days of Jotham, Ahaz, Hezekiah, kings of Judah, which he saw concerning Samaria and Jerusalem.
[2]Listen, you peoples, all of you,
    hearken, O earth and all who dwell on it!
For the Lord God desires to be a witness in your midst
    the Lord is speaking from his holy temple.

[3]For:
Behold, the Lord is leaving his dwelling place,
    coming down, to walk on the top of the mountains.
[4]Hence the mountains melt under him,
    the valleys are torn open
like wax before fire
    like torrents pouring down a steep hillside.

[5]All this is because of the rebelliousness of Jacob,
    on account of the injustice of the house of Israel.
What is the rebelliousness of Jacob?
    Is it not Samaria?
What is the injustice of Judah?
    Is it not Jerusalem?

[6]Therefore I am making Samaria (a heap) a place for planting grapevines.
    I am pouring her rubble down into the valley;
        her foundations I am laying bare.
[7]All her carved images will be shattered
(everything given to her as harlot's fees will be destroyed by fire),
    and all her idols I am going to lay waste
for she acquired these things as payment for her harlotry
    and they must once more become payment for harlotry.

⁸Because of this I am going to mourn and lament
    I must walk around barefoot and naked.
 I make lamentation like the jackals
    and shriek like an ostrich.

 ⁹Indeed, the blow from the Lord cannot be healed;
    yes, it is coming even upon Judah,
 it is reaching the gate of my people, even Jerusalem.

¹⁰Don't "boast" in Gath! Weep; yes, weep!
    In Dustville roll yourselves in the dust!
¹¹You inhabitants of Horntown, they are blowing an alarm for you
on the ram's horn.
    Rootberg will be uprooted.
    Lament for Standton, your standing place shall be taken from
you!
¹²How can the inhabitants of Evilland hope for good?
    Indeed misfortune is coming down from the Lord upon the
    very gates of the City of Fortune (Jerusalem)
¹³Harness the steeds to the chariot, ye inhabitants of Chariotsburg
(Lachish)!
    (That is the chief and first sin of Zion's daughter,
    for in you are found Israel's rebelliousnesses.)
¹⁴Give parting gifts to Gath's Possession (Moresheth-Gath)!
    Deceitville's fortifications are a deception for Israel's kings.
¹⁵I am again bringing an army of occupation upon you, you inhabitants of Occupationtown (Mareshah).
    The glory of Israel is coming to hide in the Refugees' Hiding
    Place (Adullam).
¹⁶No hair on your head as you howl in mourning for the children
you loved!
    Bare yourself bald like the beaked bird (the eagle),
      in mourning for your children who are leaving you and going
      into exile.

This part of the Bible is extremely foreign to us. Yet those who
have been commissioned to lead the Christian community should,
in the course of time, learn to know the entire Bible, not merely
certain well-known selections from it. Perhaps one of the reasons
why we are unable to relate much that is strange and dark in
our modern world to the task of the church is because we have
removed from sight what is shocking in our Bible. Let us therefore give our attention to what is strange and unfamiliar.

This chapter from the prophets is part of the Old Testament. We can, of course, describe the difference between Old and New Testaments as that between Law and Gospel or between promise and fulfillment; in such cases, however, we are always dealing with only a portion of the available passages. We should therefore consider the difference as being also the difference between a path and its goal: the Old Testament describes, mostly, the path (one which is, however, not without its own road signs that point toward the goal) while the New Testament clarifies the goal of God's pilgrim people (without, however, overlooking the problems en route). In general it may well be true to say that the Old Testament orients itself primarily from what is penultimate, whereas the New Testament points in Jesus to what is ultimate. This being so, we have in this chapter from Micah instruction for travelers concerning the path on which they are traveling. Let us therefore make some test probes to find out more about that path.

VERSE 1

Verse 1 presents us with the axioms according to which such a chapter is to be read. It is to be read as the word of the Lord, through Micah and during the time of three kings of Judah in the second half of the eighth century B.C., concerning Samaria and Jerusalem. According to these axioms we need to come to terms with two major points. First, we should take note of the enormous chronological and spatial gap between the audiences which heard this chapter then and those which hear this chapter now. Chronologically 2,700 years lie between Micah and us. Spatially and culturally even Samaria was not the same sort of place that Jerusalem was, just as Berlin and Bonn (the respective capitals of East and West Germany) are as different from one another as Boston is from Richmond, Virginia.[38] We should therefore guard against ahistorical, timeless expositions which refer individual specific statements here in Micah directly to present-day circumstances. Moreover, in the case of Micah's work, we must also think of the particular circumstances that obtained at that time.

The other major point (made by our introductory verse's first two items) is that Micah's word has been transmitted to us as

God's word. If it had not been heard and experienced as such, it would not have been transmitted at all. But it was preserved beyond the downfalls of Samaria and of Jerusalem, in order that it might be heard anew as God's warning word in similar situations, in new times and under other circumstances. It was preserved to be heard ever anew as the word of God; and as his word it still strikes home in actual history, changing and transforming that history. Hence we ought also make test probes to see if, despite the differences in the times, something similar is not applicable to us. For Jesus Christ has appeared in the interval between Micah and us and has told us, "If they do not hear Moses and the prophets, neither will they be convinced if some one should rise from the dead" (Luke 16:31 RSV). Let us therefore listen to the prophets!

VERSE 2

Verse 2 surprises us, since v. 1 had led us to expect something quite different.

> Hear, all you peoples, hearken, O earth . . .
> The Lord is going to be a witness in your midst.

Did we not just hear in v. 1 that Micah's sayings are directed at Samaria and Jerusalem? But now we do not get to hear sayings which are directed at them, but rather only what Micah says *about* Samaria (vv. 6f.) and *about* Jerusalem (vv. 9, 12). The same is true of chapters 2 and 3. Only in chapters 4 and 5 do we come across several individual passages that deal directly with all peoples (e.g., 4:1–4 tells about the procession all peoples make to Zion in order to effect peace there). Such passages were composed primarily by later prophets with whom Micah's ancient word struck fire again in subsequent ages. Such a voice comes to the fore also here in v. 2. According to it the peoples should prick up their ears to hear the message that Micah once addressed, in the first instance, solely to Israel. Thus we may imagine that this summons is directed at the Assyrians who had conquered Samaria in 722, and at the Babylonians who in 598 and 587 turned Jerusalem to rubble and ashes, deporting its inhabitants (as well as at the neighboring nations in general). They should all of them hear that Israel's catastrophic fall occurred solely at God's initiative. The prophetic word that had been proclaimed long before serves as evidence. With it in hand God appears at Israel's trial as a witness, to bear testimony to the international world of peoples (cf. Isa. 43:8–13). We can surmise that this new application of Micah's ancient message was kindled at the time of the Babylonian exile. From what was happening to Israel in the exile, the Gentiles (informed now by a stellar witness, the Lord himself, concerning his earlier prophetic word to Israel) should learn to recognize him who is also their Lord, their accuser, and their judge. The literary composite now comprising chapters 4 and 5 (the end result of the same long process of updating Micah's ancient message for later times as is 1:2) serves the same kerygmatic purpose as 1:2; after all, it also closes in 5:15 [14] with the warning, "In anger and wrath I will execute vengeance upon the peoples that did not hearken." This passage, so central for an understanding of the world of international affairs, takes up again the introductory admonition with which we are dealing in 1:2, addressed as it is to all peoples, telling them to hearken to God's word in Israel; 5:15 [14] expressly warns them against failing to hearken!

"Hear, all ye peoples"—at this point, then, we modern people too are expressly summoned, by the ancient text itself, to pay attention to the word of Micah and to the God who bears witness to himself in the prophet's word for future generations from all over the world (and who is thus presented to us as the witness, accuser, and judge of our deeds). In this way Micah 1:2 and 5:15 [14] become a hermeneutical key for unlocking Micah's words concerning Samaria and Judah so that we see them as a message for the Gentiles concerning God's will.

VERSES 3–4

In these verses we still have not yet arrived at Micah's prophetic proclamation concerning Samaria and Jerusalem. This section is like a song of praise placed as a prelude at the beginning of all that follows. It offers the basic presupposition for understanding Micah. A number of parallels in the older and younger songs and prayers of Israel have similar wordings (cf. Judg. 5:4f.; Ps.

68:8f.; Isa. 64:1f.). I can imagine that the later community sang it in worship after they had heard the sayings of Micah which had been transmitted to them in writing. Like all similar passages it connects two themes: God's advent and its consequences. Centuries before Micah, Deborah sang similarly, in praise of the God who had rescued her people (Judg. 5:4)

> Lord, when thou didst go forth from Seir
> > when thou didst march from the region of Edom,
> the earth trembled; rain fell from the sky.
> Yes, water poured down from the clouds.
> The mountains quaked before the Lord,
> > before him from Sinai, before Yahweh, the God of Israel.

In Isa. 64:1-3, centuries after Micah, the congregation cries out in its trouble,

> [1]Oh that thou wouldst rend the heavens and come down,
> > that the mountains might quake at thy presence— . . .
> [3]when thou doest terrible things, for which we looked not.

In all these instances a twofold event that was expected to occur every so often is confessed to be occurring: God is leaving his place of concealment and, because of that, the world is being transformed. He comes from Sinai (Judges 5), from Zion (Amos 1:2), or from heaven (Isa. 64:1), in any case from beyond the human scene; and he is intervening in the affairs of men. He, the one who was never taken into account in all the prognoses because he is the uncalculable factor, he alone determines the outcome. He makes use of what is intractable and changes what appears to be unchangeable. Granite mountains melt like wax. Men experience volcanic eruptions with their lava flows. During earthquakes valleys, once peaceful, secure and inhabited, suddenly break open with deep clefts that become increasingly more dangerous and treacherous as they are transformed into streams, which, like gigantic waterfalls, hurtle down steep cliffs toward the lowlands. That is what Israel (and also the peoples) must know in advance: the God of the prophets, the God who speaks and acts in Israel is none other than the one who, completely free, has at his beck and call all the power of the universe, particularly when earth and heaven are shaken by catastrophe. This insight is the basic presupposition for understanding all that follows. And Israel joined in confessing this when at a late date it responded to Micah's earlier harsh words by accepting them as God's words as it sang the hymn of praise in 1:3–4.

VERSE 5

Verse 5 picks up from vv. 3–4 and carries the point further. "All this," the people had said, pointing to the sad results of the catastrophe. "Why?" they had asked. And now the answer is given: "All this is because of Jacob's rebelliousness, on account of the injustice of the house of Israel." It is not sufficient merely to make a connection between God and the catastrophes; one must also connect the catastrophes and guilt. In this verse Micah's general theme is announced by an editor who, like a liturgist during a service of worship, is making a transition from the preceding hymn (vv. 3–4) to the subsequent public reading of Scripture (Micah's sayings in vv. 6ff.). In its wording v. 5a takes up what Micah himself designates in 3:8b as his commission, namely, the task of "declaring to Jacob his rebelliousness and to Israel his sin." Whoever wishes to comprehend God and world upheavals must ask the question, "Who is guilty?" Verse 5b continues to bore in, as with an auger, with that piercing question, and it hits upon the answer. The capital cities of the two Israelite states are guilty: Samaria, where the northern kingdom's political power had been marshaled to meet the prophets' opposition; and Jerusalem, Judah's capital, where its spiritual center is to be sought at the sanctuary on Zion. It is in the presence of the nations of the world, then, that Israel is here being drawn into a conversation; similarly it is in the presence of a broad spectrum of Israel's inhabitants that its responsible persons, especially those who are spiritually responsible, are being arraigned. In this way the disquieting connection between punishment and guilt is exposed. It becomes apparent that the ground on which people are supposed to be able to live their lives is being rent by deep crevasses, is melting away in streams of glowing lava. The world in which we live is being transformed into one vast charnel house, threatened by the heat of glowing lava and by torrential floods. What is happening is incomprehensible without God and God's activity, without the realization that the people who are really guilty are those to whom he had entrusted his word. Danger, God, and guilt—these three must be considered together. At any rate the prophet and those who elaborate on his word refuse to understand the inbreaking catastrophe purely as the effect of an anonymous mechanism.

VERSES 6–7

Verse 6 takes up the details of Samaria's guilt. Here at least, if not before, after the general introductory verses of the chapter, we are hearing Micah himself. He speaks as the Lord's spokesman. Hence now, for the first time, an "I" enters the scene; it is the "I" of God himself. The prophet, as God's messenger, expresses what God has to say.

> I am making Samaria a heap;
> I am pouring her stones down into the valley;
> her foundations I am laying bare.

Ordinarily such a message is introduced with "Thus saith the Lord" (as, e.g., in 2:3); that introductory formula may in this case have been sacrificed, during the process of transmitting the prophet's sayings, to the transitional verse 5 which serves to preface the latter-day reading of Micah's word at worship. In any case we now hear how the prophet threatens Samaria in the name of his God: first, he announces its destruction (vv. 6–7a); then he adds a reason, which is introduced with the word "for" (v. 7b). The threat of judgment says that God will make a ruin out of the northern kingdom's capital city. It had been the royal residence for 150 years. Omri had chosen the beautiful, rather steeply rising summit of a mountain as the seat for his government. There Omri and Ahab had built the palace complex during the first half of the ninth century, while the new buildings of a city had been grouping themselves around it. In the year 725 Shalmaneser V moved up to begin a siege which his successor Sargon II brought to a victorious conclusion in 722 with the resultant subjugation and deportation of the populace. (Sargon reports, "27,290 persons, together with their chariotry, and the gods in which they trusted I led away as booty.") If Micah threatens beforehand, "I am making Samaria a place for planting grape vines," then that means: all the glory of the royal capital with its palaces is to revert to what it once had been. On the slopes of the city now made uninhabitable the stones will be poured out toward the valley; and between the remaining foundation walls vineyards will be laid out, as in the days before Omri. In this way Micah testifies that what holds true of the cosmic catastrophes also holds true of the historical one, the appearance of the Assyrians: it is the Lord himself who is intervening at this point. Solely in this context is the reason for the catastrophe comprehensible: the reason for the downfall is Israel's unfaithfulness to its God.

> For this town was accumulated from what was paid for harlotry;
> and so it must once more become payment for harlotry.
>
> (1:7b)

Like Hosea, Micah means that Israel has faithlessly abandoned its God and prostituted itself like a harlot to all sorts of alien gods and men; so the city was built up from harlot hire, all the way up to the construction of its temple for the god Baal. The worship of Canaanite fertility deities in Samaria is attested by Hosea, by 1 Kings 16:32f., and by archaeological excavations. Life lived in unfaithfulness, in inordinate covetousness, and in avarice is life lived in betrayal of the God who liberated Israel and endowed it with a goodly heritage and set it at peace.

It is necessary to ask what sort of conclusion Micah's message, as far as we have heard it, ought to incite in our so very different circumstances. I read in the report of your superintendent[39] that the problem of whether our cities are livable is currently a genuine concern in Wuppertal and has provoked consultations of the state with the church. Something else causes us even greater concern. We had thought that, under the new political constellations of Europe and of the world, the danger of a third world war had for the time being been successfully avoided; but now, instead of war, we are hit from behind by an ever growing wave of terrorism which awaits us when least expected, in a Lufthansa aircraft or at the windows of our local bank. To cite a recent example, we read the following warning, "After the murder of our comrades in arms at Stammheim we intend to attack the fascist-capitalistic government of Helmut Schmidt where it will hurt the most. For every one of our murdered comrades we will blow up one Lufthansa aircraft in flight. There is no possibility of preventing this. Hence everyone should know that, if he boards a German aircraft after Nov. 15, he is flying with Death." Our granite mountains are melting like wax. Gigantic networks for capturing the guilty persons have had little success. The Christian community has as little chance as ancient Samaria did to steal away from the inseparable connection between catastrophe, the living God, and our guilt. What has become, at the end of the second Christian millennium, of our Lord's commission, "As my Father sent me, so I send you" (John 20:21)? To what extent have not unfaithfulness, inordinate covetousness, and avarice replaced in us thankful joy in our liberation through Christ, patience in awaiting his day, and willingness to devote ourselves to missionary service? To be sure, on Sundays tens of thousands of sermons are preached and during the week all over the world hundreds of thousands of Christian addresses are given at funerals, weddings, and congregational gatherings. But has it not been man who has enthroned himself everywhere as the supreme being and at the same time sold himself to illusions? Are we not insanely self-satisfied? Have our capital cities deserved comfortable survival? Is it still necessary to ask?

VERSES 8–16

But now at v. 8 the prophet himself comes before us. He no longer plies us with questions. He is wailing like a jackal and whimpering like an ostrich, so that on hearing it we are gripped by sudden shuddering. Why? "Because of this," he says at the very outset, and he can only be referring to the fate of Samaria mentioned in v. 6f. But why does this concern Micah, living as he does in the hill country of southwestern Judah? Is it because he is still living with a sense of Israel's unity despite its division into the two states of northern Israel and Judah? If one member suffers, do not all suffer together (1 Cor. 12:26)? Does not what happens in the East Zone of Germany in Leipzig concern us also in the West? In v. 9 that becomes more clear:

> The Lord's blow cannot be prevented;
>> Yes, it is coming even to Judah;
> it is reaching the gate of my people, even Jerusalem.

Accordingly Micah sees in what is happening to Samaria the beginning of a sinister movement that is pressing inexorably onward toward the south. As Samaria is unable to stem the attack from the north, so Jerusalem will eventually also be unable to oppose it. "It is reaching the gate of my people." Once its gate complex is conquered, the entire city falls. At the gate matters of jurisprudence are discussed and clarified in days of peace. When the gate has been hit, the heart of the city and of the state has been hit. Samaria is then only a beginning. It provides the prophet with the possibility of recognizing the hand which relentlessly continues to smite, reaching down even into Micah's home territory. The Lord's blow is hitting home!

Does not a comparison with the situation of the German Democratic Republic force itself upon our attention? There the blow has smitten more deeply than official voices wish to admit. Education for atheism is celebrating its triumphs; Christian confirmation is inexorably yielding ground to the dedication of the youth to the state; church services are shriveling more and more. Pastors are becoming dispirited; lay people do not dare come forth to be church elders. "Because of this I am going to mourn . . . the Lord's blow is reaching even to the gate of my people." We must at least ask ourselves whether the developments in our midst are not going in a similar direction and whether or not it will work itself out even more disastrously, the more definitely the external props of a subsidized church are removed. Did not, in these very days when we are meeting here, the synod of the Evangelical Church in Germany lament the fact that our chancellor in his last official message on the state of the nation no longer spoke of the church as the partner of the state?

It is not our task to make predictions. The word of the prophets, however, has been given to us, so that we may examine ourselves. In the superintendent's report I read the important sentence, "The community of Jesus Christ cannot and dare not cease to reflect on how it must structure itself to meet its task . . . i.e., its living relation with its Lord and simultaneously its active solidarity with the world." The prophetic word should also serve us in reckoning with the possibility that all the unfortunate changes are nothing less than "a blow from the Lord." The coming misfortune is extraordinarily important to the prophet, so that he mentions, along with his hometown of Moresheth, no less than twelve places in its immediate or proximate neighborhood. Sennacherib reports of his third campaign in 701, "Hezekiah of Judah who did not submit to my yoke—I laid siege to forty-six of his fortified towns, as well as countless smaller villages in their vicinity. I conquered them by means of well-stamped earth ramps, and the use of battering rams brought near to the walls, combined with the attack by foot soldiers, using mines and breeches as well as sapper work. I drove out of them 200,150 people, young and old, male and female, horses, mules, donkeys, camels, big and small cattle beyond counting, and considered them booty. Himself I made a prisoner in Jerusalem, his royal residence, like a bird in a cage."

Interpreters are divided on the question of whether Micah, when he spoke of the fate of these towns, had already seen these events of 701 with his own eyes or whether he merely saw them approaching. The latter seems to me more probable, for three reasons. First, the literary genre here is that of a great woe lament. Amos also utilized this genre for pronouncing doom (Amos 5:1ff.). Second, its connection with Samaria's fall (722) puts this passage more likely into the proximity of 722 than into the time after 701. Third, the statements seem less oriented toward events observed individually one after another than toward the names of places, half of which we can no longer identify. Micah is, it seems, interested above all else in warning the places of his immediate neighborhood to be prepared for the Lord's approaching blow.

The artistry and structure of these sayings merits respectful attention. Micah is a master at plays on words. They help to make his message unforgettable. In some cases he takes up a portion of a place name directly as in v. 10b, $b^e b\bar{e}t$ $l^e ap^e r\bar{a}h$ '$\bar{a}p\bar{a}r$ $hitpallo\check{s}\hat{u}$, "In Dustville roll yourselves in the dust." It is as if we were to say,[40] "Portland will lose its port" or "'No Parking' will be the sign plastered on Parkland." In other cases Micah works out a thought that is antithetical to the meaning of the town's name, as in v. 12a, "How can the inhabitants of Evilton ($M\bar{a}r\hat{o}th$) hope for good ($t\hat{o}b$)?" (That is something like "The place called Victoria wil henceforth be called the Place of Defeat.") Most of the time, however, Micah works with rhymes and alliteration. The alliteration in v. 16b can be imitated somewhat as follows, "Bald yourself bare as the beaked bird (the eagle) (in mourning for your children who are going away from you into exile)," or that in v. 13a as "Harness the horses to the chariot (*lārekeš*), ye inhabitants of Chariotsburg (*Lakîs*)." In English we frequently use the stylistic device of the end rhyme; the effect of Micah's use of it must have been similar to our saying things like "Tacoma will give off a terrible aroma," or "The City of Brotherly Love will become The City of The Hateful Shove," or "Fort Worth will be called Power Dearth."[41]

I am not interested in inspiring you to construct linguistically more brilliant or substantively more accurate proverbs. Rather, my point is this: prophetic language is well-honed. It is clear, unambiguous, and penetrating. As such, it is therefore language that can be remembered, not readily forgotten; a person has to have heard it only once. In our current crises, be they in church, congregation, or school, the language we use to proclaim our message dare not piddle around with generalities, four-fifths of which go in one ear and out the other without any effect. Micah is concerned with every syllable that he employs.

At the same time these word plays have no intrinsic significance. Let us be wary of imagining that they do! In fact, we shouldn't expect to find a great deal of theology in them; on the contrary, only surprisingly many dark details. Micah, however, is not using words without speaking of realities, and the one thing he is speaking about is shockingly brief and clear. The blow from the Lord is striking home, hitting its mark; it is going to strike all, every single town individually (v. 9). Everywhere lamentation for the dead and for the disaster is the order of the day (vv. 10–13). Resistance is useless; it deceives only for the moment (v. 14). The troops of the army of occupation are coming. The people, along with the youth in their prime, must go into distant exile. As David had to hide himself in the cave of Adullam, so Israel's "glory" ("His Majesty"? The ark of God? The crown treasure?) must be hidden in The Refugees' Hiding Place (v. 15). Only once in this passage, at v. 12, is Yahweh ("the Lord") spoken of, and then again, as before at v. 9, in connection with Jerusalem. "Yes, misfortune is coming down from the Lord upon the very gates of the City of Fortune (Jerusalem)." The sentence brings another antithetical wordplay, if one hears in the name "Jeru*salem*" the folk etymology "the foundation of *peace/ fortune*" because the foundation of fortune ends in misfortune. And this misfortune comes from no other quarter than the Lord of Zion.

That statement illuminates the entire landscape of places that are going to be smitten. Indeed, the fact that the misfortune comes from the Lord changes the unfortunate situation at one fell swoop. The stingily worded reference suffices. The "No!" which God calls out over his people is still much better than if he were to remain silent. According to this the situation is entirely different than it would be if the catastrophe could be traced back ultimately to Assyria, to Babylon, to political powers, and to historical developments. The prophetic saying about "the Lord" immediately allows the events to be seen in a different light; yes, it makes them different. There is such a thing as the Lord's turning toward people in a negative way. To be sure, he is acting in a negative way; nevertheless he *is* acting, and therewith turning toward them. "Misfortune comes down from the Lord." Doesn't this statement remind us of the one in v. 3 about his coming down upon the heights of the mountains? Doesn't this apply to mankind's granite-like hardheartedness which, at his step, is to become soft as wax, malleable, pliant, and usable for his purposes?

There is an insertion into the summons to lamentation at v. 13b that is theologically significant. With reference to "war stallions that are harnessed to war chariots" an explanation is added, "That is the chief and foremost sin of the daughter of Zion, for in you, O Lachish, are found Israel's rebelliousnesses" (Lachish was one of the most important fortresses that were supposed to protect Jerusalem from attack out of the coastal plain). This insertion answers anew the question of v. 5, "What is Judah's injustice and Jacob's rebelliousness?" The answer is: the chief element in this rebelliousness against the Lord is Zion's enterprise of self-defense! Precisely here is lurking a capital crime of which the institutional church is guilty: in its synods it works to a shocking extent for self-security. Must we not hear it from Micah: self-preservation is a chief ingredient in mistrust and therewith in the church's rebellious (revolutionary) renunciation of the Lord of the church? Here I am touching on one of the saddest problems of our churches. Did I say, "of *our* churches?" It would be better, I think, to see it as a problem of the one church of Christ. It should be, and become, the malleable instrument in his living hand, for that is indeed the purpose of the blow which is smiting us in a manner that makes it impossible for us to evade it.

As Micah delivers this message, something positive is already happening even though it is not noticed while the blow is being delivered. Opponents in "the establishment" now become those who share in being smitten by the same blow that strikes the rest of the people. It strikes all: Judah and Samaria, the country towns and the capital city, fortified and unfortified towns, Israel and the Gentiles, the cosmos and the human beings in it; the prophet and his hearers. What blows will still have to smite us also before we who have been torn apart find the way to one another, Protestants and Catholics, religious and nonreligious peoples, Boston and Richmond, Virginia![42]

To me it seems most important to notice in this chapter how the prophet becomes one with his hearers. Let us, in conclusion, look back once again at him in v. 8. He not only wails and whimpers; he is also walking around barefoot and naked. That means that already he is assuming the form and figure of a dishonored captive on his way to be deported (cf. Isaiah 20; 53). He suffers the blow from the Lord first, even before all the towns to whom he proclaims the Lord's blow. He does not stand above his people and their suffering. Does not the suffering prophet almost become in his day a pointer to the smitten Christ? Here nothing is said about "having pleasure in the death of the ungodly" (cf. Ezek. 18:23; 33:11). Under the impact of the blow from the Lord the prophet and his hearers become united one with one another. By suffering such a blow the battered Lord wishes to stand in solidarity with his battered community, so that it may become his community in the world anew.

Thou Shalt Not Covet!⁴³
Micah 2:1-11

The passage that we have for today's Bible study is unfamiliar, but for that very reason appropriate to the unfamiliar times and the extraordinary situation which we have now entered. The passage is not only unfamiliar; it is also difficult. It you compare the RSV translation with that of the NEB or TEV (Good News Bible), you will notice many differences.[44] The reasons for this go back to the passage's earliest formulations. In all likelihood the first written records of the prophets' proclamation were not made in an environment of contemplative quiet but rather in a very tense situation. They were therefore rough drafts, quickly put down to preserve a record of the proclamation. That is why it was not always easy for the later copyists to recognize all the words with precision. And that is why there are many types of variants, many sorts of small differences in this or that manuscript tradition, the manuscript variants reflecting prior variant paths of transmission. Many an item in chapter 2 of Micah remains dark for us to this day. When you therefore find remarkable differences in the translations, do not fret, dear friends. Realize, instead, that the word which had been proclaimed orally was transmitted under the constraints of continuing pressures. If you do that, you will then also affirm the fact that all which is essential remains unimpaired and unquestionable.

Before I read the passage, I wish to give you a brief overview of it. First of all, we have in vv. 1-5 a coherent unit in which the prophet speaks. Next in vv. 6-7—and here you quickly notice the heat of animated altercation—comes a protest from the hearers. Then there follows—most likely at the end of v. 7, but certainly beginning with v. 8—the response of the prophet (vv. 7b-10).

Finally in v. 11 we have a concluding note by the prophet. So let us read the passage. Micah calls out (2:1–5),

> [1]Woe to those who plan deeds of wickedness and disturb them-
> selves on their beds at night, hatching out evil schemes, so that,
> when the morning dawns, they may perform them, because they
> have the power to do it!
> [2]They covet fields, and seize them,
>   and houses, and commandeer them, as they desire.
> They oppress a man and his family,
>   and steal everyman's inheritance.
> [3]Therefore thus says the Lord,
> Behold, against this whole brood I am devising evil,
>   from which you are not going to be able to extricate your
>   necks.
> You shall no longer walk haughtily,
>   for it will be an evil time.
> [4]In that day they shall take up a taunt song against you,
>   and wail with bitter lamentation:
> "We've had it! We are utterly ruined."
>   "My people's land receives an alien lord!"
> "See, he is taking it out from under my feet."
>   "They are paying us out, dividing our fields."
> [5]Yes, you will have no share in the community of the Lord.

Thus Micah speaks. Then the people he has threatened defend themselves (vv. 6–7a),

> [6]"Don't preach at us!" is what they preach.
>   "Such insults are not proper topics for preaching!"
> [7a]"Do you think the house of Jacob is under a curse?"
>   "Has the Lord really lost his patience?"
>   "Is that the way he acts?"

In response Micah replies in the name of his God (vv. 7b–10),

> [7b]It is true, my words are compassionate to the upright
> [8]But you are rising up against my people like an enemy.
> You are stripping peaceable citizens of their robes;
>   you are depriving them of security and planning war.
> [9]The women of my people you are driving out from their
> cherished homes,
>   and from their children you are taking my honor forever.

¹⁰Therefore get up and go!
   There is no safety here any more!
   For the sake of a trifle you are taking possession
     of painful pledges.

Then Micah looks away and speaks to himself and to those who later read his word (v. 11),

¹¹If I were a false spirit and a preacher of lies
  and were to preach how they should be drunkards and topers,
   then I would be the proper preacher for this people.

What a great tumult swirls round about Micah! His cry of woe to selfish greed rumbles through the town, expressed by a Hebrew word we ought to become acquainted with: *hôy!* Otherwise that word was heard publicly out on the street only during ritual mourning for the dead. This means then that by using his terror-inspiring *hôy*, Micah is placing the wielders of power under God's verdict of death! Whenever a relative dies, the lament for the dead is begun with the words, *"Hôy, 'ākî,"* "Woe, my brother" (1 Kings 13:30). Whenever a king dies, we hear the words (Jer. 22:18), *"Hôy, 'ādôn,"* "Woe, the lord!" When the prophet Amos announces that the people will suffer massive decimation, he describes that approaching catastrophe similarly (Amos 5:16), "In all the streets, at all the town squares people say *Hôy! Hôy!*" It is such a rumbling *hôy* taken over from the lament for the dead that Micah now calls out over all who are still bursting with burgeoning vigor, who not only live their own lives but also know how to absorb for themselves the life and livelihood of others. It is precisely these puffed up, strutting figures who are now beset by the words of the dirge for the dead! Is it any wonder that Micah soon experiences a gigantic wave of furious protest (as we hear in what follows immediately in v. 6)? "We must shut that man up!" "Politics and economic policy are not proper topics for preaching!" Finally Micah characterizes these people by drawing a portrait of the sort of celebrity preacher they are itching to hear! "A preacher who would proclaim the glories of wine and liquor would be the preacher for these people. A preacher who would befog and befuddle their sensibilities, who would provide beautiful decoration and a pleasant background for their machinations, who would mesmerize them with visions of comfort and of 'the good life'—that would be the proper sort of preacher for this people."

What is wrong in Moresheth? To understand this, we should realize that Micah's native village lies in the borderland between Judah and Philistia. Within a radius of only six miles round about are situated no less than five military garrison cities. These we know from 2 Chron. 11:6ff. are the fortified strongholds which Solomon's son, King Rehoboam, had established: Adullam, Sochoh, Mareshah, Lachish, and Azekah. It is natural that many senior officials and officers from Jerusalem are stationed in these garrison cities. They find life pleasant in the mild climate of the lower hill country round about Moresheth, more pleasant than in the rough hills around Jerusalem where, at the higher elevation of 2500 feet, it can be uncomfortably cool in January (uncomfortable for Palestinian conditions at least, snow even falling there on occasion). But in Moresheth at a lower elevation (scarcely 1200 feet above the Mediterranean) a person has a glorious view of the coastal plain, vineyards thrive (very important for the officers!), and life is pleasant. With this background we understand how these administrative officials and officers toss and turn on their beds without really sleeping. The prophet, in fact, begins his message with the words, "Woe to those who hatch plans while they lie abed at night." They say to themselves as they fall asleep, as they awaken, or in their leisure moments (which they seemingly enjoy in abundant measure), "Here is where we ought to have a piece of property, a home, a garden! Oh yes, we even know a man who has such a place. Couldn't we latch on to that? But, no; that would be difficult to do. Instead, over there a woman is living with her children. It will be easier to get ahold of that property. (Compare v. 8 with v. 9.) Let's lay claim to it by means of our official Jerusalem seals, invoking the principle of eminent domain." They have the power (v. 1b) to apply official pressure even in the beautiful neighboring town of Moresheth. It is against them that Micah's *hôy* is directed, and that is why such a hubbub surrounds him in Moresheth and vicinity. Unquestionably what is happening is that Micah is taking sides with the victims who cannot defend themselves.

Does not tumult also on occasion surround this Nazareth Brotherhood of yours, headquartered here in Bethel, when, within any city one might wish to name, perhaps in a choice business section or in a prosperous residential area, you undertake to establish a facility or renovate a home for disadvantaged nonresidents? Or when anywhere else wheresoever you attempt to care for rural or urban vagrants, or for those who suffer from sickness but cannot find a home, or for other persons whom people don't want living in their neighborhoods? "They seize houses," our passages say, "as they please." How happy people are to purchase properties to prevent the encroachment of "bad neighbors" (the retarded, foreigners, people with big families, strangers, people with whatsoever undesirable characteristics one can name). Let all who run into difficulties in such enterprises know that they are dealing with prophetic situations; let them understand themselves from a prophetic perspective rather than from that of traditional bourgeois society. They are in good company; they are in the goodly fellowship of the prophets. Precisely when they run into difficulties, they are living in fellowship with the prophetic precursors of Jesus, whom people also resented and wanted to get rid of, saying, "This man receives sinners and eats with them."

In their quarrel with Micah the wielders of power complain, "What we do with our property is not the proper subject for religious discourse, nor is how we deal with the local population!" (v. 7). "How dare you threaten us, the leaders of our society, with expulsion from the country (as indeed Micah had done in vv. 4–5)? The house of Jacob is not under a curse; it has received the promise of blessing, not curses! In the final analysis we belong to that house of Jacob, even though we also have our faults" (they gladly grant that). "Has the Lord really lost his patience?" "God's goodness is what you are called to preach, and that you ought to preach also to us! Is not God's goodness and forbearance the main theme in all sections of the Old Testament? That is what you should preach to us!"

"Yes, indeed," Micah replies. "God speaks compassionately to the upright (v. 7b). But as for you, to whom God spoke compassionately, you have risen up like an enemy against my people (v. 8)! With your lack of regard for the weak and helpless you have

maneuvered yourselves out of the realm of God's goodness; you
have removed yourselves from the gospel (vv. 8–9). You are like
the unmerciful servant in Jesus' parable: you have experienced
God's goodness and patience, but when you yourselves travel a
bit further down that same path of compassion, your goodness
and patience disappear. What room do you leave for God's forbearance when you take possession of the pawned robe of the
least of my brethren because he cannot pay a trifling debt (one
which isn't hurting you a bit), or when you plot to take, and
then actually do take the roof from over the head of a defenseless woman and rob children of small joys?" Thus Micah ex-
pounds for us, far ahead of time, the saying of Jesus, "Woe unto
you that are rich now, you have had your easy life" (Luke 6:24).

We need, I believe, such clear and articulate commentaries on
the words of Jesus as are presented to us in Micah's prophecy. In
today's world presentations of Micah, of Jesus, of Christian social
service (*diakonie*) dare not be deprived of this theme. Christ did
not take up our guilt and sorrow so that we might, without giving our actions a second thought, treat with indifference those
who are unable to put up any resistance when they are mistreated. This is something our predecessors in Christian social
service not only knew but also put into practice: faith and love
belong together. As it now begins the second century of its work,
let the Nazareth Brotherhood be mindful of the fact that this sermon topic, which certain people wish to suppress, dare not be
missing. God is interested in our total life.

Micah becomes even more precise. When it comes to the
ownership of property, God is interested in the problems which
we have as property owners (and ownership is a problem not
only for us but also for the people with whom we live; yes, for
all mankind). God gives us our entire life in its totality; his goodness still protects all of it. He stands watch over the total life of
those who are hard pressed. Micah enjoins us to take a stand on
behalf of those who are unable to help themselves, and on behalf of those who have no lobbyists to represent them in the legis-
latures and caucuses of the powerful. Micah also wants us to take
a stand on behalf of those who are again given the lowest pri-
ority on the waiting lists drawn up by those who have influence.

Society, it seems, is still concerned with having trained laborers. A good labor force, it claims, is always needed. But old people, sick people, diseased people, rootless people, vagrants make no contributions to society. They are only a burden. That is why those who are engaged in Christian social service, mindful of the prophetic nature of their service, must act like advance scouts in a military campaign. In their preliminary survey of the scene they ought to be on the lookout particularly for those who are without advocates. They serve the entire host that follows them and therefore they should keep a sharp eye open for those who are helpless, for those whom the public has no eyes to see—to say nothing of any readiness to get involved in helping. The only honor to be gained in being advance scouts and taking the place of others is the honor of standing in the place where the prophets, these forerunners of Jesus, stood. Of the significance of this honor for the future we shall speak shortly.

Active involvement demands again and again eyes which are perceptive and the same sort of courage that Micah makes audible with his *hôy* (woe!). Micah would like to help us, the community of Jesus, to avoid becoming languid or discouraged at this task, for fatigue can quickly creep up on us. It is important to know that we live in the goodly fellowship of the prophets and apostles. In order to remain alert in faith and hope and in the knowledge of God's clear will, we should, above all else, ever examine ourselves anew. Other people are not the only ones who make mistakes. Micah, with his cry of woe, places us before two questions. It is in connection with these two questions which are directly applicable to us that I wish to clarify the individual sections in the main speech (vv. 1–5) of our passage.

These two questions are posed by the two constituent parts of the main speech: its accusation in vv. 1–2 raises the first question we must ask ourselves, "On what goal are we centering our thinking and our aspirations?" And its threat of doom, the announcement of judgment in vv. 3–5, raises the second question, "What in our world has a real future?"

As to the first, we will have understood the prophet's accusation only when we have learned to understand it as a summons to self-discipline. On what goal are we centering our thinking and our aspirations? The crime of the officers and officials which Micah's *hôy* condemns begins, most significantly, with the secret dreams they cherish as they lie on their beds. *Hôy ḥōšĕbê 'āwĕn* is how it sounds in Hebrew and the *ḥōšĕbê* means "planning, calculating, hatching something out" (v. 1a).

The first target at which the prophet takes aim is their relentless probing, their scheming, their calculating, their indulging themselves in fantasies. Back to that embryonic origin Micah traces all the subsequent evil. That is important, for this tiny beginning from which all the subsequent evil germinates (this secret planning, calculating, fantasizing) is subject to very little rational control. In sleepless nights those whom Micah is here indicting hatch out their plans. As they plan, they excite themselves to such an extent that they can hardly wait until morning to move into action. And then they move into violent action (v. 2a). Once they have succumbed to the desires of their hearts in the dark hours of the night, those covetous desires quickly take control of them. Once day has dawned, persons of no account are quickly overpowered. That is the way matters proceed. Desire is the basic evil, for the evil had already occurred when the future culprit was stealthily approached by fanciful dreams, not just when he was overcome and completely taken over by them. No wonder the Ten Commandments climax in the repeated warning: "Thou shalt not covet!" The word "to lust after" (to desire, to covet) is the word Micah takes up at this point. He takes into his hands the mirror of the Decalogue to hold it up before the people. Have you not, dear friends, noticed that in the Ten Commandments no key phrase is repeated as much as is this one: "Thou shalt not covet!" The warning applies to our coveting persons as well as things: do not covet your neighbor's house, his wife, his associates at work (male or female); do not covet your neighbor's cattle, or his ass (today we would say, his tractor, his washer-dryer, his Mercedes-Benz) or whatsoever other sorts of cattle or asses we are able to covet.

The danger of covetousness begins in leisure hours; then our self-control must also begin. I expressly say "our" (yours and mine), for here the proverb applies, "Resist the beginnings." What thoughts concern us as we fall asleep, as we awake, or in our sleepless hours? Do we know the daily medicine for maintaining good health in our psyche? Do we take that medicine regularly? Yes, we know about a lot of things today, but medicine kept in chests or in drawers doesn't do much good unless we actually take it. The prescription we know: praying when we go to bed, "All praise to thee, my God, this night for all the blessings of the light. . . . Keep me, oh keep me, King of kings, beneath thine own almighty wings. . . . Oh may my soul in thee repose and may sweet sleep my eyelids close, sleep that shall me more vigorous make to serve my God when I awake."[45] By praying such hymn stanzas we can nip temptation in the bud. It is a matter of overcoming, at its earliest stage, whatever arouses psychological sickness, that most sinister of the viruses in the lives of modern people. Only if we ourselves have practiced self-control and taken the proper medicine for ourselves will we be able to pass it on to others. Let me say it in another way: the word of God and the response to it in prayer are what we must have constantly at our side; that is the loaded pistol we keep ready against the surprise attacks of covetous thoughts.

> All-holy Lord, in humble prayer
> we ask tonight your watchful care
> And pray that our repose may be
> A quiet night, from perils free . . .
> From evil dreams defend our sight,
> From all the terrors of the night,
> From all deluding thoughts that creep
> On heedless minds disarmed by sleep.

One thing is clear: when such praying, the traditional praying of Christendom, ceases among the bulk of a population for an extended period of time (and into the future, without any reversal of the trend), then a brutalizing derangement takes place in the psyche of a people, one with which no psychiatry can cope. What a boon it is when the opposite occurs: when a person is so liberated personally that he is able to perceive other persons' needs. Recently an elderly lady in New York unstintingly and effectively helped a young German woman who was in deep trouble. And when the young German was so overcome by this unexpected help that she asked, "How can I pay back what you have done?" the elderly American answered, "By helping the next generation." In this little episode a bit of freedom from covetousness shines through (also a tinge of the desire to merit thanks). In payment for the help and love we have received in such rich measure we must transmit help and love to the next generation, to those who are lonely and isolated in the extended family in which we live.

Perhaps Micah is getting at the worst sore spot of our age when he indicts covetousness as the root of the evils he is attacking. Today's skeptical younger generation is, as we know, an affluent group. It has become not only a generation which is pleasure-addicted, pleasure-sated, pleasure-bored; it has also become a generation that demands many things. Moderation is not only a personal virtue; it is precisely what a rational analysis of our present world tells us is absolutely necessary if life is to continue. For moderation, in conscious protest against what is the unchallenged rule in our demanding society, is the soil on which love can grow. The desire to become ever more wealthy causes, however, all sorts of enormous problems in both public and private realms. As I see it, it was one of the wisest politicians of our day who said, "Let us finally decide what it is that we want to have grow in our midst before we decide how much growth we need." We must decide what shall grow: covetousness or the renunciation of affluence, income or outlay and involvement, giving or receiving. Which of these is the more blessed is the one which we must decide to practice, be it demand for what we desire or attentive perception of where there is need which we can alleviate. That is the first thing which the prophet Micah can prompt us to do in our day. As we listen to his indictment of those who plan and covet on their beds, let us examine what it is that our thoughts center on, and what is the target of our aspirations.

The second question which vv. 3–5 prompt us to ask is: What in today's world has a real future? Micah confronts his day's avarice and disdain for human beings with a sharp word from his God. He removes the veil so that our vision may penetrate the foreground and behold the determining facts at the depth of reality. Such is the task as well as the opportunity given also to those who live with Holy Scripture: they are enabled not only to see through the immediate realities of the foreground but also to gain a view of the totality of all realities involved. How do things look then when the veil has been removed? To those who plan evil on their beds the prophet says, "Thus says the Lord, 'Behold, I am making plans. . . .'" The word which had been the key in v. 1 is taken up here in v. 3, "I, the Lord, am planning." And in point of fact he says, "I am busy, planning evil, now that you are busying yourselves as you lie abed with coveting what is evil. Behold, I am planning to bring evil on this brood of evil-planners. I am planning evil from which you will not be able to extricate your necks." They will be forced to wear a monstrous yoke. These mighty lords and masters will be driven away as slaves of the Assyrians who already stand at the entrance to Syria-Palestine. "You will have to travel into slavery." While men make plans for evil, God is already far ahead of them in making counterplans.

That is the totality of realities involved! We are not masters of our future; God is, and he alone. What determines the future is not our desires or our demands. One thing alone is completely sure as far as humankind's future is concerned: we humans can only ruin our future by selfish coveting. That becomes completely clear in what vv. 3–5 say about the connection between coveting and its consequences for the future. They will lose their ability to walk erectly (v. 4 says that in so many words). Observers of the world situation have come to realize the truth of this statement for our world as a whole. If we, for example, do not now keep the Third World in mind in our political and economic thinking, if we do not foster a genuinely fraternal common life with developing nations and regulate our desires for consumption accordingly, then we are at this very moment being forced into a yoke from which we will not be able to extract our necks. If we do not decisively moderate our consumption of energy, then we are undermining the possibilities of the coming generation. Micah's unambiguous message is valid in such a comprehensive way that he himself could not even have come close to guessing at in the eighth century before Christ.

Let us return to his reference to interhuman relationships and therewith to the specific area of Christian social service. In plain words he is saying: whoever takes from those who need help the place where they might live will find that he will himself be driven away from the place where he resides. Whoever refuses support to a ruined person will himself one day cry (v. 4), "We are completely ruined!" There is no room here for cheap grace. If the prophet urges anything, it is this: grace is costly! People should not say, "This is an Old Testament retribution idea which has no place in the New Testament age," for in the Sermon on the Mount (Matt. 7:2) Jesus himself proclaims with a shrill voice, "With the judgment you pronounce you will be judged. And the measure you give you will get." In advance of his time, Micah takes up Jesus' lament for the rich who have become poor in the lament he places into the mouth of his latter-day dispossessed real-estate speculators. Whoever abandons an elderly person to solitude will soon find himself utterly desolate.

The prophet makes us consider most seriously the fact that our selfish greed cannot guarantee the future, but only misbuild it. But it is just possible that we can be freed from lovelessness, from harshness and indifference, and thus from unrealistic dreams of gain by this combination of the prophet's sharpness and Jesus' goodness (a goodness which also has its own sharpness, as the saying from the Sermon on the Mount indicates). If that happens, then we can begin to bless our future. Dear friends at Bethel, with his harsh message the prophet would like this very morning to begin to put this process of liberation into motion, so that we may know that the future is determined solely by the all-inclusive planning of our God. Despite all the things we see in the immediate foreground, this determinative factor of his activity should become evident for us when we view the situation from prophetic perspective. All who are engaged in Christian social service (*diakonie*) should accept Micah's "woe!" as a liberating message: you gain more possibilities for the future if you use the possibilities you have for the sake of others. You gain more time if you use it for others. To recover these simple rules is what we are urged to do on this very day.

In conclusion I want to remember our fellow workers, brothers and sisters who are busy at jobs where they are not expendable and who therefore cannot join us here at this time of catching new breath, because they cannot leave the needy people they are serving. That sort of obligatory service in which every one of you shares in some way is usually wearisome, especially if it must be extended over a long period of time. There is a Bible passage which I wish to send to such absent brethren, namely Eccles. 3:13, "It is God's gift that a person take pleasure in all his toil!" Dear friends, take this passage along with you for those times when you too will be engaged in toilsome, extended, difficult service. We pray that such service of yours may be the gift which God has prepared and planned for those in need. Let all brothers and sisters know that, quite unlike the celebrity preachers of comfortable pleasure, who are really singing the song of deceit, wind, wine, and liquor, they have been personally included in the great history of God's love, the history which includes many tender branches in which his life pulsates. That life goes out from Jesus and has its forerunner in the Old Testament prophets. Let us therefore take our place in the midst of the tumult round about Micah—that tumult continues—adopting the perspective of the prophet Micah and taking the right side. We have seen where the battlelines are drawn. Let us take our place on the right side and advance toward the real future, the approaching reign of God.

The Gathering and the Breakout:[46]
Micah 2:12–13

[12]I surely intend to gather you together, all of you, O Jacob,
   I want to gather all that is left of the people of Israel.
I intend to bring you together
   like sheep returning to the fold
like a flock in its pasture
   so that the place will be noisy with multitudes of people.
[13]He who breaks open breaches is going up ahead of them;
   they will break through the gates and escape.
And their king is going before them,
   the Lord is leading the way.

The two parts of our text bring two messages for the two different situations in which we modern Christians can readily find ourselves at any given time. We may find ourselves among the dispersed and scattered or among those immured and confined. Both parts expound our Advent promise, "Behold, your king is coming to you!" What does that king intend to effect in our midst? He intends to gather those who have been scattered and to lead forth into freedom those who have been imprisoned.

The first saying applies to those who have been scattered in all directions and who have been almost annihilated. Do we not recognize the situation of contemporary Christianity in the prophet's portrayal of the scattered Israel of exilic times? Are we Christians who live in a pagan environment not similarly dispersed? If you are not experiencing this dispersion personally, think of those who are, to their great sorrow! Does not the danger threaten that entire congregations will be ground to pieces? Is it not true that all that is left of Christianity in many of today's families, student bodies and crowds on the street are solitary individuals who consider Christ their Lord. Has not the process of individualization progressed so far in the last two or three generations as to make us Christians no longer feel at home in "Christian lands"? Well-established congregations have been decimated; only a remnant survives.

The word of the prophet reminds us that this current phase in the history of God's people is not unique. In this situation God's promise is as valid for us now as it was when it was first formulated. "I surely intend to gather you together; I want to gather all that is left." Yes, I am making a new beginning, just as I am now beginning a new year of grace for you in the midst of the world's old evil year. I am tearing you away from the powers of dissolution. I am gathering you together. Our gathering here this early morning, dear friends, as a small group in this immense old church also receives its life from this powerful promise. No individual remains isolated at "a lost post" (as happens in a war when a lone soldier must be abandoned at an important but hopeless position). The royal shepherd takes each one of us out of his or her isolation. That means that we are called to take decisive steps to curb the centrifugal forces which tend to scatter everything in all directions. This promise will not spare us sad moments of depression. But it is not our analysis of the current attrition which determines the future but his word, "I am gathering; I am bringing together; I am uniting." What we can expect is a joyous noise, the commotion of a gathering people. As our text puts it, "the place will be noisy with multitudes of people."

The second part of our text addresses a different situation. It refers to an encircled and besieged city, or to imprisoned captives. How can one get out of the narrow cell, against whose walls one can only batter one's head or bruise one's limbs? We think of Prof. Ahn in prison in Seoul. To those who are in such straits where, it seems, one can only run circles around one's own self, the message comes, "He who breaks open breaches is going up before them; then they too will break out. They will break through the gate and escape; their king is passing on before them; the Lord is leading the way!" Twice it is emphasized that he will pass on "before them" and once, "he is leading the way." The breakout into freedom occurs only from following him. But it *does* occur, as people follow him! Let us take this promise home with us for those hours when we are depressed and we despair because of our weakness, our tendency to succumb to temptation: "Our leader has broken out before us; our king is going before us; he is leading the way for us." The fact that we are imprisoned and besieged by the old evil foe is a truth, but only a penultimate one; the ultimate truth is this, "he is breaking open breaches in the walls of our prison."

Thus all of us may experience again what it means that Jesus Christ comes to us as King. Await it day by day. He is gathering us from the dangerous situation of dispersion! He is opening the door of our prison for us (the prison is being opened from the inside!), the prison in which we sinners had been locked.

We pray:[47]

> Sin's dreadful doom upon us lies;
>   Grim death looms fierce before our eyes.
> Oh, come, lead us with mighty hand
>   From exile to our promised land.

Against the Prophets Who Lead
My People Astray:[48]
Micah 3

Resistance and Accommodation in Micah's Day and Today

Hear from the prophet Micah, chapter 3:1–12.

¹And I said,
>Listen, you leaders of Jacob,
>>you rulers of the house of Israel!
>Is it not your responsibility to foster justice?—

²ᵃ   you who hate what is good and love what is evil,
³ᵃ   who eat the flesh of my people
>>and break their bones in pieces—

²ᵇ   who tear the skin from off my people's flesh
>>and the flesh from off their bones,

³ᵇ   who chop them up like meat for the cooking pot
>>like steaks for the frying pan.

⁴ If they then cry unto Yahweh,
>>he is going to hide his face from them at that time
>>>because their deeds have been evil.

⁵Thus Yahweh has said concerning the prophets who lead my people astray:
If they have something to bite with their teeth, they cry, "Salvation,"
>but if a person refuses to give them what they demand, they declare a holy war upon him.

⁶Therefore it shall be night for you—without vision,
>darkness for you—without instruction from me.
The sun is going down upon the prophets
>and dark shall the day be over them.
⁷Then the seers shall be disgraced,
>the diviners will have nothing to say,
they shall all veil their mouths
>because they receive no response from God.

⁸But as for me, I, by contrast, am full of authority (i.e., Yahweh's
power), justice, and courage,
> to declare to Jacob his rebelliousness
> and to Israel his delinquency.

⁹Listen to this, you leaders of Jacob,
> rulers of the house of Israel,
who abhor justice
> and twist what is straight,
¹⁰who build Zion with blood
> and Jerusalem with injustice.
¹¹Her leaders give judgment for a bribe;
> her priests interpret the law for pay;
> > her prophets give their revelations for money.
Yet they lean upon Yahweh and say,
> "Is not the Lord in our midst?
> No disaster shall come upon us!"
¹²Therefore because of you
> Zion will be plowed as a field,
Jerusalem shall become a heap of ruins,
> and the temple mount will be given over to the beasts of
> the forest.

IMPORTANT PROLEGOMENA

Permit me to make two preliminary remarks which will clarify
what I intend to present.

1. The Old Testament prophets are most certainly not to be
identified with today's clergymen, not even if the clergymen call
themselves Protestants. Only on rare occasions will today's or
tomorrow's clergymen function as prophets. What concerns us in
this lecture is the relation of a true to a false prophet. This relation is, of course, to be noted if we wish to equip ourselves to distinguish false messengers of the gospel from true ones. It depends on what criteria we use for identifying what has ultimate
authority and what leads astray.

2. In our consideration of this topic we shall permit ourselves
to be guided by the report of the controversy which has been
transmitted to us by Micah of Moresheth. It is the first conflict
of this sort in which the actual criteria that the prophet used are
set out before us (and thus it goes beyond the report of Elijah's
conflict with the prophets of Baal). A century later, in the trial of

Jeremiah such criteria will become even clearer. But in the main the criteria which Jeremiah will use in his conflict with his opponents correspond to those Micah uses in our chapter. Therefore we take as our point of departure the first classic controversy within the prophetic circles of the eighth century, the one described for us in Micah 3.

Two other things must still be clarified if we are to understand this chapter. First is the question, Is the chapter a unit? It is, significantly, introduced by the brief notation, "And I said," which marks a new section over against the preceding chapters 1 and 2. Further new sections come at v. 5 ("Thus has Yahweh said") and at v. 9 ("Listen to this, you leaders . . ."). One might therefore possibly conclude that we are dealing with three originally separate prophetic sayings. But on closer consideration, one is struck by the fact that the address in v. 9 corresponds exactly to that in v. 1 and by the further fact that in the third saying (at v. 11) the prophets (to whom the second saying in vv. 5–8 was addressed as a separate group) have been included in the accusation along with the leaders of Jerusalem who had been addressed already in the first saying. Accordingly what was at least intended by the present written formulation of Micah's message about the prophets is that these three sayings are to be understood in connection with one another; their themes obviously belong together, and they most likely originated in an appearance of Micah's at a gathering of the Jerusalem leaders. The written formulation goes back to Micah himself: "And I said" (v. 1a).

The second question is, why does Micah of Moresheth appear in Jerusalem? That the "leaders" who are addressed are responsible in Jerusalem and for Jerusalem is clear from the accusation in v. 10 ("they build Zion with blood") and from the threat in v. 12 ("because of you . . . Jerusalem shall become a heap of ruins"). A hundred years later at the trial of Jeremiah (26:18) elders from the rural areas of Judah recall this saying of the man from Moresheth against Jerusalem. But what is "the man from Moresheth" (thus Mic. 1:1 and Jer. 26:18) doing in Judah's capital? Moresheth lies twenty miles southwest of Jerusalem in the lower hills of Judah, 1200 feet above the coastal plain of Philistia, nine miles east of the Philistine city of Gath, whence it got its alternative name, Moresheth-Gath (Gath's Possession), in keeping with an older border line. This border village's connections with Jerusalem are easily clarified. For no less than five of the fortress cities constructed from the time of Rehoboam onward (2 Chron. 11:7–9) lay within a radius of six miles from Moresheth; that means that Jerusalem officials and officers were constantly coming and going in the vicinity of Moresheth. Furthermore, these garrisons in the neighborhood make a lively traffic likely between Micah's home and Jerusalem. That traffic included members of the families from the region who were dragged off to the capital Jerusalem as conscripts to labor on the estates of civilian and military officers or on official construction projects there (v. 10). Micah frequently calls these fellow countrymen of his "my people" in contrast to "those people there" (the Jerusalem people, 2:11), often in very striking contexts (3:3; cf. 2:8, 9; also 1:9 and 3:5). Last but not least, it was for the sake of these oppressed kinfolk of his that the man from Moresheth may well have been summoned before official commissions in Jerusalem to render an account of his activity.

VERSES 1–4, MICAH'S MESSAGE TO FELLOW ELDERS

With this background our first saying becomes understandable (vv. 1–4). It portrays the same social stratum in which (as we will see afterward in vv. 5ff.) the prophets are also active. As mouthpieces of the God of Israel the prophets are not to restrict themselves to some sacred retreat far off the beaten path, just as Micah is not to allow himself to be cooped up in such a ghetto. To what social stratum do they belong? In v. 1 (and v. 9) Micah addresses the "leaders" and "rulers." These are most likely the leaders of the ancient historic clans and families, elders who are supposed to make decisions in matters of jurisprudence and who are active in the administration of the city. Let it be noted that Micah is not thereby addressing the king or the senior court officials (as least he is not addressing them with the official title *śarim*, "governors" or "chiefs"). This apparently is not because as an insignificant commoner from the province he was shy in court circles, but, more importantly, because for him these elders are the people who dealt directly with the poor. In any case he addresses those who are responsible as the natural functionaries in ancient Israel's clan federation (cf. Judg. 11:6, 8, 11).[49] What does he have to say to them? Three things.

First he sets forth briefly and clearly the criteria he will use in measuring their performance. The leaders in Jerusalem are expected to know what is binding legal order (*mišpaṭ*). With a rhetorical question he refers to what must be taken for granted, "Isn't it true that, if anyone, you are responsible for knowing and practicing what is valid justice in Israel? Life in accordance with justice is expected to be your concern!" But, when measured by this criterion of legal order, they themselves fail the test!

Hence there follows immediately (and this is the second point) an accusation with its characterization of their style of behavior. First, there is a general accusation, "They hate what is good and love what is evil."[50] In a very simple way the function of "justice" is thus clarified: it is to discriminate between good and evil. Such discrimination between good and evil, and, in connection with it, between love and hate is well known in the contemporary prophets as well as in sapiential speech. I need refer only to such passages as Isa. 5:20 "Woe to those who call evil good and good evil!" or Amos 5:14f., "Seek what is good and not what is evil. . . . Hate what is evil and love what is good; establish justice in the gate!" In wisdom literature the contrast of good and evil occurs often, e.g., Ps. 34:14a (RSV), "Depart from evil and do good. Seek peace, and pursue it!" (see also 37:27) as does the love/hate antithesis, e.g., Prov. 1:22; 9:8; 12:1 (RSV) ("Whoever loves discipline loves knowledge, but he who hates reproof is stupid"); 13:24. Such simple, clear language was most likely familiar to Micah from his background in the Judean country towns and the gatherings of elders (since they were teachers and judges in the families); it seems equally appropriate for the heads of clans in Jerusalem. At this point Micah is already accusing the Jerusalem leaders of what he later in v. 9b calls "abhoring justice" and "twisting what is upright." He uses religious terminology as little as he uses complicated presentations of evidence. Justice according to Micah means rescue for those who are endangered, help for those who have been hurt, surcease for those who have suffered violence. Micah illustrates that by means of a contrasting portrait of injustice.

In vv. 2–3 he uses a drastic metaphor to make things crystal clear. The responsible persons arrange celebrations at which the poor are butchered; they tear the skin from the flesh of the poor, the flesh from their bones; they chop up the flesh like steaks for the frying pan. Such is the gruff peasant language of this man from the country.

When we are confronted with coarse expressions like this, we should guard against suspecting that we are dealing with a false prophet (just because of the rough language involved). As a matter of fact, the false prophets remain much more formal and courteous in their terminology (e.g., their expressions in 3:5, "salvation" and "declare a holy war"); they prefer traditional expressions. The true prophets, however, were never very prim. By means of the metaphor about the cooking pot and the frying pan into which the people are being cut up piece by piece Micah indignantly declares that these mighty lords are exploiting the commoners to satisfy their personal desires. What these metaphors mean is expressly said in other sayings. In 2:1 the woe is raised against those "who plan evil on their beds." There one sees the officials in the fortress cities round about Moresheth disturbing themselves as they fall asleep, dreaming, "Oh, how nice it would be to settle in this region permanently! How can I get ahold of a piece of property here? . . . Oh yes; over here is a man whom we might dispossess; but no, over there is a widow whom we can get rid of with much less fuss."[51] No sooner does the dawn arrive than the dreamers go about putting their sinister plans into action; "after all, they have the power to do so" (2:1b). They take possession of the property they want by using their official Jerusalem seals. Micah had probably observed at firsthand the results of the ensuing coercive measures that were taken time and time again in the vicinity of Moresheth. How can one then expect the officials to treat the conscripts who must do forced service in Jerusalem! "They build Zion with blood!" (3:10). If someone doesn't work readily enough, he is beaten bloody or even strangled (cf. Jer. 22:13–17). Such brutal realities may well lie behind the coarse metaphors of the prosecutor from Moresheth (3:2f.).

No matter what may be rightly said in criticism of the neglect in political discussion today of the Bible's social justice message, this must remain clear: witnesses from the Bible like Micah emphasize the fact that the true preacher is also a champion of the helpless who are being oppressed and mistreated. At the same time, of course, we must note that Micah did not organize the oppressed in a movement of resistance toward their masters. He does not place himself at the head of protest marches or demonstrations; rather, he addresses the guilty directly, mincing no words.

The accusation is followed by a reference to (and this is the third point) the *consequences* (v. 4). The time is coming in which they themselves will cry to their God from trouble and—he will not listen to them. Toward them his countenance will remain dark. Thus they will reap the harvest of their evil deeds. Persons who close their ears to God's demand of justice for the helpless will themselves remain without a response from God when they are themselves dependent on God's listening to them. Those who do not wish to hear God's word on behalf of others will no longer be able to hear it for themselves. The only thing which is not delineated in detail is the historical catastrophe in which such bitter experiences will occur.

Perhaps the reference in v. 4 to an absence of any response from God and to his hiding his countenance already reminds us of the failure of the prophets (of which we will hear more in vv. 6f.). Be that as it may, in what follows Micah turns expressly and directly to the prophets.

VERSES 5–8, THE DELINQUENCY OF
MICAH'S FELLOW PROPHETS

What task is rightly theirs? First of all, as a matter of principle, none other than that which Micah recognizes as his own task. Otherwise Micah could not compare them to himself in v. 8. The prophets, then, have much less to do with the interior duties of worship than do the priests to whom such duties were entrusted. Rather, their attention is supposed to be directed to exterior and public affairs: questions of peace and war, of social health and social ills. Above all, they must seek "the answer of the Lord" to specific questions about justice and injustice, about the good or evil effects of specific types of activity. The fact that according to 3:7 the prophets will receive no divine revelations seems to be the presupposition for the fact that the voice of God has become silent also for these public officials (cf. what was said above on v. 4). The man from Moresheth considers these prophets his colleagues in Jerusalem.

What he has against them he mentions immediately: they lead people astray! The prophets are themselves the misleaders. What does the expression "lead astray, mislead, seduce" mean in this context? The Hebrew root (*t'h*) can have two meanings. For one thing, it can mean "to wander about lost" as when (Gen. 21:14) Hagar wanders about lost in the wilderness of Beersheba; in Exod. 23:4 the word describes an ass which has run away and got lost. In its second meaning the word can describe the reeling and staggering of a drunken man who cannot see straight, to say nothing of walking straight; "Priests and prophets reel with wine!" (Isa. 28:7). To lead astray (as the causitive *t'h* hiph. indicates) then means in the original Hebrew, "to cause someone to wander about lost or to be so drunk as to be incapable of going to the desired direction." If Micah calls the prophets "those who lead Jerusalem astray," then he is saying that it is they who are responsible for the fact that God's people no longer know and no longer are able to find their proper path and their proper goal. It is possible, to judge from 2:11, that the concept he has in mind is total inebriation. For there he sarcastically paints a portrait of the sort of preacher who would be popular with these Jerusalemites: "If a false prophet and a preacher of lies were to tell you how to be drunkards and topers, then he would be the proper preacher for this people."

True messengers differ from false ones in that the one group is able to help people in a sober manner to travel the right path to the right goal, whereas the other group gets them fatally drunk so that they can recognize neither path nor goal. The line of demarcation between "true" and "false" may well cut directly across both lines that are currently drawn up for battle, the establishment people and the revolutionists. Both can be sober helpers of the oppressed, the injured, the mistreated; or, conversely, both can be so completely intoxicated with the idealistic picture they have of the past or of the future that they lead the present generation astray.

Our look in the direction of the Jerusalem "prosperity preachers" is, according to 3:5, in itself already a look in the direction of what is causing this loss of path and goal.

"When they have something to bite with their teeth, they cry, 'Salvation!' But the person who refuses to give them what they demand will find that they will declare war on him." If we are to grasp this saying so crucial for our main question, a few details must be explained first of all. What is meant by the expression, "when they have something to bite with their teeth"? We must, it seems, recall the preceding metaphor: the prophets join the Jerusalem leaders in feasting on the flesh of the poor, who are being chopped in pieces for the frying pan. If the prophets need "payment for services rendered," they simply sieze pieces of real estate or levies of conscript labor, both of which have been (illegally) made subject to their coercive measures. Their ostentatious contributions to those who twist justice and hate what is good guarantee what such prophets will proclaim, "Salvation!" That means that these prophets proclaim peace and affluence to those who have themselves already increased their own affluence and with whom they have made a rotten peace.

In individual cases there seem to have been exceptions, for v. 5b speaks in the singular of a prophet who "refuses to give them what they demand." The usual translation here is that of Luther, "He who puts nothing into their mouths receives the preachment that a war will come."[52] But *'al pîhem* does not mean "into their mouths" but "according to their mouth, their say-so, their command or wish"; in Gen. 41:40 Pharoah says to Joseph, "All my people shall order themselves as you command (*'al pîcā*), i.e., will obey, at your command" (cf. Gen. 43:7). According to this, these prophets make certain demands; if, however, someone hesitates, possibly in order to refuse, then "they sanctify war against him," i.e., they formally threaten him with the inauguration of a state of war.[53]

An exposition of such details can explain how the prophets came to lead Israel astray, so that it now staggers along, finding neither its path nor its goal. Self-interest prompts what they preach. What comes out of their mouth depends on what has first gone into it. If their hearers batten them, they get to hear pleasant messages of good; if, however, someone upsets them, he gets to hear a message of doom. Micah's main complaint therefore is that these prophets let their audience determine their message;

the stance their hearers take over against them determines what they say. These prophets are not false prophets because they preach salvation; they are perfectly able on occasion to proclaim war. In fact, as false prophets, they vacillate between opportunistically indulging and sternly opposing their hearers, oscillating like a pendulum between accommodation and resistance. Hence just as accommodation to selfish interest cannot be the hallmark of a true prophet, so mere resistance to the hearer cannot be proof of true prophecy.

What the misleaders preach is merely a reaction to audience response and audience behavior. Later on Jeremiah will supplement this insight by another: viz., by strengthening the wicked on their evil way, the false prophets prevent them from repenting (Jer. 23:14, 32; cf. also on the topic of "leaders as misleaders" Isa. 3:12; 9:16; also 1:17). Here we have a model for the pastor who is determined "to get along with his people."[54] Also in such a case (as with any false prophet) God is merely the fifth wheel on the wagon, whereas in the case of a true prophet God is the wheel that drives all the wheels (cf. E. Busch, *Karl Barths Lebenslauf*, 102, 115).

What is the result when audience stance determines a prophet's text and theme, and personal gain and pleasure become the preacher's dominating concern?

Micah's response in v. 6 is given in direct discourse,

> Then it shall be night for you—without vision;
>   darkness for you—without revelation!
> The sun is going down upon the prophets,
>   and dark shall the day be over them.

Since they have directed their eyes and ears solely to their audience, and consequently away from their God, they do not consequently expect the clarifying, illuminating word from their God; and they will not receive it. Persons who have wanted to stagger around in drunkenness by day will, on sobering up, lapse into a night in which they will be unable to find their way any more. Unexpectedly judgment overtakes them in the form of a darkness in which no one can see the next step. "Night darkness . . . the setting of the sun, a dark day," these are all metaphors to express comfortless bereavement. Hence (v. 7), great grief is going to descend upon the prophets who had promised themselves pleasure from their hearers. But because they really have nothing worthwhile to tell the Jerusalem leaders about God's justice, they end up in disrepute and painful disgrace (Luther, "They are ruined"), unable to say much, and intimidated (Luther, "They have become objects of scorn"). At this point reference is made to their resorting to the rites of mourning (cf. Ezek. 24:17, 22): they veil their moustaches. *Śāpām* refers to a moustache in distinction from a *zāqān*, the beard of one's chin and cheeks. Here the point is that the false prophets veil their mouths because they have nothing more to say, "for there is no response from God!" God has become silent for those who expect everything from their audience. They are not even winning the honor and respect of these hearers to whom they devoted such steadfast attention. They are also in disrepute with them, since it is also because of them that the leaders in Jerusalem are now without God's word (v. 4) when in their perplexities they cry out to God. God's silence therefore is not the result of his allegedly having fallen asleep (as was the experience of the prophets of Baal, 1 Kings 18:27) or of his having died (as is the case with the gods of the modern world). God's silence in this instance results precisely from wrong expectations by those who should be his messengers. Frightened by Mic. 3:7, John Calvin summons the readers of his commentary to pray, "Almighty God, shine forth so brightly by thy word that we be not overtaken by the darkness of avarice!"

After Micah has placed a future of darkness and disgrace before his well-fed prophetic colleagues in Jerusalem, his own prophecy takes a surprising turn. At v. 8 he places himself in direct opposition to them as their counterpart. With special emphasis at the beginning, he says,

> But as for me, on the contrary—I am filled
> with authority, justice, and courage,
> to declare to Jacob his rebelliousness
> and to Israel his delinquency.

What amazing self-confidence! To understand its basis and its goal, let us consider the wording in detail!

"I am filled." What does that mean? First of all, the man from Moresheth's personality is like an empty jar, a hollow space—like a container which can receive grain, oil, wine or whatever from without, retain it, and then, in turn, pass it on to others. In 1 Kings 7:14 a metalworker is presented as one who is *"full* of wisdom, understanding, and skill in the art of casting bronze." We would say he was *gifted.* Similarly in Deut. 34:9 Joshua, after his ordination by Moses, is *"filled* with wisdom." "To be filled with" means then in these similar contexts "to be endowed, gifted by God with." To his great pain, Jeremiah discovers how difficult it is for a human personality to be filled by God, particularly if the person is to function as the Lord's prophet,

> I am full of the wrath of Yahweh;
> I am weary of trying to hold it in.
> (Jer. 6:11)

What fills him is a sort of fire which cannot be held within but which must finally be hurled forth.

> I sit alone, because thy mighty hand is upon me,
> for thou hast filled me with indignation.
> (15:17)

Being filled with the wrath of the Lord, a wrath that needs to be expressed, is what thrusts the prophet into solitude and therewith into an independence, at least over against men.

This "being filled by God as a prophet" transforms a person into an individual who, in this new solitariness, is self-assured over against others but still does not live from his own resources and is therefore not really independent. Such a person lives entirely from the endowment given him. What is it that fills Micah to the full? Three things. "Power/authority" is the first gift mentioned. This power of his to put in an appearance, country bumpkin that he is, before the prominent people of the royal capital is not a power that Micah developed out of his own resources. As in Isa. 40:29, "The Lord gives power to the faint and strength to him who has no might" and in v. 31, "They who wait on the Lord renew their strength." So the power spoken of here is the power to continue opposing very influential power brokers with a resistance that seemingly has no prospect of success. (The gloss to the word "power" explains pertinently, "It is the power of Yahweh's Spirit").[55]

Justice (*mišpaṭ*) is the second gift. This catchword refers back to v. 1b. It means "the sense of justice" which should have guided the leaders of Jerusalem but which they had perverted. It fills Micah with full authority and gives him direction and orientation in his work.[56] The third gift is *geḇûrāh*, almost a technical term from ancient warfare. A solitary warrior needs to have *geḇûrāh*: readiness to engage in combat against others with a sense of self-confidence. A messenger needs courage to relay the message even in the camp of the enemy. It makes Micah capable of the coarseness of his drastic accusations (vv. 2f., 5). All in all, the question as to what is the basis of Micah's self-understanding is clearly answered here: it is this commoner's having been endowed with full authority.[57] A true messenger will never show cringing diffidence.

Micah's endowment corresponds to what the New Testament calls *exousia*, the very characteristic which, according to Matt. 7:29, the crowds saw as distinguishing Jesus from the scribes with their circumstantiality and casuistry. Paul also boasts of such full authority (2 Cor. 10:8), as one who "boasts in the Lord" (v. 17); such *exousia* makes his letters appear, even to his opponents, "weighty and powerful" (v. 10). So the basis of Micah's self-understanding is this endowment of the weak with strength, with an uncorruptible sense of justice in the midst of a confused situation, with self-assurance even while resisting the highest authorities. The brief sentence (Mic. 3:8) is something like the report of a prophet's call, something of which we do not otherwise hear in Micah.

We may then learn to distinguish true from false witnesses by asking, Who is filling their mouths? God, or those who listen to them? What gives them direction and orientation? God's law, or men's influence? To whom do they accommodate themselves? Whom do they oppose? What needs to be noted today as always is the fact that the pressure of massive opposition can change a witness into a misleader just as much as the influence of the few who sit at the center of world power. Israel's ancient sacred law saw the danger of bribing a judge as coming from two possible directions: from enticing money and from the presence of a noisy multitude (cf. Exod. 23:2, 8 in the section of the Book of the Covenant on the duties of judges); both can blind those who see. The chief question always remains the one which also must be addressed to those who are supposed to make their appearances as messengers of Jesus Christ: Who is filling their mouths? The basis of all authority can only be he, he alone.

And yet we must now also consider the other question: What is the goal of a prophet's being endowed with authority? The goal is public accusation and indictment: "to declare to Jacob his rebelliousness and to Israel his delinquency."

To do that requires, of course, special authority, if one is to unmask the Jerusalem leaders as rebels against the God of Israel (the word *pešaʻ* for "transgression" is the word used in 1 Kings 12:19 for revolt). Micah has to use the appropriate word for describing wandering from the right path and the right goal (*hāṭāʾ* means: to miss the mark, the bull's eye, as in Judg. 20:16; Prov. 8:36). What does Yahweh want to be done with the rebellion and disorder in Israel? It should be publicly indicted (as the word *higgîd* indicates). That means: defection and straying from the God of justice should be lifted up on high, placed before people as on a billboard, so that it cannot be overlooked; it must be publicly proclaimed loud and clear, so that no one can fail to hear about it. That is what "proclaim" means. Note how limited Micah's task is: the prophet must stay on the trail of those who are wrong. He need not speak a syllable about salvation; he need issue no summons to repent. Whatever else is to be proclaimed has legitimatizing truth and power only if this primary thing occurs at the proper time, at Micah's own moment of truth, viz., that what is injustice in God's sight is openly exposed. That, Micah says, is the goal of his vocation. That is what his "self-understanding" consists of. The presence of such advertisement of crime is what distinguishes true from false proclamation.

VERSES 9–12, EXPOSING GUILT AND PROCLAIMING DOOM

How Micah's exposé of crime and guilt was carried out is indicated by the concluding section of this chapter. After Micah has legitimated himself (v. 8) by referring to the authority he had received, he again addresses, as in v. 1, the official representatives of the magistracies and describes their twisted relation to justice (vv. 9f.; cf. vv. 1–3). In what he says, two things are new: one of them in the accusation in v. 11 and the other in the threat of doom in v. 12.

The indictment in v. 11 accuses the leaders, secular as well as spiritual, of one and the same capital crime: the judges decide for a bribe; the priests interpret the Torah for pay; the prophets proclaim according to the money they get paid. Verse 5 already had told us that, when it comes to the response of these prophets to questions addressed to them, outcome corresponds to income. Now, at v. 11, this is exposed as part of the general malaise in all the leaders.

What makes such activity rebellion against the God of Israel? It is not that Micah contests the principle that laborers (including judges, priests, and prophets) deserve payment for the work they do. Micah knows that the ancient seers were rightly paid for their work with bread or cash (1 Sam. 9:6ff.). But in the situation under discussion something entirely different is to be pilloried. Everywhere, among royal court officials, in administrative and judicial fields, among the city's entrepreneurs, reimbursement has become the dominant factor. Ways and means are not adjusted in accordance with what is just for the protection of the weak, but according to the financial calculations of the powerful. Grants to priests and prophets come to function as bribes. The cost of public service is not what determines the service cost; rather, the amount of payment he receives is what guides the course of an incumbent's service.

In sum, the accusation is this: money speaks louder than God. That is what happens in a society which is fascinated by prosperity and its continual increase. In all circles the principle of "making a sharp bargain" gains a strength that not only makes it coercive but also produces a unity which is all the more destructive. Income growth is the chief slogan. It subtly threatens to influence the way every office is administered. God and the hurting neighbor are pushed aside in day-to-day operations by the determinative force of rising demands and claims. That is why it is all the more cynical when these same people lay claim to God's protective presence by means of Ps. 46:6f., asking, "Is not Yahweh in our midst?" Employing pious slogans like "A mighty fortress is our God" to express their self-security, these puffy-cheeked culprits reject the prophet's warning, saying, "No evil shall befall us!"

Just where is God's presence now? In the temple, or in the word of justice and of doom? In the institutions of the powerful, or in the witness who is hot on the trail of injustice and need? In the religious guarantees of security, or in the announcement of fatal catastrophe? Micah's response becomes unequivocal in his concluding threat (v. 12),

> Therefore because of you
>   Zion will be plowed as a field,
> Jerusalem shall become a heap of ruins,
>   the temple mount will be given to the beasts of the field.[58]

Because of you! The leaders of Jerusalem are the sole instigators of the approaching catastrophe. They who should be proclaimers of the word about God's helpful justice are the last ones to live up to their responsibilities. Now is the critical time: when the people in authority, the priests, and the prophets continue without God's response (cf. vv. 4, 7). Their defection from the word is what is causing the members of the establishment and their institutions to totter. What is making Jerusalem a heap of ruins? The prophets' dependence on men of influence! Waiting for the word to come from the wrong direction is what is letting the temple mount become an uninhabitable wasteland. The person who delivers himself up to merely human interests or to his own pious need for peace of mind is the person who is causing the house of God to become a lair for the beasts of the forest. Please note, respected hearers, that it is precisely those who circle around the pious affirmation, "The Lord is in our midst," who are the chief culprits. It is also precisely in this activity of judging them that the God of Israel shows himself to be present as the God of his word of justice. As such he plays the same role here that he plays when he speaks his eternal yes to the crucified one, who took upon himself all the judgment of guilty men. Only in him does God open for us the gate to life in the midst of well-deserved judgment. This new life, however, is at the same time life lived in solidarity with the least of his brothers, that is, with the least important brothers he has.

Even a century after Micah, at the time of Jeremiah, this threat against Jerusalem still rumbled in the ears of the elders and resulted in Jeremiah's acquittal (Jer. 26:17–19). How about us? Have we understood the distinction Micah makes between true and false prophets? Are we indeed able to understand it? If I am to face up to Micah's threat against Jerusalem, I know of only one question that is decisive for our understanding: what would we think, say, and do if we were to relate the announcement of catastrophe upon Jerusalem to our own national church (folk church, *Volkskirche*) and its structures? I am certain that it will be, at the very latest, the present generation of theological students who will have to reckon with something like this. What would then be ultimate for us: money, or God? Would we then quickly change our vocations, our programs of studies so as not to lose out on "an education for the future"? Or would we then allow ourselves, all the more decisively, to be filled by the uncorruptible word which shows itself victorious particularly in the rubble it brings about? Would we then look past Mic. 3:12, past the ruins of parsonages, church buildings, and financial guarantees in the direction of Mic. 4:1–4 (Jerusalem as the highest mountain)? Would we then, from the midst of fields scattered with Jerusalem's ruins, look toward the new Zion which transcends all nations? Would we then, from that place, await with suspense the word of the Lord which has been authenticated on Golgotha, the word which causes swords to be beaten into plowshares? The conditional clause of such a hypothetical question (if this should happen . . .) does *not* seem to me to be formulated correctly when it is made to refer to a situation that is contrary to the facts (if this were to happen . . .). Only when we accept the judgment of death and the promise of complete liberation unto life will the false prophet in us be unmasked. None of us will live through the experience with less equipment for our task than what Micah had. The human personalities in which we live our lives need to be filled with the gifts of authoritative power, with a sense for justice, with courage, and yes, with the power of the Spirit of the Lord who said, "Without me ye can do nothing" (John 15:5).

Zion's Future:[59]
Micah 3:9–5:14

What will become of Zion? What will become of the people of
Zion? What contribution do Zion and its people make to the welfare of the peoples of the world? This complex of questions is
dealt with at no place in the Bible at greater depth and breadth
than in Micah 4–5. The two chapters contain at least ten individual sections, which are connected solely by their common
structure as prophetic announcements of the future. Considered
individually, they are remarkably different in form and content—
at points even contradictory. For instance, 3:12 and 4:1ff. stand
in crass contradiction one to the other; for alongside an announcement of approaching total catastrophe for Jerusalem stands an
announcement of Zion's elevation to the ultimate pinnacle of
world peace. Micah's threat to Zion in chapter 3 is one of the
most severe announcements of judgment anywhere in prophecy.
It seems to have evoked the polyphonic and dissonant choir of
voices we now hear in chapters 4–5. Before attempting to trace
the appearance of these voices and of their various themes, we
will have to concern ourselves first of all with that original saying of Micah, the one (3:9–12) which the subsequent process of
compiling ensuing oracles made its point of departure.

Before doing that, however, I wish to call your attention to an
interpretative hint we owe to the final editorial addition that was
attached to the Micah traditions. It prefaces at 1:2 all the Micah
material with the following surprising summons,

> Hear, you peoples, all of you,
>   hearken, O earth, and all that is in it!
> Yahweh is a witness in your midst,
>   the Lord from his holy temple.

It is surprising that the nations are summoned to listen because in what follows in chapters 1–3 oracles for Israel only are voiced, especially oracles directed against Samaria and Jerusalem. This means that the peoples of the world should find in what is directed to Israel God's own personal witness also to them. Only in the subsequent chapters 4–5 are the nations again mentioned explicitly, and then again also in connection with the Zion theme. These sayings close, significantly, in 5:15, after an oracle at 5:10–14 which again addresses only Jerusalem, with a bitter threat of wrath upon those peoples who, in disobedience to the summons at the beginning, "do not hear." The interpretative hint of these outermost editorial brackets at 1:2 and 5:15 is rather clear. The nations misperceive Yahweh's dealings with Israel, if they stand aloof, keeping their distance from Israel, its history and theology. In what God says and does to Israel they should perceive a message that applies also to them. The church which exists in the midst of all the various peoples of the world should show itself as an intelligent representative of these peoples by comprehending precisely this summons. Attention that is merely historical (that of polite spectators at an exhibit in a museum) does not lead to understanding. In the Lord's message about Zion, the church should therefore not only recognize an essential part of its own prehistory; it should also (setting a good example for the nations) recognize that message as a warning and as a relevant guide for its own journey through the present into the future.

Let us hear then the basic oracle in which Micah's proclamation of chapters 1–3 reaches its climax, 3:9–12.

> 9Hear this,
>> you heads of the house of Jacob,
>>> you rulers of the house of Israel
>> who abhor justice
>> and pervert all equity,
> 10who "build" Zion with blood
>> and Jerusalem with wrong.
> 11Her leaders give judgment for a bribe,
>> her priests teach for hire,
>>> her prophets divine for money.
>> Yet they lean upon the Lord and say,
>> "Is not the Lord in our midst?
>>> No evil shall come upon us!"

¹²Therefore because of you
    Zion shall be plowed as a field,
        Jerusalem shall become a heap of ruins,
           and the temple mountain will be given over to the beasts
           of the field.

(I read the second last Hebrew word *lᵉbahᵉmôt* as in 5:7; cf. Lam. 5:18 "Mount Zion lies desolate, jackals prowl over it.") The Old Testament has no more devastating oracle than this. After all, God's proper habitation, people believed, was on Zion. And now we hear that it will be levelled with the ground. It will become a heap of ruins, over which jackals will prowl. This saying impressed itself on its hearers so deeply that the elders of Jerusalem quoted it from memory a hundred years later at the trial of Jeremiah (Jer. 26:17–19). To them Micah provided a precedent for Jeremiah's doom oracle against the city and the temple. The elders also recalled the fact that in those earlier days King Hezekiah did not condemn Micah, but repented. On that occasion the recollection of Micah's oracle saved Jeremiah's life. Thus the hard saying continued to function in Israel. And so it is designed to be heard in the church made up of persons from all nations of the world, and to continue to be effective on its trajectory into the future.

What is Micah's accusation? It is directed at the incumbents of various offices, those who are in positions of honor. When their stance is examined, the accusation is threefold. First, they pervert justice and build Zion with blood (vv. 9b–10). Workmen are misused, their just wages denied them (King Jehoiakim is a later example of this, according to Jer. 22:13–17). Second, they are accused of greediness. Judges, priests, prophets are united in one prime concern, the concern for profit, contributions, money. Nothing concerns them, as they go about the duties of their offices, as much as the question of their own advantage and their personal income. The income they receive determines the outcome of their deliberations. Despite all this they appeal to Yahweh—that is the third accusation. When the prophet pronounces judgment upon them, they put their piety out on parade. "Is not the Lord in our midst?" they ask, quoting from their hymnbook (Ps. 46:6). But such "certainty of faith" is unmasked by Micah as hypocrisy, because they are really basing their future on their own contrivances.

"Hear, you peoples, all of you." That is the superscription that stands also over this oracle. Do not at least the churches, living as they do in the midst of the various peoples of the world, examine themselves as to (*a*) what they are doing in the cause of justice for dependent persons and (*b*) what role their involvement in the possession of property plays in the society in which they live? The touchstone of genuine faith will be whether those in positions of responsibility keep the prophet's word in their hearing: "Because of you Zion shall be plowed as a field; Jerusalem shall become a heap of ruins, and the temple mount will be given over to the wild beasts of the field." Even our national churches ought to reckon much more seriously than heretofore with the fact they will no longer be national, that their buildings will become ruins and their sanctuaries assigned to other uses. They ought (together with and on behalf of their people) permit the reason for the catastrophic decline to be exposed: the God of Israel, the Lord of the church, is determined not to be found apart from the least of his brethren. (This was presented to me unforgettably in my first semester here at Bethel in the summer of 1931.) The prophet opens our eyes to the fact that no sacred locale guarantees either God's presence or a secure future at that place. Solely in his judging word does he remain present, determining the future also in these accusations and in the heaps of ruins.

This dark saying of Micah comes from the eighth century. We saw already in Jeremiah 26 how it had been hovering over Jerusalem for a century and more. Hence it was remembered in the days of the Babylonian crisis at the beginning of the sixth century. "It is coming now! Now! Now!" is what the later disciples of Micah say. It is they whom we hear in the threefold "Now" (Mic. 4:9, 11; 5:1) with which reference is made to the approaching crisis of Babylon's conquest of Jerusalem. Only by passing through a complete fulfillment of this word of judgment can there be an entrance into the new age. That is the message of these sayings which begin, it seems, at 4:8 and come to their climax at 5:2 and 5:4. In 4:8–5:4, therefore, we see a nucleus of sayings which take up the message of Micah's original dark saying (3:9–12) and carry it along through times of frightful fulfillment.

(1:2)		3:9–12	4:1–7	4:8–5:4	5:5–14	(5:15)	
E		Micah's	Then	The Nucleus	Then	E	
D	B	Original	Sayings	of Now	Sayings	D	B
I	R	Saying		Oracles		I	R
T	A					T	A
O	C					O	C
R	K					R	K
I	E					I	E
A	T					A	T
L						L	

Encompassing this nucleus of "Now Oracles" (4:8–5:4) on either side is a broad band of other sayings. They speak of the more distant future of Zion and its people. In contrast to the nucleus' four Now Oracles, these sayings on either side are introduced by "Then, at the end of days" (4:1) and similar expressions ("that day" in 4:6 and 5:10, "and then" and "then" in 5:5, 7, 8). Whereas the Now Oracles travel a path of suffering, the main theme of the "Then Sayings" is that path's ultimate goal. If the nucleus of the Now Oracles originated in the time when the Babylonian crisis fulfilled the original doom oracle, the band of Then Sayings which surround that nucleus on either side most likely come from postexilic times. The former deal with Zion's and Israel's fate; the latter, for the most part, with the fate of the nations.[60] The outermost brackets which we noted at 1:2 and 5:15 bring all these sayings to the attention of the nations.[61]

Thus the collection of prophetic oracles in chapters 4 and 5 come to us as the documentation of a tremendous amount of ongoing theological wrestling concerning Zion's and Israel's future in the midst of the world of nations as that future is experienced in various different phases of history. Zion's crisis incited consideration of Zion's significance; the church's crisis likewise incites renewed consideration of what the church is. This collection of sayings permits us to see how Micah's original oracle of judgment (*a*) accompanied Jerusalem on its journey into its future and (*b*) was in turn accompanied by other oracles from the prophet's disciples as they passed through successive catastrophes and were led to the expectation of an ultimate future. Thus these chapters not only offer us the preliminary study for "an ecclesiology in miniature" but also accompany those persons in the international world of peoples who are ready to listen as they pass through very dark stretches of their history. Above all, these chapters incite expectation.

The process of editorial compilation which gave this material its final shape has placed immediately after the announcement of catastrophe in 3-12 (in breathtaking juxtaposition) the great oracle 4:1–4, which designates Zion as the ultimate goal toward which all people travel in their journey through the stars to their ultimate destinies. Mic. 4:1–3 has a parallel in Isa. 2:2–4. There this oracle also follows on the heels of an oracle of judgment for Jerusalem. The parallel indicates that the process of editorial compilation was concerned not only with presenting Micah's original oracles but, beyond that, also with providing prophecy's full range of witness concerning Zion and a guide for Israel and the nations as they travel on their path through history to their goal. Whoever contemplates the deadly guilt and the ruinous downfall of the holy city should also hear immediately thereafter the following paradox,

> ¹But in the latter days it shall come to pass
>> that the mountain of Yahweh's house shall be established as
>> the highest mountain, raised up above the hills.
> Peoples shall flow to it; ²many nations shall come and say,
> "Come, let us go up to the mountain of Yahweh,
>> to the house of the God of Jacob,
> that he may teach us his ways and we may walk in his paths."
>> For out of Zion shall go forth instruction,
>> Yahweh's word from Jerusalem.
> ³He will judge between many peoples,
>> and shall be the judge for mighty nations.
> Then they shall beat their swords into plowshares,
>> and their spears into pruning hooks,
> Nation shall not lift up sword against nation,
>> neither shall they learn war anymore.
> ⁴They shall sit every man under his vine and under his fig tree
> and none shall make them afraid.
>> Thus the mouth of Yahweh of hosts has spoken.

Please note, first of all, the connection between 4:1ff. and 3:12. The catchword, "the mountain of (Yahweh's) house," in v. 1a (cf. v. 2a) refers back to 3:12, as does the mention of Zion and Jerusalem in v. 2b. It is precisely that heap of ruins which becomes the peak most attractive to all peoples of the world. It is precisely the city which had been reduced to a wilderness which becomes the source of ultimate world peace. That—and nothing less than that—is written into the "family history" of a ruined Israel, of a disintegrating, faltering church. We should keep the point in mind: the place of well-deserved historical catastrophes and the place of the promise of ultimate peace are identical! We note that in the promise there is no reference to Israel, its leaders and teachers. A mission emanating from God's people is not even hinted at. Yahweh himself and Yahweh alone establishes something entirely new, something that appears in the midst of the world of peoples coming from the direction of Zion. He establishes new realities.

If we view this "great-expectations oracle" of ours in the context of both the preceding oracle 3:9–12 and of the continuation of the history of Zion in the Christ event at Jerusalem, then it is perfectly clear: despite God's people's guilt, salvation comes to the international world of the nations from the direction of Zion; it comes from Zion's Lord. In the verdict of judgment which Jesus took upon himself before Jerusalem's gates, the foundation is laid for the peace which is valid for all. The abrupt contradiction between 3:12 and 4:1 is overcome only by what comes from the direction of the crucified one. On the other hand, 4:1ff. places us into the tension of an existence between what has already entered the world from the direction of Jesus and what is to be expected for the international world of nations and their ultimate peace from the direction of the promise of 4:1ff. This tension prompts faith to live in hope. This unambiguous promise should make clear the direction in which the church is to travel as it moves in the midst of the nations. By itself this promise gives anyone sufficient motivation for undertaking the study of theology or ministry in the church of the crucified one. This promise alone gives sufficient motivation for listening with careful attention, during the dry periods of the bleak present, to him who established on Zion his enterprise of peace for all.

But what about the people of Zion during the long, frustrating intervening interim? We still behold military activity, heavy with tragedy. That is also what Israel had to take into consideration most soberly as it experienced what contradicted this promise. The next oracle is vividly agitated by this reality.

> All the peoples (still) walk
> each in the name of its god;
> but we walk
> in the name (at the instruction) of Yahweh our God.
> **(4:5)**

Perhaps a certain note of resignation is to be heard as it is here stated that for the present the peoples are not yet thinking of linking their destinies to the pilgrimage to Zion. They are still by and large living lives of self-justification, instead of recognizing their guilt; they are still seeking protection in their own security measures rather than in following the crucified one; their pride must still experience God's opposition, while his grace waits for them to humble themselves. "All the peoples still go their own ways, each in the name of its god."

But that should not prevent the humbled community of Zion which lives in the midst of the world of nations from resolutely setting out for itself on the path of following the Lord of Zion. The church is engaged in thinking about the future of the international world of all peoples precisely to the extent that it not only speaks but also lives in accord with the voice which comes from Zion. Precisely when the peoples of our world continue to engage in war, the people of Zion should travel the path of peace; "but we will walk in the name of the Lord our God." To participate in what is indicated in the words "but we"—that alone, I repeat, provides adequate motivation for undertaking a vigorous study of theology, i.e., for seeking to know the God of Zion more clearly. Thus humans become witnesses of the future. Otherwise humankind has no future.

In the next oracle (4:6f.) the goal is even more distant. The pronouncement is addressed to the community that has survived the painful catastrophe announced in 3:12. That community, after the burning of Jerusalem, is in danger of succumbing to sheer depression as a beaten, dislodged company. To these hopeless survivors the message is shouted,

> ⁶In that day, says Yahweh,
>   I will assemble those who limp.
>   I will gather those who have been dispersed
>   and those whom I have brought into disaster.
> ⁷And those who are lame I will make a remnant;
>   those who are wounded I will make a strong nation.
> The Lord will be king over them
>   on Mount Zion from this time forth and forevermore.

This is addressed, then, first of all to the exiles, persons who had lost all those things that make for political stability: their territory, the institutions of an independent nation, and even their central sanctuary, the temple with its well-ordered worship of God. How can a structure that has been blown apart like that continue to exist in world history among the nations? The fact that it has nevertheless continued to exist and still exists permits us to gain some inkling of the actual sustaining power of the prophets' promise and of its ability to create an effective history in the future. In view of this experience which its predecessor has had with the promise of its God in a hopeless situation, the Christian church should perk up its ears, even where it has become, or is becoming a people who limp, who are wounded, decimated. What still remains its hope? The "I" of its God, who still addresses precisely those who are languishing amid unmistakable signs of external and internal dissolution. Precisely this is his hour for a new beginning. "Those who limp I will make a remnant." Despite its doleful connotations, the word "remnant" is here a concept of salvation, of promise fulfilled, of survival assured. The "remnant" is the community of those who have been liberated from the prison into which God's judgment had put them. Its synonym in v. 7a is, surprisingly, "strong nation," the same expression used at 4:3a for the superpowers whom God is leading toward peace. Now, however, wounded Israel is raised to the height of the superpowers. Only as a people battered and wounded but also rehabilitated by Yahweh does the people of God become "a superpower." Its wounds are actually its strength. That fact the lame and the halt should grasp firmly.

Verse 7b moves from Yahweh's speaking in first person (vv. 6–7a) to a statement about Yahweh (third person). This addition underscores the fact that Yahweh shows himself on Zion "from this time forth and forevermore" as king over his community, which was formerly scattered and languishing, but now is gathered and invigorated. So the community that has been rescued by way of catastrophe is already an advance token of God's ultimate dominion, a dominion to which all people are called.

How does this royal rule of Yahweh take place? The passage 4:8–5:4 tells how it will take place for "the daughter of Zion" (4:8, 10, 13); the verses 5:5–14 add a description of how it takes place among the nations. At v. 8 we turn away from peering far into the distance (toward the ultimate) in order to focus on what is nearer and penultimate for the community that suffers in order to learn the next steps it is to take through its afflictions. Verse 8 strikes the dominant tone,

> And you, O tower of the flock, hill of the daughter of Zion,
> to you the former royal rule shall come,
> the kingdom of the daughter of Jerusalem.

Zion's title here is strange: "O tower of the flock"; it can hardly refer to a specific place; rather, it seems to describe devastated Jerusalem in which, after the fulfillment of the judgment announced in 3:12, only flocks move about. The former royal rule, the former glory of the royal residence has disappeared! But, according to this promise, it will show itself as a preview of what will come in the future. It will return, coming, however, only by way of bitter times of trouble. That sad route is described by the subsequent three oracles in three different ways. They all challenge the hearer to say first, "yes" to a painful "now," viz., to the hour in which the doom announced in 3:12 is historically fulfilled by the Babylonians in 598 and 587. One of Micah's later disciples calls out first of all, entirely in keeping with his old teacher (4:9–10),

> 9Now why do you cry aloud?
> Is there no king in you?
> Has your counselor perished,
> that pangs have seized you like a woman in travail?

¹⁰Writhe and groan, O daughter of Zion, like a woman in travail,
    for now you shall go forth from the city;
and dwell in the open country;
    you shall go to Babylon.
There you shall be rescued;
    there the Lord will redeem you from the hands of your
    enemies.

The troubles resulting from Jerusalem's fall are clearly recognizable here. With deep irony inquiry is made concerning the whereabouts of the king (Zedekiah had fled at the last moment). Outside the city in the open country groups of Babylon-bound deportees will be organized. There first (in Babylon), there (the word is repeated twice) Zion's God will show himself as redeemer and liberator—in the midst of his people's deepest humiliation.

The second oracle of the Now nucleus reminds one of the same time of siege with its opening words (4:11–13),

¹¹And now many nations are assembled against you.
    They say, "Let her be profaned, let our eyes gaze upon Zion
    with joy at her misfortune."
¹²But they do not know the thoughts of Yahweh,
    they do not understand his plan,
    that he has gathered them as sheaves for the threshing floor.
¹³"Arise and thresh, O daughter of Zion, for I will make your horn
iron and your hoofs bronze!
    You shall break in pieces many peoples, in order that you may
    dedicate their gain to Yahweh and their wealth to the Lord of
    the whole earth."

This oracle places before our eyes the city of God: under siege, the nations' choking hands at her throat, brutally mocked. But the nations' plan has long since been reversed in the thoughts of the Zion community's Lord: those who gathered to destroy Jerusalem are gathered for their own demise. The paradox can hardly be put more strikingly: the threshed daughter of Zion will herself thresh the peoples.[62] But she does this neither by her own power ("*I* will make your horn iron . . . and bronze" says the Lord), nor for her own gain and glory ("that you may dedicate their gain to Yahweh and their wealth to the Lord of the whole earth"). Thus is pictured with the ancient world's typical vividness how the current situation of those besieged by the superpowers will be changed. If in the subsequent history of the Zion community Jesus bears the guilt and judgment not only of Israel but also of the nations, then the new Zion community has only to overcome the nations as a messenger of reconciliation and thus be able to bring their treasure to the reconciler.

The third Now Oracle in our characteristically Old Testament "Brief Prolegomenon to the Doctrine of the Church" pushes much further in the direction of the messiah Jesus. It also begins, first of all, with the community's current time of troubles, 5:1-2, 4 (with an afterthought inserted at 5:3).

> [1]Now scratch yourself to pieces in lamentation,
>> O daughter of robber bands!
> Siege has been laid against us.
>> With a rod they have smitten the ruler of Israel on the cheek.
> [2]But you, O Bethlehem Ephrathah, who are little among the clans of Judah,
>> from you shall come forth for me he who is to be ruler in Israel,
>> whose origin is from old, from ancient days.
> [3](Therefore he gives them up until the time when she who is in travail has brought forth; then the rest of his brothers shall return to the people of Israel.)
> [4]And he will step forth and as a shepherd shall feed his flock
> in the strength of the Lord
> in the majesty of the name of Yahweh, his God.
>> And they shall dwell securely
>>> for then he shall be great
>>>> to the ends of the earth.

Let us note first that this well-known oracle, like both those that preceded it, is addressed to the battered and guilty community. The daughter of Zion had become a "daughter of robber bands" (this title recalls the violence and greed of the leaders of the Zion community which was pilloried at 3:9ff.). The command that she scratch and disfigure herself in lamentation and thus perform the ritual of contrition and repentance, reminds us (as does the wordplay *tithgōdᵉdî bath gᵉdûd*) of Micah's own artistic language (he formulates similarly at 1:10–16).[63] It is, in fact, by no means excluded that the wording of this entire oracle originates with him; for the announcement of the coming ruler's origin from

Bethlehem more likely also goes back to a native Judean like Micah than to any of his successors. If, in fact, an original authentic Micah oracle at this point is the kernel of the Now Oracle nucleus which begins at 4:9, then we can also understand that nucleus' introduction at 4:8 as a parallel to its original Mican model in 5:2 (parallel both in its theme, the renewed royal rule "going forth" from Bethlehem and "coming" to "the daughter of Zion," and in its adversative introduction: "but you, O tower of the flock," paralleling "but you, O Bethlehem"). The situation of Micah's original oracle one would have to imagine to have been Jerusalem besieged and its sacrosanct ruler being profaned by Sennacherib. The situation of the later parallel 4:8 (also 4:9 and 4:11) would then be the catastrophe of 587. In any case this oracle is also addressed to the people of God who are ripe for catastrophe.

But it is precisely to this people that the Messiah is announced. However, instead of coming out of the dynasty of the sons of David in Jerusalem, he comes out of Bethlehem, the unprepossessing and militarily insignificant place in Judah (it was little among the clans which contributed levies to Judah's citizen army). God's royal rule in Zion (4:8) comes to its fulfillment through the shepherd king from Bethlehem (5:2, 4). Bethlehem reminds us of the Israelite monarchy's humble beginnings. Thence came in the hoary past the erstwhile despised youngest son of Jesse. So when its great leaders are first buffeted and then deposed, Zion should think back to its origin in ancient days. Despite its Lord's lowly origin, it should be certain that he will step forth with divine authority as the royal shepherd (v. 4a; the insert, v. 3, again reminds us of the difficult interim of the exile). "Step forth and feed"—what does that mean? It means that, in defiance of the entire situation, he will protect and defend Zion so that it need not fear; he will take care of it and nourish it, so that it will not waste away; he will lead and guide it, so that it will have before it an open road that will bring it to the goal.

The goal is described in the words, "she will dwell." This means that all confused wandering about and all painful being-driven-about will cease. We are reminded of the promise in 4:4 about each person "dwelling under his own vine and fig tree," i.e., in complete peace. And the extent of the shepherd's royal dominion, "to the ends of the earth" (5:4b) also reminds us of the universal viewpoint in 4:1–4. The passage that follows surveys once again the route by which it will travel into the end time (the *eschaton*). In the passage, vv. 5–6, the unit v. 5a and v. 6b differs from the unit inserted into it, vv. 5b–6a. The subject of the former is the shepherd of v. 4,

> 5aAnd then he will be Lord of peace . . .
> 6bhe will deliver us from Assyria, when it comes into our land
> and treads upon our soil.

Even amid the dangers of their history the shepherd will succor his people. The subject of the inserted statements, on the other hand, is "we." And the statements latch on to v. 6bβ ("Assyria, when it comes into our land and treads upon our soil").

> 5bThen we will raise seven shepherds against it (Assyria) and
> eight princes of men.
> 6aThey shall feed the land of Assyria with the sword and the land
> of Nimrod with the drawn sword.

According to this insert the hard-pressed people undertake once again, it appears, to protect themselves with drawn swords. If we pay attention to the New Testament (as the canon within the canon that provides the ultimate frame of reference for all of what is said here), it is clear that what is old and long since obsolete (vv. 5b–6a) is to be nicely differentiated from the promise of the new in the old (v. 5a and v. 6b). Self-protection by means of violent action gives way to sheer expectation, expectation of the shepherd from Bethlehem who will come with ultimate authority.

The two subsequent oracles in vv. 7–8 place us before a similar variety of expectations.[64] It is a question of the people of God's ultimate function among the nations. Verse 5:7 reads,

> And then the remnant of Jacob shall be
>   in the midst of many peoples
> like dew from the Lord,
>   like showers upon growing plants,
> which hope not on men
>   nor wait for the sons of men.

The "remnant of Jacob" is again the community which was rescued as it passed through well-deserved judgment. Its universal importance for the whole world is described in the word picture about the dew, which says two things. First, dew falls unobtrusively. Unlike a downpour, it is hardly noticed; and still it moistens everything so completely that, e.g., during the completely rainless months in Palestine it bestows on vineyards vigorous prosperity. Thus the remnant of Jacob will be among the nations: unobtrusive, hardly noticed, and yet extremely effective. Second, for people of antiquity dew had a thoroughly puzzling origin; it certainly did not come from the gardener. So it is described as what is not expected to come from men. The Zion community's worldwide effectiveness is apparent in the fact that it receives spiritual vitality as well as political and social success from its Lord alone, not from human potentates.

An abrupt parallel to this oracle about the dew is the shocking oracle in 5:8,

> And then the remnant of Jacob shall be in the midst of many peoples
>> like a lion among the beasts of the forest,
>>> like a young lion among the flocks of sheep,
>> which, when it goes through, pounces on them
>>> and tears them to pieces, and there is none to deliver.

For our modern sensibilities this oracle cannot be harmonized with the one about the dew. Yet nothing about it, either in its style or in its context, points to an author different from that of v. 7. In its native Old Testament context it does supplement the oracle about the dew. Alongside the community's mysteriously effective function of bestowing blessing is placed the picture of the lion, a promise of the invincible superiority of Jacob's remnant. In that respect this oracle also corresponds to the promise which the New Testament community has received. If, however, its hope of invincibility is explained by the lion "who, when he goes through, pounces on the prey, tearing it to pieces, with no hope of rescue," then this feature is fulfilled not, in the first instance, by what has occurred with the advent of Christ but by what our earlier eschatological oracle promises in 4:1–4 and also in 5:7 about the future peace among nations coming out of Zion. Perhaps the oracle attached to v. 9 is to be understood as a petition, one which points to the fact that the conquest of the opponents, as a punitive judgment, is left to God alone. For we hear in 5:9,

> Lift up your hand, O Lord, against your adversary,
>   so that all your enemies shall be destroyed.

But even as a prayer, it belongs to those Old Testament prayers against the enemies which have been superseded by 4:1–4 and from which the New Testament community should learn to do the very opposite (to aid its enemies).

The last lengthy oracle (5:10–14) leads us back to the point from which we set out, insofar as it shows that God's judging activity is in the first instance directed not against foreigners, but against the Zion community itself. That it is directed against Zion is underlined by the fact that the introductory formula of 4:6 ("in that day, says Yahweh") is taken up in 5:10 (after 4:1 "and then, at the end of days"):

> ¹⁰And then, in that day, says Yahweh,
>   I will cut off your horses from among you
>   and I will destroy your chariots,
> ¹¹And I will cut off the cities of your land
>   and tear down all your strongholds.
> ¹²Then I will cut off the magic charms you use
>   so that you shall be without soothsayers.
> ¹³Then I will cut off your idols and sacred stone pillars from your midst,
>   so that you will bow down no more
>   to the works of your hands.
> ¹⁴(And I will root out the images of the goddess Asherah
>   in your land and destroy your cities).

In this passage the judgment of 3:12 and the promise of 4:1–4 about Zion being the source of world peace are skillfully combined. Four times the series of statements in vv. 10–13 begin with the execration formula, "I will cut off," except that these statements are here directed not against individual culprits who endanger the existence of the community (as in Lev. 17:10; 20:3, 5, 6) but against the objects of false trust, objects from which the entire community must be liberated by one great act of purgation. God deals with his people most harshly. "I will cut off . . .

destroy . . . tear down . . . root out." What is struck down by this purge? Two conveyors of power are mentioned, which then and now continually endanger God's people in their existence in the presence of God and therewith in their service among the peoples of the world. First mentioned are the instruments of political and military power (vv. 10–11): chariots and strongholds, designed for offensive and defensive enterprises. Mentioned second are the religious means of guaranteeing self-security that were customary in Israel's world: magic charms, soothsayers and other religious paraphernalia. Both are included in the expression "the work of your hands" (v. 13b). The sole purpose of God's hard-hitting purge is, according to v. 13b, "so that you will worship no more the things that you yourselves have made." Israel had not been mentioned, not with a single syllable, in the earlier promise (4:1–4) that the nations will make their pilgrimage to the dispenser of peace. Now the compilers of the tradition supplement that viewpoint by adding here at the end of the collection: only through God's activity of destruction within his own community does the community become the place of peace where all defensive and offensive concentrations of power have been destroyed along with all means of carrying on occult religious practices which are to guarantee its independence and security. Precisely by being stripped of its power Zion is equipped for trusting its God-given call to promote peace. The nations will be overcome only by an Israel that has itself been purged.

Up to this point the oracles of our collection referred mostly to Israel. And yet the oracle which functions as the initial bracket of its final edition, 1:2, showed us that the nations should direct their attention to all the subsequent oracles. The final bracket (5:15) underlines that last point once again with a certain amount of coarse harshness, employing the "I style" of the preceding Yahweh oracle.

> And in my great anger and wrath
> I will execute vengeance on the nations
> if they have not hearkened.

Here at the end of the collection three things are set forth with a firmness and directness characteristic of the Old Testament.

First, the reason for universal confusion in the world is exposed. When the founder of peace from Zion is unrecognized and despised, then the wrath of God is at work in tumultuous turbulences. Even in the New Testament it is impossible to bypass Christ and still escape God's wrath. Only in him has that wrath been swallowed up. Second, this final statement intends once again to prompt the nations to hearken. Hearkening or failing to hearken, that is the point where the decision is made between salvation and damnation, peace and war, rescue and catastrophe. The future is what is at stake in such hearkening or failing to hearken unto God's work and word to Israel and in Israel. Theology is relevant only as an introduction to such hearkening. Third, the direct and indirect summons to the nations to hearken is directed toward very diverse stretches of the path which Zion travels in its history and is intended therefore to influence the most diverse phases of that history: those who are self-secure in the midst of injustice receive the announcement of catastrophe; those who cringe in utmost danger experience new hope. Precisely by passing through its own tests of suffering Zion is equipped to be the witness to, and forerunner for, the God who lifts up those who have been humbled and gathers those who have been dispersed. Let us not forget: it was precisely the time of stress that made the remnant of Jacob a refreshing "dew" from the Lord for all peoples (5:7). Its final task in history is this: to begin, despite everything, the journey through the stars toward the goal where all swords and spears will be recast into plowshares and pruning hooks.

Clear Principles:[65]
Micah 6

On the twentieth of January, 1977, just over four months ago, Jimmy Carter took office as the president of the United States of America; on that occasion he placed his hand, as is customary, on the Bible while taking his oath of office. Do you know, dear friends, to what passage he had opened the Bible? He told us at the beginning of his inaugural address, "To take my oath of office I put my hand on the timeless passage of the ancient prophet Micah." And then he read Mic. 6:8 (KJV), "He hath showed thee, O man, what is good; and what doth the Lord require of thee, but to do justly, and to love mercy, and to walk humbly with thy God?" A change of presidents is a milestone in the life of the United States. A similar sort of turning point should occur in the life of every person when he asks the question anew (and permits himself to be told the answer again), "What is really good for a person (for me, for my fellow citizens)?" Let us conduct a little quiz, in the hope that the result may foster a change of government in our lives! Let us ask ourselves the question, "What, in our opinion and that of our average contemporary, is really good for us humans?" I would almost like to have you each write your own answer on a piece of paper (or, if you prefer, come up with an answer in your mind).

What is good for a person? What is good for a human being? The more honest we are, the more diverse our answers will be in this area. All right! What have we written down? "To have plenty of money and lots of vacations!" Or, "to accept all that is enjoyable in life with thanksgiving." Or, "to be in charge of a large personnel staff." Or, "to be able to do our work without having to depend on others." Or, "to be able to demonstrate exceptional accomplishments." Or, "to hear nothing; to see nothing; simply to be able to rest, to rest, nothing but rest." What is good for a person? To enjoy life? To win the game of life? To enjoy undisturbed quiet? Or . . . ? What do you think?

All right. After this spiritual sitting-up exercise, we now join Jimmy Carter in opening our Bibles to the concise answer in the book of the prophet Micah. And we go about making ourselves face up to this answer, because science, technology, and politics do not give us an answer. Yet the answer which we first consider likely, then adopt as our own, the consequences of which we are finally prepared to live with—that answer is vitally important not only for each of us personally (and not only for a consideration, like today's, of "Christian Social Service from Prophetic Perspective") but also for politics, yes, for all thinking that is done in our scientific and technological world. The prophet's answer is shocking already in its introduction, "It has been shown you, O man, what is good and what the Lord requires of you."

According to this statement what is good is "what the Lord requires of you." "The Lord requires"—is that thought alien to us? alienating? disturbing? What does it call to mind? It straightforwardly tells us that we humans have not created ourselves; none of us is able to do that. Even when humankind is considered only as part of creation, by itself it is unable to know what is really good for itself. Must not its Creator tell that to it? What is good for my watch is something my watchmaker knows, not my watch. But does the Creator tell us what is good for us, his human creatures? The context of our chapter shows that God is engaged in an important conversation with his people. In fact, the entire Old Testament bears witness to the conversation God carried on with ancient Israel. And the New Testament, with the advent of Jesus, draws all humanity into this conversation. Micah 6 shows at the outset how God's conversation with Israel takes place before the forum of creation, for vv. 1–2 begin thus,

Hear ye what the Lord is saying:
"Arise, plead your case before the mountains
and let the hills hear your voice!"

(What magnificent mountain scenery now appears on the stage!)

Hear, ye mountains, how the Lord is going to present his case,
　and listen, ye foundations of the earth,
for the Lord has a case against his people,
　and he is going to bring an accusation against Israel.

Two things are to be noted in this gripping introduction.

1. The earth's heights and depths are enlisted as witnesses.
God's conversation with his people takes place before a global
forum. Today we recognize that the question about what is good
for humanity affects the cosmos, the world of creation. Where in
the depth of the earth should we bury atomic waste for the next
thousand years? Our answer to the question about what is good
has worldwide consequences, no matter whether we deal with it
as individuals or as groups, no matter whether it is a question of
oil from the North Sea and its present consequences or the last
barrel of oil that can be supplied by Iran in 1993. Today we must
be aware of the far-reaching consequences of any decision we
make about what is good for us.

2. What is good is a matter in dispute between God and his
people. God is bringing accusations against his people and, what
is more astounding, he is seeing himself accused by his people,
for that is the way the disputation begins in v. 3. "What have I
done to you! In what respect have I demanded too much of you?
Answer me!" Old Testament form critical exegetes like myself
categorize what we are dealing with here as a sort of speech in
self-defense. God is here speaking to his people like a defendant.
"What have I done to you; in what way have I demanded too
much of you?" The questions presuppose that Israel had been
raising accusations against its Creator, yes, is even in the process
of renouncing all ties with him. The Lord's demand that Israel
give answer, that it undertake honest self-examination remains,
however, without an echo of response from Israel. Overburdened,
exhausted humanity no longer gives any response to God. Do you
not see, dear friends, how God is at great pains in his concern for
humankind? He presses Israel even somewhat tempestuously, because he is waiting for his people's answer. But humankind no
longer knows how to speak with God. Having become silent in
God's presence, humanity has nothing more to say to him.

But, marvel of marvels, God continues to carry on his conversation with obstinate, uncommunicative humans. That is something Israel experienced anew a thousand times over, in spite of its obstinacy and of its pitiful situation. Here he reminds his people of what he had done for them (v. 4), "I brought you up from the land of Egypt; I redeemed you from the house of bondage." The situation is not that Israel's God has oppressed and overburdened Israel; rather, God is the one who has rescued Israel from being oppressed and overburdened, and has led it forth to freedom. Furthermore, he reminds Israel of the fact (v. 4b) that his divine sovereignty has not been exposed to uncertain religious speculations; rather, at the critical hour he legitimatized human messengers, "I sent before you Moses, Aaron, and Miriam." Why precisely these three? The Targum (the late Aramaic paraphrase of the Old Testament that was regularly read in the synagogues) explains why these three persons are mentioned. He sent Moses as revealer of God's will, that Israel might learn what was right. He sent Aaron as the atonement-making priest, who should free Israel from the burden of guilt when the people failed to live up to God's will. And he sent Miriam to be the special teacher of women.

Furthermore, v. 5 says, "Remember, O my people, how your God intervened when you were in danger. Balak intended to bring curses and ruin down upon Israel, but despite that Balaam had to call out blessings upon Israel." At critical junctures, "from Shittim to Gilgal" (Shittim being the last camp in Transjordan and Gilgal the first one "this side of the Jordan") God made it possible for them to take the decisive steps. To what purpose does God recall all these events? Verse 5b answers, "that you may realize what the Lord did in order to save you." In the examples mentioned, the prophet is presenting only a prelude to what would happen in the New Testament. God's goodness climaxes in his sacrificing himself for all, as this is presented to us step by step in the life of Jesus. So it is not a matter of fantasizing or speculating about God—not even a minute is spent on that here. The gods which result from philosophers' fantasies and speculations are stillborn. It is rather a matter of reading from the events of history what authoritative messengers have certified to be God's saving deeds for Israel and for humankind.

What is good for humans? Let us, in view of all that will follow, first keep in mind the fact that Israel is to keep clearly in view God's past deeds of salvation. In fact, God is wrestling with his people in this debate in order that those acts of his may be remembered. Otherwise every answer to the question, "What is good for humankind?" will be wrong. Those who forget what God has done to remove the burden will be overburdened. Those who deny their Creator end up being uncreative and exhausted. The Creator is not discontinuing his creative activity for us and in us. Hence Luther's translation of the first item in v. 8 says that what is good for humankind is "to keep God's word." Luther means that humanity should keep clearly in view the saving acts of God to which the biblical witnesses testify.

Before examining in detail the neatly polished answers in v. 8, however, let us listen to a single voice that is heard in our chapter after the prophet's reference to God's good guidance of his ungrateful people. Here we again note, as we did yesterday[66] when we became acquainted with the tumult surrounding Micah, that the voice of a prophet who transmits God's summons to his people never remains a solitary voice. We hear in vv. 6–7 a voice which responds. It is a solitary, hesitant voice, "With what dare I come before the Lord, and bow myself before God on high?" A solitary individual is grieved by Israel's repudiation of God. He poses the counterquestion, "What then is it good for humans to do in God's presence? What is good in view of the final uncompromising standard?" That is the ultimate question. This individual, with an almost monstrous escalation of zeal, tests out the possibilities: "A whole burnt offering in which a bullock goes up in flames as the offering?" In that case the entire capital investment is sacrificed and nothing is left over for human enjoyment. "A one-year-old calf?" In that case an especially precious possession is sacrificed. "Thousands of rams?" Something like that occurs only at such magnificent celebrations as Solomon's coronation, 1 Chron. 29:21, when thousands of rams were sacrificed. That is something only a king can afford, and then only on special occasions; in that case a fortune is sacrificed, one that would support a normal family for a long time to come. "Countless streams of oil?" Oil, olive oil! We have little conception of what olive oil meant for the people of antiquity with its varied uses—as human sustenance, providing the decisive supplement for promoting bodily vigor; as protection of the skin against sunburn; and as antiquity's equivalent of modern beauty care. Shall this precious gift be expended to no avail?

At the climax of the possible offerings is the gift of "the firstborn, one's own son." Abraham had been released from the obligation of sacrificing his son. In the present context it is seemingly considered the highest type of sacrifice for a misspent life. We note that what is here exaggerated to an almost pathological extent is religious readiness and awe-inspired risk in approaching God, total submission to the Lord of heaven. In each of these cases sacrifices are proffered; renunciation is exercised; surrender to God takes place. Nothing is kept back for humans or gained for them. Such religiosity as is here expressed by the solitary voice demands respect. But our individual voice goes no further than asking the question, "With what then should I dare to come forward?" He asks it with great uncertainty. The famous answer comes only later. And when it does come (v. 8), it will not accept any one of these suggestions. Such renunciations or sacrifices for God's sake do not belong to what is good for humanity. Stating the matter thus in negative terms is in itself already something not unimportant. But if one is to state it positively, one must ask, "What then is good?"

Now there follows in Mic. 6:8 the famous answer which humans dare never cease considering. It is worthwhile pricking up one's ears for every single word here. Even the introduction is important, "It has been told you, O man, what is good and what the Lord demands from you." "It has been told you!" Ever since Moses and the prophets it has been told. Nothing new need be said to answer the questions as to what is good for man. Instead, what has been told should be heard anew. Jesus said, "If they do not hear Moses and the prophets, neither will they be convinced if someone should rise from the dead" (Luke 16:31). You, dear friends, know this reply to the rich man's concern in the parable about Lazarus. Accordingly, this is what is good for humankind: to discover anew that what has already been proclaimed is what has a future. To proffer that is what the church, the Christian community, and the brotherhoods dare never become weary in doing. These groups do not have to be ashamed of listening again to what had been said long ago, as they travel on their way into the future. "It has been told you, O man." At this point it is no longer the people who are addressed, as in v. 2 ("he has a case against his people") or in vv. 3–5, where "my people, my people" are addressed in so many words. Rather, it is the solitary person who posed the question in vv. 6–7 who is being addressed. Every individual must gain clarity about what is good for humanity. Only then can an authentic community grow, a new type of human, who is able to withstand mass psychoses induced by life lived in subjection to tyrants; this growth always begins with the individual's listening and gaining certainty. That becomes completely clear in the life of Jesus and in the call he gives his disciples to follow him, but we see it already here in the Old Testament. No one should therefore be concerned about the extension of our work of Christian social service to include broad areas. The Brotherhood (and now I am going to make my final point about the expression "it has been told you, O man," an expression which we must inscribe on our memory)—the Brotherhood lives from the watchfulness of every single individual of its members.

Similarly every individual lives, in turn, from the supporting social group to which he belongs. There is a reciprocity here, in which neither of these two beats of the heart dare be missing. But the individual person, the human being who has been called by God, *does* have something more pressing to do, for the present, than concerning himself with others; he has to listen to "what the Lord requires of you." The word "require" is a bit harsh for what is meant by the original; it might be better translated, "it has been told you what the Lord seeks of you, what he expects of you." The idea is that he stands before your door and expects you to let him enter. With his question about what is good, a person is not directed to depend on others (not to mention depending on the majority or the masses). A person first stands alone before his waiting Lord. That makes a person independent, able to stand on his own two feet; that also makes him a worthwhile member of society, of the brotherhood into which God fits him, providing he is listening to what the Lord expects of him.

PRACTICING JUSTICE (DOING WHAT GOD
HAS COMMANDED)

What does God expect? There follow the three famous classical
answers, which Jimmy Carter discussed in his own way. The first
is translated by Luther (as we have already noted), "to keep
God's word." We saw that this translation is justified insofar as the
remembrance of God's foundational deeds of salvation and of his
rescuing help is the presupposition of all that is good for humankind. Stated in terms of its content, that is the foundation, as we
saw in vv. 3–5. When we investigate the original Hebrew formulation, however, then we find that it expresses simply and clearly
what was also available to President Carter in his English translation and what the Zürich Bible's translation also provides,
namely, the Lord requires of you nothing more than "doing justice." The expression here "doing justice" is not a general statement about "God's word that must be kept." Instead it means,
"effecting or putting into operation a just social order," i.e., fulfilling the commandments, practicing a just order of activity.
What that means in practical terms is: actualizing the will of God
in one's own environment or vicinity, the will which was entrusted to Israel at Sinai.

What is therefore now being considered is what is good for a
human to do. That sounds simple. But it is everything else but
self-evident; it implies the total change of governance in a human being's life, when what has become old and traditional is
heard anew. It means guiding one's activity not according to personal advantage, not according to personal comfort, not according
to the desire to dominate, but according to God's will as that is
formulated, for instance, in the Decalogue. That is what is good;
otherwise people get into hopeless confusion. We do not have the
time now to mention many concrete illustrations, but one can be
added as a supplement to what was said yesterday.

One of the brothers called my attention to the fact that yesterday[67] I improperly omitted from comment a sentence from Micah
2. Given the great number of statements in that chapter, such an
omission is understandable. He was thinking of the part (2:9b)
where the injustice of "a society which is hostile to children" is
pilloried. I did, of course, refer to the fact that women of the peo-

ple were being driven off by those who were dominated by a desire for power and were being separated from their beloved children. But I did not expressly explain that it is precisely the beloved children who are protected by Micah. The prophet's accusation is "You are robbing them of my honor forever." Particularly in our society where hostility to, and unconcern for, children is rife, we ought to point out what is to be done, both as to what is just and as to what is commanded. What does this mean, however, "From their children you are taking away my honor forever"? What is "my honor"? At this point one thinks of Ps. 8:5, "You have crowned man with glory and honor." It is particularly the common man, the person who is in need of aid who is adorned by God with glory and with honor, something that shows itself in his independence and sovereignty within nature. But at the same time "my honor" can remind us that children also should be God's honor by praising him (Ps. 8:2). In any case that is how Jesus understood it when he referred to Psalm 8 in Matt. 21:16, "Out of the mouth of infants you have prepared praise," since they were honoring and magnifying him. This reference to children is a necessary supplement, and I invite you all to continue the search in these texts for other references to "doing justice." Since Micah seldom gets a hearing, scarcely once each hundred years, you have the opportunity of making a number of pertinent discoveries.

In what follows (vv. 10–12), the prophet scourges damnably false measures and weights as well as lying tongues. So we see he is now taking aim at the merchants. How up-to-date the Old Testament is (v. 12): "(Jerusalem's) rich men are full of lawlessness and broad strata of its inhabitants tell lies." Aren't we also suffering from periodic price fixing by industry and commerce on the one hand and on the other by a disastrous increase of theft in our stores and university libraries? Theft by one group is justified by an exorbitant increase in prices by the other, and vice versa. On the one hand enticing advertisements fail to describe merchandise adequately while on the other hand, lying is defended by deceivers as justifiable self-protection. In this respect our cities and townships are disaster areas. On all sides the danger threatens that "good is called evil and evil good," a condition which receives Isaiah's woes (5:20), as we heard yesterday. Thus individuals lose their sense of direction and society is being ruined, while no one objects. It is devastating that such extenuations of lawlessness are passed off as political or psychological necessities. Theft can no longer be called theft; lying is no longer lying. Thus we are thrust out into uncertainties and, psychologically, exposed to life in a veritable no-man's-land. Community life is devastated when people imagine that they are living by themselves and are able, by themselves and by arbitrary methods, to level things out or confuse good and evil, without having to live in the presence of their Creator and Liberator. The Christian community has the task of setting an example of living with new clarity and with clear principles, and of illustrating what is really good for humans, putting into practice in their own little world the wholesome will of God, his statutes for a just order. That means in plain words really getting to know the Ten Commandments. What can be expected, however, by those who order their lives according to personal advantage the prophet describes a bit later. In vv. 14–15 he says without mincing words,

14You shall eat
  but not be satisfied
What you put aside
  you will not be able to save.
What you save
  I will give to the sword.
15You shall sow,
  but not reap
You shall tread olives,
  but not anoint yourselves with oil;
You shall tread grapes,
  but not drink wine.

There is a real future then only for one enterprise: actually putting into practice the good and justice-bent will of God in the world in which one lives. That is why this is what is good for humanity. The clear answer of the Old Testament should not be put out of focus by shifting attention to the New Testament and our present situation. Christ does not eliminate the force of God's commandments; if anything, he makes them even more radical. When he forgives sins, he presupposes that sin is sin and that a new beginning cannot be made without forgiveness and triumph over guilt.

FOSTERING COMMUNITY SOLIDARITY (LOVING MERCY)

The first description of what is good ("doing what has been commanded") is continued in 6:8 where a second answer is added to the question about what is good for humankind. It is translated by Luther "to practice love." Actually this is not a second item; rather, it is to be understood only as a clarification or commentary on the first. For to put God's will for justice into practice is, in essence, "to practice love," since that is the goal of his commandment; on it the entire law hangs. At this point it is also worthwhile to investigate the original wording. For us a translation like "to practice love," or "to love," has become too bland, too ambiguous. In the original the word is *hesed.* (Yesterday you leared the word "*hôy,*" "woe!"; your Hebrew word for today is *hesed.*) I prefer to translate it as "sense for community solidarity" or better "sense for shared community."

What is meant becomes clear from several examples. When, according to Joshua 2, the harlot Rahab bids farewell to the Israelite spies whom she has hidden in her house, she says, as she lets them down by a rope from her house on the city wall, "Now then, when you come and conquer Jericho, remember that I showed you *hesed*" (v. 12). This is not "love" as we understand that word, nor yet "kindness"; rather, she means, "I have shown that I have made common cause with you, that I have practiced a sense of community solidarity with you." A second example is in 1 Sam. 15:6 where Saul smites the Amalekites, yet spares the Kenites who led a nomadic existence within Amalekite territory, because when Israel came up out of Egypt, the Kenites showed Israel *hesed,* i.e., declared their solidarity with them. They joined forces and made common cause with Israel; they practiced a sense of shared community. This is the purpose served by all commandments: they are to enable people to continue to experience wholesome community with God and also to strengthen wholesome community among men; that is what was intended.

Hesed occurs in the well-known refrain in the Psalter (e.g., Ps. 118:1, a refrain often used today as a prayer at meals), "Give thanks to the Lord, for he is good and his 'mercy' endures forever" ("mercy" is how Luther translates it, but the original is "his *ḥesed* endures forever"). I prefer to translate, "Magnify Yahweh, because he is gracious, he is bound to us forever." *Ḥesed,* therefore, refers to the relationship of being bound together, be it God bound to man, or man to man. *Ḥesed* establishes community; it refers to the goodwill which aims at shared community. The Old Testament clearly says that God's statutes for a just order are not fulfilled when all that happens is that punishment is inflicted according to correct procedure; only when broken community is healed for all involved does God's justice reach its goal. That is why Christians, above all, should see to it that the meting out of punishment be more in accord with the Old Testament (which implies that it be also more in accord with the New Testament). What is needed is not the passing of laws, but the restoration of new community, of living in community solidarity with those who have become liable to punishment. As far as our "migrants" or "nonresidents" are concerned (about whom there is fortunately a lot of discussion here in Bethel), the church ought to remember that in its first stages it led a nomadic existence in the society of that day; we are thinking of Israel's journeying through the wilderness after the exodus. The New Testament still understands Christians as God's pilgrimage people. Bodelschwingh spoke of "our highway brothers." Because they share the same nomadic social structure, "nonresidents" should be related to the Christian community as fellow travelers. To make a thorough study of their situation and to help in concrete ways will be one of the important tasks of this particular Nazareth Brotherhood of ours.

One more point. The word which we translate as "judge" has the basic meaning of "deciding, conciliating or mediating"; in the Old Testament "mediating" and "judging" are identical. Law proceedings should serve the purpose of reestablishing disturbed community. For the attainment of this goal God's statutes for a just order are what is good for man. God's expectations are directed toward this goal, rather than that the cause of one party ought to be pressed against another or that someone's own righteousness ought to be established in God's sight. Remember how the solitary voice in vv. 6–7 considered the possibility of bringing various sacrifices into the presence of God. But that is *not* how you dare come before God; before him you dare appear only with your neighbor, the one with whom you have gained a new solidarity by sharing a common life together.

It is astounding to note the practical ways which the Old Testament's regulations for a just social order suggest for overcoming hostility between persons. Let me mention at least Exod. 23:4–5 (RSV). "If you meet your enemy's ox or his ass going astray, you shall bring it back to him. If you see the ass of one who hates you lying under its burden, you shall refrain from leaving him with it, you shall help him to lift it up." Such was the ancient commandment in Israel. By means of it the practice of community solidarity was fostered. The lawgiver knows how difficult it is, once relationships have been broken, for one protagonist to make contact with his foe, his antagonist, the person who hates him. But here the trouble which a poor ass gets into becomes the bridge for approaching the neighbor with whom one is on such bad terms; the helpless ass and the ox that got lost—they now make it possible to take up new relations with the enemy to whom the animals belong. Today we would say: let the automobile accident of the fellow with whom you no longer are on speaking terms be an opportunity for renewing relations. Look upon the loss which he is suffering as an opportunity for you to begin anew a common reconciled life together.

In this way even the Old Testament leads us to exercise ourselves in community solidarity and community sensibilities. Already in the Old Testament the new righteousness involves more than mere conformity to laws; it comes into its own in the way persons relate to one another. What is good for human beings is not therefore "loyalty to a party program" (a point which must be underlined today), nor "surrender to some social theory" (theories which promise paradise for our grandchildren make life for our contemporaries a veritable hell), but rather, "paying attention to the contemporary of ours who lives before our very own eyes," above all to those who are weak, who have been cheated, who need help. Fostering community solidarity is what is needed. Such a bond of faithfulness is good for humans. By means of it a

wholesome orientation is achieved, an orientation which is in accord with God's will rather than with one's own advantage.

WALKING HUMBLY WITH YOUR GOD

The third thing that is good for us humans is "walking humbly
with thy God." But this last item is not something separate from
the first two. Instead, it points to the driving force that makes it
even possible for persons to foster new community and to direct
their will according to God's deeds and commands. What is
meant by "walking humbly with thy God"? The adverb "humbly"
indicates a good deal of what is meant. It warns against pride and
arrogance, for, as Prov. 11:2 (RSV) says:

> When pride comes, then comes disgrace;
> but with the humble is wisdom.

The servant who walks humbly does not place himself above his
master. In turn the person whom the Bible calls master maintains
a faithful relationship toward those who have been enslaved,
cursed, and endangered. Today people often support "education
for dissent." Such activity is wholesome insofar as people are
thereby educated in theory and practice (citizen initiative) to do
independent thinking, decision making, and acting. The apostles
learned this from Jesus. "We must obey God rather than man,"
they say as they disobey the Jewish magistrates, as we learn in
Acts. We can find this, however, also in the Old Testament, e.g.,
in connection with the Hebrew midwives in Exodus 1. They were
supposed to kill the Hebrew women's male children. But they
did not obey the command of the state because they feared God.
Because of the disobedience of these women, God's people came
into being—something we should not forget. Or, to cite another
example, from Numbers 22, King Balak summoned Balaam to
curse Israel. This curse could have had disastrous effects; but
Balaam could not, dared not, pronounce a curse. God employed
an ass to prevent that. Balaam disobeyed the king of the Moabites.

"Education for dissent" is a necessary thing insofar as it is
based on the fear of God. Disobedience to human authority is
good for humans to the precise extent that it arises from unconditional obedience to the good Master of all humans and to his

word and not from pure belligerency and lust for controversy. To say it another way, dissent is good insofar as it arises out of deep humility, the will to submit to man's Creator and Liberator. From that source arises a new style of living, a new way of acting out of dissent. The new life-style is a part of humility in the presence of God. It brings a new life up out of the waters of baptism.

But the Hebrew word for this third description of what is good contains a bit more than is expressed in our word "humility." *Haşĕnēă* denotes attentiveness, thoughtfulness, watchfulness. What then is good for us humans? *"Haşĕnēă leket 'im 'ĕlōhêkā,"* i.e., "to live attentively, thoughtfully, watchfully with your God." It would take a lifetime to exhaust the implications of this expression. This third description of what is good does not refer to humility as an ethical posture of being ready to accept a lower social ranking (to say nothing about it being what it is often understood to be, an inauthentic pose, a false posturing of submission). What is meant is the attentive sharing with God in the journey on which he is traveling, "attentive journeying together with your God," what the New Testament calls "following Jesus." Psalm 123:2 (RSV) rewrites and paraphrases it thus, "As the eyes of servants look to the hands of their master, as the eyes of a maid to the hand of her mistress, so our eyes look to the Lord our God."

A final point we still must make is to emphasize that Mic. 6:8 speaks about attentive traveling "with your God," i.e., with the God whose kindly disposition you know from Old and New Testaments. He means for things to go well with you; he is liberating you; he created you for a lofty purpose; he is breaching walls before you; you may therefore attentively travel with your God through the breaches which he has opened in the very walls that you cannot take by storm, but against which you can only batter your head to no avail. So the third description is full of meaning and includes within itself also all that was said in the previous two descriptions: doing what was commanded and fostering a sense of community by watchful, attentive traveling with the God who opens before you his own path for your benefit.

Jimmy Carter expressed the hope at the end of his inaugural address "that when I end my term of office as your president, the people of our nation may be able to say that it was not in vain that we recalled the words of the prophet Micah and renewed our striving for humility, mercy, and justice." We include that in our intercessions, I am sure. But as far as we are concerned, each of us experiences a change of government daily. What will we do with the remainder of our lives? Each morning we can celebrate a coronation festival in which our old Adam is dethroned and another ruler ascends to be our Lord. Let's compare this to what you wrote at the beginning of today's address in answer to the question, "What is good for us humans?" May we find at the end of our consideration that we have ourselves affirmed what Mic. 6:8 wishes to impress on us, "It has been told you, O man, what is good and what the Lord seeks of you, namely, to do what is commanded, to foster the sense of community, and to attentively travel with the God who is constructing your way for you."

Confusion and Forgiveness:[68]
Micah 7

This chapter takes us on a long journey. It picks us up in its first verses at a place where we hear about truly chaotic conditions and it leads us far into the distance to a place where in the last verses we hear a great hymn that praises God's faithfulness. Today then we ought to allow ourselves to be led on this path out of great distress to a confidence that is even greater. When we view our lives from the perspective of the prophets (the perspective in which they really stand, no matter whether or not our vision of them is clouded), then we are also able to recognize the various stages of the journey we are making through the rough but actual realities of the world in which we live.

STAGE ONE (7:1–7): DESPAIR, CONFUSION, ISOLATION

At the beginning of the journey on which the chapter takes us we hear the sounds of someone who is grieving over bitter disappointment (vv. 1–4),

> [1]Woe is me! For I have become like a person who goes out into the field
>> after the summer fruit has been gathered,
>> after the vintage has been collected
> and—there is no cluster to eat,
>> none of the early figs I love.
> [2]The godly have perished from the earth.
> There is none upright among men.
> They all lie in wait to murder,
>> each hunts down his kinsman.
> [3]They are expert at doing evil.
> The official makes demands.
>> The judge desires a bribe.
>> The great man makes arbitrary decisions.
> They twist matters as they wish.

⁴The best of men is like a brier;
    the most honest like a thorn hedge.
Yet the day is coming
    that your watchmen have seen,
then you will be punished;
    then confusion is going to begin.

"Woe is me; I am like a hungry man who goes out to the fields and vineyards after the harvest has been completed." For people of antiquity a comparison that begins like this is vivid indeed. By common custom poor people may enter fields and vineyards after the harvest to glean; and ordinarily they always find some good things left. But now we hear of a person who looks and looks, still hoping to find a few grapes or a small fig, but finds absolutely nothing: no cluster of grapes, not a single fig, no tasty morsel, not even a tiny tidbit to bring some joy to his heart. Among the great promises of 4:4 we had heard "they shall sit every man under his vine and under his fig tree, and no one will terrorize them anymore." But now? That whole promise seems to have evaporated. In chapter 7 the lamenter's fruitless search is immediately interpreted as the metaphor that it is: he is not looking for a fig or a cluster of grapes. He is searching among humankind but finds no one from whom he can gain even a bit of help, a bit of support. No godly person exists anymore! No upright person among humans! What the ancient prophet Micah once made the subject of his lament (in chapter 2 and, almost even more clearly, in chapter 3), that same grievous condition this lamenter now finds reoccurring in the Jerusalem of his day. Even among the officials who are supposed to help and to create order, there is no help. Instead of helping, they are making demands; instead of providing even some small bit of aid, they want people to fill out forms. They are engaged in the business of making a profit for themselves instead of supporting those who need support. On top of it all, in any personal contacts they make, they are ruled by their whims, with the result that basic issues are not dealt with. Even when you deal with the best of them (v. 4), you tear your garment as on a thornbush and rub yourself raw as on a thorn hedge.

Do people have similar experiences today in our midst? Is their search in their surroundings for a dependable person also fruitless? Do they experience bitter disappointment in all available officials, in all the standard institutions? When the prophets include in their message those who voice very bitter disappointment, it is as if they still want to tell even the very last of those who have become fainthearted and resigned that here in this part of the Bible, in the word of the prophets, they may find a companion in suffering who is willing to take them along on the path he is traveling. The ancient Jerusalemite whom we hear in v. 4b is certain of one thing, viz., that the society in which one hunts down the other (as v. 2b puts it), will not escape the day of judgment, of punishment. When that judgment hits home, people from that society will not know where they are coming from or where they are going to in a chaos which they themselves have created and in which they are being consumed. But that is no comfort! For the time being things will get ever worse. This solitary lamenter not only fails to find support in the public sector (to say nothing of finding genuinely fraternal brothers in the covenant). What is worse, in the private sector he finds himself entirely isolated and encircled by hostility. Not even his friend or the wife in his bosom can be trusted (vv. 5–6),

> ⁵Do not believe your neighbor,
>   or trust your closest friend.
> Guard the door of your mouth
>   even from her who lies in your bosom.
> ⁶For sons treat their fathers as fools;
>   daughters oppose their mothers;
> the daughters-in-law quarrel with their mothers-in-law,
>   and a man's enemies are the members of his own household.

This particular passage was taken up by Jesus (Matt. 10:35f.) because the disciples who follow him must endure the opposition of even the closest family members. And the worst result is that a person's foes become members of his family, as is said at the end of Mic. 7:6.

Whoever has to live through something similar—and it is good that Scripture effectively prevents us from prettying up the situation—that person should first of all soberly examine his own share of responsibility for his plight. But he should also realize that he is not alone in experiencing this period of living with public and private disappointment and adversity; instead, he is standing in a chain of predecessors within the people of God. Yes, he should realize that his own situation of complete isolation is also dealt with in Scripture, and that in this situation he should set a watch over the gate of his mouth, as v. 5b puts it. He should post a guard before the door of his mouth so that nothing comes out in the presence of those who are false that is itself born of false hope (also so that no mistaken lament is sent to a mistaken address). Above all else we should learn from our predecessors here in the Bible to direct our eyes in the right direction, for as the speaker in v. 7 now says (despite his public and private disappointments),

> But as for me, I am directing watchful eyes to the Lord;
> I am waiting tenaciously for the God of my salvation.
> My God will hearken to me.

Even this total isolation of his is not yet the ultimate end, as it is in the case of the person who sees only half of reality and who considers man the final authority. This mistake is the weak spot of our twentieth century: it considers man the final authority; for a person with such limited vision the onset of this isolation does indeed spell the end. But the prophetic voice of our text reminds us of him who is sovereign Lord also of the so-called last station at the end of the line where everybody has to get off; that is why the voice says, "I am waiting tenaciously for the God of my salvation." That is the new highway that leads forward into open country. The first Hebrew verb here, "to hope," means something like "to climb a high tower and peer out, examining the horizon and the surrounding land to see if there is anything of God's help to be seen." Beside it stands another verb, also translated "hope" but meaning something like, "tenaciously enduring and expectantly waiting." That is how Isaiah (8:17) speaks of himself in the days of God's hiddenness, "But I will wait on the Lord who is hiding his face from the house of Jacob and I will peer with watchful eye toward him."

In the Book of Micah we hear further, "My God will hear me." Thus the person speaks who finds no one anywhere round about who will listen to him or trust him. Let us note that the expectation that God will help is not voiced at a time of euphoria. It does not grow out of pleasant experiences, or out of having had one's prayers heard (something that does happen, but is not happening to this person at this time). Rather, as a result of prophetic experience, resistance to the gathering darkness is asserting itself. Disillusionment and isolation in the human community must not, and dare not, end in hopeless despondency. Because of the reign of God the King a "But as for me" dares rise up against it. When sight can, for the time being, see nothing, faith has its assignment: it is to peer forth, to persist, and to tenaciously await the response of God's intervention.

STAGE TWO (7:8–10): CONFESSING SIN AND HOPING FOR ACQUITTAL

At v. 8 the text leads us into the second stage of our journey, now that the first stage of bitter disappointment has ended in v. 7 with "But as for me" and has climaxed in the expression of confidence, "but my God will hear me." We read in vv. 8–10,

> 8Rejoice not over me, O my rival,
> Though I have fallen, I am now getting on my feet.
> Though I sit in darkness,
> yet the Lord is my light.
> 9The Lord's anger I must bear
> (for against him have I sinned)
> until he takes up my case
> and executes justice for me.
> He will lead me to the light;
> I will see his salvation.
> 10My enemy will see,
> shame will cover her,
> who was always saying to me,
> "Where is the Lord, your God?"
> My eyes will gaze down upon her.
> There she lies trampled
> like mud in the streets.

As in vv. 1–7, here also a voice is heard speaking in first person singular ("I"). But it is more than the voice of a single individual: a personified city is speaking. At v. 11 we shall recognize this very clearly, for there mention is made of walls that are being rebuilt. It is the voice of Jerusalem that we hear in vv. 8–10, the voice of the city of God, of the city which was threatened with doom in 6:9ff. and which, since chapter 3, had to experience the prophet's specific word of judgment. Here therefore we are no longer listening to a single person who sees himself as distinct from many other individuals, as in vv. 2–6; here, rather, the city of Jerusalem is set over against its external foes, here personified as its rival. Verse 8 mentions this rival's malicious joy at Jerusalem's misfortune. Obadiah 11–14 pictures the situation even more clearly. There Edom's malicious joy at Jerusalem's fall is the background. The neighboring peoples' malicious mockery is expressed in the question, "Where is its God? Does that band of losers pretend to be God's people? It has been conquered just like all the other peoples!" The prophet Micah himself had announced that most harshly,

> Zion will be plowed as a field;
> Jerusalem shall become a heap of ruins;
>> and the temple mount will be given over to the beasts of the forest.
>
> (3:12)

The sequence of elements in this text takes the isolated individual of 7:1–7 with his public and private problems into the larger total community with its continuing problems caused by external foes. But even in this community he finds no place of refuge. We must still hear the mocking laughter directed against the community of God which is inwardly corrupt and externally helpless if we wish to get a full understanding of what follows: "Where is he, the Lord, your God? Does that defeated horde pretend to be a special people chosen by God?" Maliciously taunting, the Edomites stand at Jerusalem's gates and ask, "Just where in this city is the helpful power of God evident? And just where, outside of it, is the Lord's protection against the superpowers evident?" The Jerusalem community offers, it seems, absolutely no help to the solitary individual; rather, because of the entire situation, it burdens him all the more.

Let me pose a question: Is not this isolated person's disillusionment with God's community relevant also for us? The picture which God's community currently presents depresses many a person much more than it helps them. Yesterday we heard something about that when the key word "institution" came up for discussion.[69] That is why the voice of that community of Zion is all the more disconcerting. With admirable composure and objectivity Zion says to its triumphant counterpart, the foe, the rival who considers it a hopeless case,

> Rejoice not, my rival, over me.
> Though I have fallen, I am now getting on my feet.

What is the source of such expectations? The answer is,

> Though I sit in darkness,
>   yet the Lord is my light.

Nothing is concealed here. The fall in darkness has occurred. The brotherly love one might expect from the New Testament is missing. And yet, when that has been said, not everything has been said. There is something that the foe who mocks so maliciously from without is unable to recognize, viz., "In the midst of darkness the Lord is my light." With the help of this light the one who has fallen can survive the darkness. Yes, is not this light the dawn of a new creation despite chaotic conditions, just as the first day of creation called light forth to serve in a chaotic world, so that the subsequent works of creation could be seen? Had not the prophet himself drastically announced the city of God's demise (as, for instance, in 3:12)? Yes, and the one who has fallen does not forget that, for she says in v. 9,

> The Lord's anger I must bear,
>   for I sinned against him.

Because Jerusalem's sin and God's anger are acknowledged, the foe's laughter, we may expect, must quiet down and become less raucous. For the city of God's catastrophic fall is but a proof of God's sovereign dominion over it. What produced the present trouble was not the foe's desire, but the word of God proclaimed through the prophet. For these two things belong together: God's people and the living God. Thus we are led further on our journey, out of the stage of disappointments and anxiety into the stage of thoughtful reflection on the question, "What is the underlying cause of the present situation?"

In this connection, dear friends, we ought to give some thought to our own crumbling national church (folk church, *Volkskirche*). Only an acknowledgement of the wrath of God which we have deserved can give us the extremely important answer to that question so we realize that even amid her external decay this community is exclusively in the hands of her Lord. All the statistical data, all the depressing observations we make about it are connected with the Lord of the church. It is not because evil foes have taken over or because certain laws of history continue on their irreversible ways that the darkness has become so great, but because God's people stand solely in the presence of their lord with no choice of evading him. All of this peering out toward hope (spoken of in v. 7), this awaiting him and his response—all that is of no avail to the church unless it first of all sees the searching eye of God resting upon it. His disputation with the church is continuing, i.e., the Lord's legal case with us, his covenant people, as v. 9 makes clear. For it is particularly in this lawsuit that he does not let go of us whom he has called. We are always included, particularly today, in this dramatic lawsuit. Look at the Jerusalem of that day in its catastrophic situation! "The Lord's anger is to be borne" (that is said here so very harshly) "until he takes up the case and his disputation with us anew."

Here in the middle of the Old Testament the certainty breaks through that a renewal of the trial is going to lead to acquittal— to a new brighter stage, one in which salvation, rescue, and liberation will be experienced. So in v. 9 the community of Zion says,

> I intend to bear the Lord's anger
> for I sinned against him
> until he takes up my case
> and executes justice for me,
> until he leads me out into the light
> and I see his righteousness.

Then even the laughter of the mocking foe will disappear. Up to now that rival could ask, along with scoffers of all ages, "Where is he, the Lord, your God?" and say, "Don't pester me with your stupid and irresponsible talking about God!" But now Jerusalem will see that foe trampled to the ground "like mud" (v. 10).

Here the Old Testament's thinking about retribution is expressed, the sort of thinking which, insofar as it is a wish, must disappear in the shadow of the cross. But what should not disappear is the certainty, here expressed in Old Testament terms, that it is easy for God to make the rich small and poor and the poor big and rich, and thus to humble the scoffers and to raise up those who have been scoffed at. Let us keep this clearly before our eyes: such certainty dare never lead the New Testament people of God to despise their enemies or to take vengeance on them; after all, it is out of pure mercy that we have been taken from the world of pagan nations into the sacred history of salvation which God first established with Israel. The certainty of the foe's fall remains valid only when it bears witness to God's power and God's freedom, a freedom to continue his trial of the guilty until it ends with their salvation.

In the second stage of the journey in this chapter (a stage which we just traversed in vv. 8–10) the basic progress achieved was that the city of God learned to (1) know that it has been delivered up solely to its God for the present as well as for the future. It also learned how to (2) face up to God's lawsuit against it with both hope and recognition of guilt. The path into the future (vv. 11–13) does not lead out of the stage of despair, confusion, and isolation (vv. 1–7) except by way of the second stage (vv. 8–10) which involves joining the existing community in confessing sin and thus in facing up to the trial God is carrying on and in hopefully awaiting from him the ultimate verdict of acquittal.

STAGE THREE (7:11–13): A NEW PROMISE FOR A NEW DAY

In what follows hope is mightily strengthened by means of the prophetic statement in vv. 11–13. This prophetic statement is designed to respond to the city of God's statement in vv. 8–10. Unfortunately the Zürich Bible translates it wrongly (putting it in the first person singular: "*my* walls," "*my* boundaries" in v. 11 and "they will make a pilgrimage to *me*" in v. 12). But the original employs the second person ("*your* walls," "*your* boundaries" and "they will make a pilgrimage to *you*"). Accordingly what follows here is an address to the community. In it the same sort of dialogue is again presupposed which we already learned in a different way in earlier chapters.[70] Now the community (an individual member of which had at first been confused in his isolation but which now faces up to the court trial with contrition and thoughtful reflection) gets to hear the following prophetic voice (vv. 11–13),

> [11](Daughter of Jerusalem), the day is coming for rebuilding your city walls;
>> then your border will be enlarged—
> [12]that day when they will come to you
>> from Assyria to Egypt,
>> and from Egypt to the Euphrates,
>>> from sea to sea,
>>>> from mountain to mountain.
> [13]Then the earth will be devastated
>> because of its inhabitants,
>>> on account of the fruit of their deeds.

The third stage of the journey on which this chapter is taking us is one in which Jerusalem is permitted to receive a new word of assurance, of promise. To meet Jerusalem's situation in that day the prophet becomes very precise. He places two prospects before Jerusalem in vv. 11–12.

First, it will receive new city walls. "Your walls will be rebuilt" after having been first razed. Second, the deportees will return from all parts of the world. That means that the city of God will be protected (by walls) and strengthened (by the returnees). Perhaps v. 11b adds that the area of the city will be considerably extended; but the text is a bit obscure. An exact translation is: "Your frontier will be moved far into the distance." That implies a considerable enlargement of the community's territory. In Zech. 2:4–5 we hear that after the return from exile walls of stone need no longer be built around the city of God: they would be too small anyway to encompass the multitudes of people and beyond that, the magnificent promise says, the Lord himself will be a fiery wall around about her and will thereby show himself glorious. In this way then one may look at the meager announcement here ("your frontier will be moved far into the distance"). It means, "You will be both protected and strengthened!" That is given as the promise of a new future for despised Jerusalem and its confused inhabitants, those in the city of God who are disillusioned.

Alongside the promise to Jerusalem there appears in v. 13 a general threat to the rest of the world, one which we can read only with goose pimples, "Then the earth will be devastated because of its inhabitants, on account of the fruit of their deeds." Ancient Israel already knew in its day that the rest of the nations were by no means beyond God's activity but were included in God's just management of affairs. Of that we shall hear more shortly. For the present, however, let us hold fast to the fact that those who hear this proclamation are being prepared to reckon with very specific changes in the circumstances of the world in general and of God's people in particular. In any case, faith must get out of its head once and for all the idea that it may reckon with a "changelessness of current circumstances." Precisely when we are inclined to doubt whether things can be changed—and many of us are acquainted with the despondent resignation which despairs because circumstances cannot be changed when they ought to be and when we would so like to see them changed—precisely then we should become certain, and remain certain, of the fact that in the world not everything is going to stay unchangeably in its accustomed place; that is what we ought to receive from vv. 11–13 as a prophetic assurance, valid in its own right and also corroborated by experience.

STAGE FOUR (7:14–20): PRAYER AND PRAISE

The fourth stage of our journey through this chapter will tell something more (something ultimate) about how these changes will come about. Verses 14–20 introduce us to the "how" of these changes and do so in a noteworthy manner. They differ from all the preceding verses in that they assume the form of prayer. If in vv. 1–7 and a bit differently in vv. 8–10 we heard an individual person lamenting and confessing, and if we heard a prophet giving a promise to this suffering individual in vv. 11–13, now in vv. 14–20 a group is heard, a "we" which directs itself to God in prayer. The community that had been listening to the prophet's word (vv. 11–13) now responds with prayer to God. God's promise has encouraged it to speak to him about the troublesome situation that is still continuing.

First of all, the community presents very precise wishes, in view of its future (vv. 14–17),

> [14]Shepherd thy people, O Lord, with thy staff,
>> the flock of thine inheritance,
>
> who dwell alone in the underbrush
>> in the midst of a garden land.
>
> May they find pasture in Bashan and in Gilead
>> as in the days of old.
>
> [15]As in the days of thy exodus from Egypt,
>> let us see wonderful deeds,
>
> [16]that the peoples may see and be ashamed
>> despite all their superiority,
>
> that they may lay their hands on their mouth
>> and their ears become deaf.
>
> [17]They shall lick the dust like a serpent,
>> like those who crawl in the dust;
>
> they will crawl out of their prisons with trembling;
>> to thee, the Lord, our God,
>>> may they come in fear and be obedient to thee.

Let us note how the community first of all describes its troublesome isolation in v. 14; it "dwells alone in the underbrush." We remember the vexatious isolation of the lamenter in vv. 1–6 and the foe's mockery of the solitary city of God in vv. 8–10. Now the Lord is invoked as shepherd. With his strong staff he should get them out of the underbrush and lead them to better pasture land. Bashan and Gilead are the two regions which had ancient Israel's best grazing land. And that is what they signify here: the best pasture. The international political situation makes an enlargement of Israel's *Lebensraum* unlikely. But God's people takes its direction not from the realities of current international politics, but from God's earlier deeds (recall 6:8, "It has been told you"). So the petition is made, "Let us see wonderful deeds as in the days of thy exodus from Egypt."

"Wonderful deeds" refer to events that are really unexpected. "Let us experience what we no longer dared to expect!" "As in the days of the exodus!" The history of God's people began with what was improbable or at least with what was, speaking in terms of the international political situation, unlikely. This is also something which we learned yesterday[71] for our community: throughout its existence it has always begun with what is entirely unlikely. But it is from precisely such beginnings that faith expects God to lead once again into the incalculably vast expanses—to Gilead and Bashan. According to vv. 16–17 the nations will become astonished, awestruck in spite of their own superiority, in their amazement losing both hearing and sight (that is what is meant when the text says, "they will lay their hands on their mouths and their ears will become deaf"). For they will experience not only, as v. 13 announces, the humbling hand of God, but they will also on their part humbly and respectfully approach the God of Israel and enter his service.

With this hope the Old Testament suppliants already point, as they pray, in the direction of the New Testament fulfillment. The final goal God wants for the nations is not devastating judgment (though that is one of the stages through which they also pass, corresponding to the stage in which he judges his own covenant people); rather his ultimate goal for all of them is their integration into his liberated people. It is the sight of that people's liberation which leads the nations beyond amazement (v. 16), beyond humble submission (v. 17), to calling at their own initiative on the God of Israel and to entering his service. "To fear the Lord" means "to honor him as God and to be obedient to him." Do you notice, dear hearers, how, as its conversation with God proceeds, Israel's position over against hostile people changes? Verse 10 still expressed the cold thought of vengeance: the rival who had despised the daughter of Jerusalem is herself trampled in the streets like mud. That was a bad message. In v. 13 the text had clearly stated, "The earth will be devastated because of its inhabitants, on account of the fruit of their deeds." But now, as the conversation with God continues, a different view of the Gentiles is intimated by vv. 16–17, and what is expected is their movement toward the God of Israel. "They shall lick the dust like a serpent"; the word picture here is to be understood from its background in rites and ceremonies of submission to conquerors. An act of submission and of adoration is meant. They will kiss his feet (cf. Ps. 2:10–11). "They will crawl out of their prisons with trembling" (Mic. 7:17). This is an Old Testament prelude to the New Testament expectation that the peoples will come to Christ. Whenever a severely tempted community brings its problems with the future before its God, then its desires are clarified, its hopes transformed and purged, to make them fit in all particulars the current environment. The closer the community moves toward its God, the more it leaves petitioning behind and enters the realm of adoration.

That is the decisive final step in the praying that constitutes our chapter's fourth stage. It is the step out of petitioning into adoring. It occurs in vv. 18–20 in a way that prompts us to speak of it as a high point among Old Testament expressions of the certainty of faith. Indeed, to voice a personal opinion, nowhere in all of the Bible do I find equally powerful and exultant statements about what we call the forgiveness of sins.

> [18]Where is there a God like you,
>   who takes away guilt
>   who passes over transgression
>   for the remnant of his inheritance,
>   who does not hold his anger forever,
>   for he delights in steadfast love.
> [19]He will again have compassion upon us,
>   he will tread down our iniquities.
>   Thou dost cast into the depths of the sea
>   all our sins.
> [20]Thou wilt show faithfulness to Jacob
>   thy steadfast love to Abraham
>   as thou hast sworn to our forefathers
>   from the days of old.

Suddenly deep amazement overwhelms the suppliants who exclaim, "Who is a God like you!" The rhetorical question magnifies God as the incomparable one, "Who is a God as you are God?" Stop a moment, dear hearers, and ask yourselves this question, "What is so incomparable about the God of Israel?" Is it his power? His sovereign majesty as Creator? His judgment and righteousness? His hiddenness? His universal dominion? The community which has listened, suffered, and prayed itself into his presence gives an entirely different answer, one that is unequivocal, and yet at the same time valid for the whole Bible. Its answer comes in no less than seven separate statements which, however, always say in seven different ways one and the same thing, namely: the God of Israel is incomparably great in this respect that he forgives sins.

But now everything depends on this expression (the forgiveness of sins) not becoming an empty formula, for it is one which we perhaps know all too well. Our hymn (vv. 18–20) bears witness to the truly transforming and renewing power of God's incomparable deed. But we have really understood the transforming power of the forgiveness of sins only if we retain what precedes it in the Book of Micah: the community's great trouble that resulted from God's judgment, its submission to God's righteousness, and, during the disputation God carried on with it, its petitions for freedom in the future. Once the forgiveness of sins becomes certainty, everything becomes new. New freedom arises solely through forgiveness; and when men are forgiven, then freedom begins its powerful transformations. Let us hear about this by weighing, as it were, each one of these seven statements on a scale so delicate that it could be used for weighing gold.

"Who is a God like you, who takes away guilt!" is an exact translation. This bearing, carrying, taking away is a greater deed than all God's deeds of might and power. It is the marvel of man's complete exoneration and emancipation. As the New Testament put it, "He carried our sins away/He bore our sins up to the tree of the cross" (1 Pet. 2:24).

The second sentence is "He passes over transgression." This means that he does not consider our rebellious uprisings worth any further consideration. He lets our sin lie in an out-of-the-way place, while he himself accepts us and takes us along with him on his journey.

The third statement, "He does not hold his anger forever," means he lets go of it; anger has only a temporary, transitory function.

What delights God in the long run is mentioned in the fourth statement, viz., "his steadfast love," his relationship of faithfulness. The Hebrew word *ḥesed* refers to his loyalty to the covenant, his sensitivity to community solidarity, yes, his desire for shared community that is stronger than everything else, a desire that even his transitory anger must serve. Anger corresponds to this steadfast love as three does to a thousand, because his anger endures for three or four generations, but his steadfast love unto a thousand generations (Exod. 20:5–6).

Verse 19 brings, first of all, the fifth statement, "He will again have compassion upon us." The Hebrew word here does not refer, as does *ḥesed,* to the covenant (the steadfast faithfulness or loyalty, the sense of community solidarity); rather it refers to the inner, heartfelt compassion a mother feels for her helpless child. In Hebrew the root is related to the word for the womb in which a child is carried, or to the bosom in which a child is protected. According to Isa. 66:13 God comforts us as a mother comforts her child. He accepts helpless man unconditionally. That is how his compassion works. The sinner is accepted despite his inability to help himself. That is what compassion means.

The sixth statement is even clearer, "He treads down our guilt." The Hebrew word *kābaš* for "tread down" refers to a wild and violent stamping to pieces. What the word picture here refers to is perhaps the stamping out of a consuming fire which was about to set a person ablaze, as the fire of sin does. God treads down our iniquities. The forgiveness of sins means nothing less than that dangerous, life-threatening fire is extinguished.

The seventh statement brings a final climax, "Thou dost cast all our sins into the depths of the sea." In Exod. 15:5 we hear concerning the Egyptians who pursued Israel, "The waves covered them; they went down into the depths like a stone." As the foe went down like a stone, so sin, our foremost foe, sinks into the depths of the sea like a stone. Let us note that the determining categories here when the forgiveness of sins is being discussed, are those of the exercise of power, of conquest over foes! The Lord displayed himself as victor, as the victor over the Egyptian army on Israel's behalf; similarly forgiveness is an act of surpassing victory which completely transforms the entire situation. Sin is humanity's deadly enemy—that is the presupposition here. When that foe has been hurled into the depth of the sea, life's circumstances are entirely new. Sin can cause no more trouble; it has been entirely removed.

Verse 20 sums up the certainty that has been emphasized already seven times,

> Thou wilt show faithfulness to Jacob
> and thy loyalty to Abraham,
> as thou hast sworn to our forefathers
> from the days of old.

Reference is now made to the very first beginnings of the people of God, the first of which we know was the promise to the patriarch Jacob, and even before him, to Abraham. Preceding everything that Israel could achieve or ruin was the word of God's unbreakable faithfulness, his promise to the forefathers. Through Jesus, his cross, and resurrection at the center of history that word of promise has been sealed for Israel and, at the same time, put into effect for all peoples. It is in force and valid! Before I was born, this fundamental principle of the forgiveness of all of our sins was put in force as the end of all our disputations with God and of all of God's disputations with us.

When the burning fire within has been stamped out and our sins sunk into the depth of the sea, then our community and each of its members experiences the legally valid end of God's dispute with us. That means nothing less than this: the final judgment, the last judgment has already been validly anticipated. Everyone can join in singing the sevenfold hymn. What has become of our lament? We can hardly be, or ever become, any more lamentable than we were described in vv. 1–6. But we forlorn individuals of Stage One have been led, already in the midst of our world's confusions and daily vexations, past the stage of petitioning to the jubilation of the hymn and we have thereby been completely transformed.

Calvin concluded his commentary on the prophet Micah with the words, "Thanks to these last three verses, O Lord, we do not have to hesitate to flee daily to Thy compassion."

Thus we can be liberated from bitter despair to renewed activity and industry in Christian social service (*Diakonie*).

UPDATINGS

"Certainty of Faith" and
Public Responsibility:[72]
Micah 2-3

About ten years ago numerous Christian groups at the universities began to involve themselves in vigorous social and political activity. In the process not a few lost their specifically Christian dynamic and became appendages to non-Christian movements. About five years ago the winds began to shift: from secularity to religiosity, from public to private activities, from action to meditation. But even after this shift many were slow to perceive their specifically Christian task in the world in any definite way. Today we are asked, How may we avoid the false alternatives of either a private "certainty of faith" or public responsibility?

The answer can be only this: by clearheaded reflection on what is genuinely Christian. What is genuinely Christian is not some neutral position or some special program, but a special person, Jesus Christ, who has manifested himself in our midst as the one who liberates human beings from all the powers of evil with the full authority of God. This Jesus Christ we learn to know solely in the Scriptures of his witnesses. "Scripture Alone"—this motto is intended to protect Christians of all ages from being dominated by alien voices, alien motivations, and alien goals in their social and political involvements. But equally as important is the other motto, "The Entire Scripture." This second principle protects us from dangerous half-truths and one-sidednesses, e.g., from the spiritual inbreeding which, secluded in a pious ghetto, frets about appearing in public.

The prophetic writings belong to "The Entire Scripture." They can be of immense help in our current dilemma, for the voice of the prophets is the voice of accusation, of threat, and of promise. Jesus' disciples again and again recognized that their master was fulfilling the basic model of the Old Testament prophets. If we in turn are to gain a clear understanding of Jesus and his will, we must listen carefully to the voice of the prophets. If we therefore want to do what is specifically Christian in the current situation, we ought, first of all, to call to mind the path-breaking biblical voices by means of which God has opened up a new history for humankind. Such "memory can take up the battle against the excessive power of the factual, can divert the pressure of existing facts, can knock a hole through the wall of 'what works,' of what has been effected, can make us free of the present, and can open the way to a better future" (Hans Küng, *On Being a Christian* [Garden City, N.Y.: Doubleday & Co., 1976], p. 121).

Let us then open up our Bibles to the prophet Micah. Chapters 2 and 3 are for me some of the most moving chapters in the Bible. They present us with two versions of the certainy of faith: the one, that of the prophets; the other, a pseudocertainty. We will have to examine the question of which of the two we have so far been favoring and what the prophetic verdict about this is.

The prophets' certainty of faith rarely offers us a detailed self-portrait. We learn to know it only indirectly. In other respects also it is much less concerned with itself than with other people. We read the first saying that Micah proclaimed in public, 2:1-5:

2:1–5, MICAH'S MESSAGE OF WOE TO THE LEADERS

¹Woe to those who plan injustice and monstrous deeds,
  as they disturb their sleep at night on their beds,
    so that, when morning dawns, they may perform them
    because they have the power to do it.
²They covet fields, and seize them,
  and houses, and commandeer them.
 they oppress a man and his family
  and steal everyone's inheritance.
³Therefore thus says the Lord,
 Behold, (against this entire brood) I am planning evil,
  evil from which you are not going to be able to extricate your
   necks.
You shall no longer walk haughtily
(for it will be an evil time).

⁴In that day they will take up a taunt song against you
and wail with bitter lamentation,
"We've had it! We are completely ruined! (My
people's land receives an alien lord! How he is
taking it out from under my feet!)
They are dividing up our fields!"
⁵Therefore you will have no one to give you a share of land in the
community of the Lord.

It is clear that the prophet is here speaking publicly. Even the initial cry "woe!" (*hôy*) is a public cry. Imagine, dear friends, how this cry rumbled through ancient Israel as part of the ritual observance whenever anyone died. The lament for the dead sounded across squares and through streets with the words, *Hôy! Hôy!* This is a cry that no one can fail to hear. That is how the prophet begins. In doing so he is dealing with the culprits publicly as if they had already fallen victims to death and were lying in their coffins. While he is crying "woe," these very same fellows are still strutting along full of health and vigor, for it is clear from what follows that the persons whom Micah is addressing are public figures. They are those "who have the power" (v. 1b, literally, "who have things in hand," i.e,. who have human beings at their disposal). In actual fact Micah is most likely referring to the Jerusalem officers and administrative officials who represented royal authority in the fortress cities in the vicinity of Moresheth.[73] What concerns Micah are also matters of public concern: what is happening to ancient, long-established inhabitants in the vicinity, to the people and their property, and to the administration of justice (v. 2). Finally, the consequences that Micah announces are also public: masters are to become slaves; the large land-owners are to lose their land. So it is clear that the prophet is aware of the role of "public responsibility"—responsibility in social, political, economic, and legal affairs.

But just where in this passage can roots of the certainty of faith be seen? They are seen most clearly in 2:3 at the transition from the accusation (vv. 1–2) to the threat (vv. 3–5), "Therefore thus says the Lord." Micah does not remain silent about the fact that he had learned the will of God concerning this matter. In sharp

contrast to v. 1b he says in v. 3a, "Those who plan evil are themselves already being exposed to a corresponding plan of God."
"You plan. Yes, you make plans there on your couches where you
disport yourselves while hatching out your schemes. You are
doing the planning; but God is already busy making his plans for
you." Those who bring force to bear upon defenseless people,
their houses, and fields, will themselves be delivered up irrevocably to alien forces (v. 3b) who will dispossess them (vv. 4–5).
By virtue of his certainty of faith the prophet knows that God is
going to resist greedy and violent caprice. Micah proclaims this
as God's word, and he does it in a way which is so clear that no
one can fail to understand what he means.

Prophetic certainty of faith also manifests itself in v. 2, though
less obviously, for with the word "covet" Micah is referring to the
ninth and tenth commandment (Exod. 20:17a,b), which also
deals with our fellowman and his property. "Thou shalt not covet
thy neighbor's wife, manservant, house, cattle, ass. Thou shalt
not covet! Thou shalt not covet!" In the entire Decalogue no
other prohibition is thus repeated. The commandment against
coveting, however, does occur twice. That keyword is repeated
also here in Micah. Similarly the word pair here, "steal" and "oppress," is one which harks back to ancient legal terminology and
is in fact attested in Lev. 19:13; there, as here, it is bifurcated
as a prohibition outlawing the use of force against persons and
against property. The prophet does not actually cite that passage,
but it is obviously the word of God in which he is living. It is, in
fact, the presupposition of the public accusation he makes in v. 1.
As he cries out about these crimes, he does not explicitly refer to
God by name. Rather, he exposes the beginnings of coveting in
the nighttime planning and in the violent execution of these plans
at the break of dawn. It is important for Micah to let the ancient
prohibition shine into these culprits' situation.

In sum, prophetic certainty of faith is not narcissistically busy
first of all with itself; instead it manifests itself when it expresses
God's will even where there is no specific reference to God's word
but where current lawlessness is exposed for what it really is and
the afflicted find support in their need. Two distinctive features

characterize public responsibility that is born of prophetic certainty of faith.

First, the public indictment of violence (made in the prophetic accusation) is not made in a general or abstract manner, but in specific terms. Concrete crimes are tracked down, beginning with secret coveting and scheming and ending with violent performance. "Conditions" or "the system" are not pilloried but rather the persons who are responsible for their deeds.

Second, the public threat (in the prophetic announcement of doom) tells the guilty culprits themselves in direct speech (vv. 3–5) that they will experience the evil of their deeds in their own bodies and possessions and that they will be unable to evade God's judgment. In order to oppose them, the prophet does not try to assemble those who are afflicted and are suffering, with a view toward addressing them or perhaps summoning them to resist. In this respect Micah would be happy with our friends at Göttingen who did not assemble some sort of mob as they could easily have done, but addressed themselves directly to the responsible minister of state.[74]

Terrorists' acts of robbery and murder (increasing among us and alarming the entire world) need to be brought under the strict discipline of the obedience of faith. Taking our cue from this portion of chapter 2, we must take up two questions: Where are the origins of the current wave of terrorism? and, To whom are we to address ourselves?

But before we discuss these and other questions in a more precise and practical manner, let us first listen to the prophet's opponents who would exclude such questions completely from any discussion whatsoever. Their protest against Micah has been transmitted to us in the following series of statements (2:6–7a):

2:6–7a, THE OPPONENTS' COUNTERATTACK

6"Don't preach at us!" is what they preach.
  "Such topics are not proper topics for prophetic discourse!"
    "That insult doesn't apply to us!"
7"Do you think that the house of Jacob is under a curse?"
  "Has the Lord really lost his patience?"
    "Is that the way he acts?"

Those are fragments from a passionate argument. Apparently Micah is the center of a tumultuous dispute. The imperatives and the rhetorical questions here show how vehement the disputation has become. Whoever, like Micah, must get involved in public problems will inevitably get involved in public disturbances. We see various factions confronting one another.

"Don't preach at us!" they preach. "Sermons should not be preached on such topics!" Micah, it seems, is not the only one being attacked. Other targets are his colleagues, people like Isaiah or his disciples. Who are the attackers? They apparently also "preach"; they could well be other prophets, as we will get to know them better at 3:5. But the statement "That insult, that calumny doesn't apply" may well be a statement made by the wielders of power themselves. A coalition of church and state arrives on the scene as one united front to oppose the prophet and his friends.

What do the members of this coalition want? First of all, they want nothing less than the prohibition of free speech. What they are really aiming at, however, is Micah's sermon topics. As far as they are concerned, economic and political measures, problems of real estate, the duties of incumbents in public office, are not fit subjects for sermons. As they see it, the dangers of foreign policy, the enslavement and deportation of prisoners, and the exappropriation of property are subjects that do not fit with Israel's expectations of the future. Therefore they reject what they consider insult and outrageous abuse.

Behind all such opposition is the conviction that a prophet ought not leave the sphere of religious themes. What Micah says allegedly stands in opposition to the sacred traditions of the faith. That, in their view, speaks of the election of a chosen people (not of infamy), of blessings for Israel (not of a curse), of God's patience (not impatience), and of his deeds of salvation (not of punishments). In 3:11 Micah once again cites his opponents' conviction, "Is not the Lord in our midst? No evil shall come upon us!" For those who are here quoted, confidence in Yahweh's helpful presence stands without question in opposition to Micah's expectation of catastrophe; Yahweh's salvation stands in opposition to the evil that is threatened. "Stick to religious topics! Stay with statements that inspire confidence! Don't talk about everyday matters! Remain in the sacred realm in which God's name is adored!" Where, dear friends, would we now be if Jesus had restricted himself to the religious realm according to the model proposed by Micah's opponents?

But is not the certainty of faith that is here speaking in opposition to Micah a peaceful and joyous certitude of faith and of confidence, a confidence which is based, for instance, on Ps. 46:7, "The Lord of hosts is with us; the God of Jacob is our refuge"? Micah's opponents are citing a line from their hymnal! Is not an exemplary certainty of faith alive and well in their statements, every other one of which explicitly appeals to God ("Is not the Lord in our midst?" "Has the Lord really lost his patience?")? Indeed what is expressed in every single one of their statements is trust in God despite all disagreeablenesses! The tenor of the statements here in 2:6–7a and afterward in 3:11 bears witness to a rejection by believers of everything that causes insecurity. Faith is here burrowing, so to say, into its underground nest and is not permitting anything to lead it astray, not even prophetic accusations or prophetic threats of doom. Let worldly affairs run their course, they say! (And worldly affairs do precisely that when no one speaks up in opposition, as we heard yesterday.[75]) The heart of the church, they say, beats in the sanctuary. Such are the convictions of the second type of certainty of faith, one which confronts the prophetic certainty of faith with eloquent, incontrovertably pious-sounding statements.

The burning question is, To which side do we tilt? Do you not note, dear friends, that the decision which must be made is between two types of certainty of faith? Can it be denied that Micah's opponents most likely stand close to certain evangelical types? Please consider the possibility, dear friends, that Micah most likely stands more in line with groups in the World Council of Churches! But, above all, let us examine ourselves, for that is the real point. What sort of certainty of faith do we practice?

Let us hear Micah's response? It begins at 2:7b.

2:7b–10, MICAH'S PROPHETIC RESPONSE

⁷ᵇTrue, my words are compassionate to the upright.

Micah does not in any way wish to impugn God's compassion. It
is indeed valid for the person who permits his or her entire life to
be thereby raised up, guided, impregnated, liberated.

⁸But you have risen up against my people like an enemy.
  You are stripping peaceable citizens of their robes,
    unsuspecting travelers who are disinclined to put up a
    fight.
⁹The women of my people you are driving out from their cherished homes,
  and their children you are depriving of their honor forever.
¹⁰"Get up and go; there is no safety here any more!"
  For the sake of a trifle you are taking possession of painful
  pledges.

Micah makes the self-styled pious people face up to hard facts.
God's goodness does not permit itself to be used as a cover for
evil, as a theatrical mask used to exploit and trick people. His
faithfulness is eminently valid for all who are afflicted, i.e., also
for those whom Micah's opponents meet with such hostility. In
the New Testament this answer of the prophet gains the form of
the statement, "Faith without works is dead." (James 2:17, "So it
is with faith; if it is not active in deeds, it is by itself dead.")
James is also concerned in the very context of his statement with
the exploitation of the poor by the rich. Paul says the same thing
in a different way in Gal. 5:13, "Be careful lest your freedom
open the way for selfishness; instead, serve one another in love."
Thereupon vv. 19–24 contrast the fruits of the Spirit with the
works of the flesh (love, self-control, and faithfulness over against
enmity, selfishness, and dissension).

Two things should be noted about Micah's criticism of the false
certainty of faith. First, his approach is by way of his immediate
surroundings. He speaks of hostility "against my people" (2:8)
and of the eviction of "women of my people" (2:9); he says they
"eat the flesh of my people" (3:13); and "they lead my people
astray" (3:5). Throughout he is referring to his kinfolk in the im-

mediate and proximate vicinity, for whom he knew he was responsible, perhaps even as an elder.[76] Second, he closes his response to the opponents in 2:11,

> If I were a false spirit and a preacher of lies, saying,
> "I am going to preach to you of wine and whisky"—
> then I would be the proper preacher for this people!

He thereby unmasks that presumed certainty of faith which says, "Is the Lord not in our midst?" "Has the Lord really lost his patience?" He unmasks it as nothing else than gross hedonism. When Micah makes these two points—and he is speaking about his immediate surroundings, unmasking its inordinate desire for enjoyment—then, as I see it, two further questions are posed to us today.

First, Where is the place that we should first of all perceive our public responsibility? As the Christian Student Movement in Germany, do we not share, most definitely and most prominently, in responsibility for our universities and schools of higher education? Last evening we heard about driving our cars with bright lights or with parking lights.[77] In driving school I learned that in between these two possibilities there is such a thing as driving with lights dimmed (which is my practice, as I hope it is of everyone else's, when driving in town). As for driving through the land of our responsibilities I am not excluding the use of bright lights on occasion to see far ahead in the distance; nor am I recommending driving with parking lights, but rather with lights dimmed. We ought not overlook our immediate surroundings ("my people"; "my kinfolk"), our fellow students, the fields of specialization in which we are working, and the institutions of higher learning in which we live.

Is it not our responsibility to give attention to justice and injustice in our day-by-day surroundings? Dare we overlook what is happening in our immediate vicinity when violence and oppression take over, when fellow students suffer? Dare we overlook what is happening in our committees and student groups, or what has to be done and suffered by staff personnel, by teachers, and even by boards of regents? Must we not, when we consider the questions of the beginnings of terrorism, also think of ourselves? Was it not especially the religious students who withdrew from public discussions at the universities into irresponsible isolation?

I refer also to such a problem as that of the strike which will be a great concern for us in the coming semester. I dare to make an unequivocal statement about that, on the basis of a decade of reflection. The reason for the strike that has been formulated presents considerations worth reflecting about. If legislation proposed in Baden-Wuerttemberg includes the elimination of general student government committees, aspects of that plan must be considered and discussed, as our friends in the Christian Democratic Union have already done in talks with the present governor and secretary for education. The minister of education in Rheinland-Pfalz is strongly opposing any such prohibition of student involvement. The arguments pro and con must be objectively weighed.

Another sore spot is the problem of law and order. Certainly violence must be eliminated from the institutions of higher learning. But whether a special legal code serves peace at such schools better than the general law which is valid everywhere is a problem that must be publicly examined. Finally the burning question of the limitation of the period within which students must complete their programs of study needs attention. Those who protest the adoption of any such legislation must contemplate the fact that admission of new students is often being blocked for a surprisingly long time by students who stay on and on. Above all, we must consider how to deal with problems which would arise when difficulties surface because of the new limitations, perhaps by a better advisory system or by specific curricular reform. For this we need the positive cooperation of students in the various schools and divisions. These problems must lead to discussion, studies, decisions, and action. But one thing these problems do not demand, and that is a strike. A strike is not a helpful way of dealing with these matters. I would like to declare this unequivocally! It is nonsense to respond to the problems of higher education with strikes. That amounts to nothing more than boycotting one's own education and development as well as that of fellow students. It is understandable only for people who basically do not want to help others progress; rather, they want to persist in a continual negativism. Instead I want to urge you, dear friends, to appeal regularly to those who teach to agree on a suitable time for a fair, deliberative discussion of the problems and a consideration of how progress can be made with some prospect of success. A strike, by contrast, only enlarges the problems. I refer to this as an example of the necessity that we not continue to practice irresponsible withdrawal and permit affairs in our sphere of work to run their course without taking a definite stand here and there wherever we recognize problems.

The second question is this: Are we not in danger of the false certainty of faith which, to be sure, employs pious words, is faithful to the traditional faith, and also expects God's goodness for itself in the future, but which, without being aware of it, enriches itself at the expense of others rather than helping them, permits thinking to circle around self-satisfaction rather than conscientiously raising the question about the will of God in the social and political world around us, and which enjoys Christian celebration among familiar acquaintances instead of practicing the difficult business of doggedly tracking out public suffering in the name of God? If we follow the prophet, like Micah we will get into hand-to-hand combat. That cannot be avoided. Did our Lord avoid it? With his statements Micah is well able to point to the path on which one follows Jesus. According to their "Guidelines" students in the SMD (Christian Student Movement in Germany) intend to help one another shape their entire lives in the light of Christ.

The third chapter of Micah makes clear what tasks we can undertake. Let us hear first 3:1–4:

3:1–4, AGAINST MICAH'S FELLOW ELDERS
¹And I said,
Listen now, you leaders of Jacob,
you rulers of the house of Israel!
Is it not your responsibility to know justice?
²ᵃyou who hate what is good and love what is evil,
³ᵃwho eat the flesh of my people
and break their bones in pieces—

²ᵇwho tear the skin from off my people's flesh
   and the flesh from off their bones
³ᵇwho chop them up like meat for a cooking pot
   like steaks for a frying pan.
⁴If they then cry unto Yahweh,
   he is not going to give them an answer;
 he is going to hide his face from them at that time
   because their deeds have been evil.

Here, first of all, the main type of public responsibility is mentioned by the name of "justice." Micah does not say, surprisingly, "God's justice! God's commandments!" Naturally that is what he means. But he apparently also means that we should not always have God's name on our lips. There is, it seems, such a thing as using the name of God too often. After all, Micah's opponents mention him more than Micah himself. "Justice" is what Micah calls for. That is paraphrased with very simple words as "loving what is good and hating what is evil," in contrast to those who hate what is good and love what is evil (3:2a). (That conflict of values must be reckoned with now as much as then.) Micah exposes the criminal manner in which the privileged classes in Jerusalem exploit the labor conscripts from the country. The upper classes enjoy themselves and enrich themselves at the expense of the common people. They humiliate and ruin helpless persons.

How is it with us? Right now many people are busy in the post-capitalistic world as well as in that of socialism with attempts to give a more human face to these conflicting social structures, to assure more justice for all, to overcome class hatred through cooperation, to guarantee that the weakest member of society will be cared for, to practice coexistence, and to preserve and foster human dignity in penal as well as regular vocational situations.

And now, in the midst of this process in which very much still remains to be completed, out of impatience or despondency, terror is rearing up among us in a form which, without giving its actions a second thought, can unconcernedly eliminate four persons in order to kidnap one so-called capitalist. Then the person abducted is abused in a manner in which no employer would dare treat his employee. Then murder is celebrated as "execution" after it is too late for any regular court to impose the death penalty. In a brutal way, "capital punishment" is carried out using the word "execution." In reaction voices can be heard—and I ask you all to consider them as well—asking that these kidnappers be delivered up to the masses whom they allegedly wish to liberate. There are already groups who are ready to shoot one of the Stammheim prisoners for every day that Hans Martin Schleyer continues to be held under terrorist arrest—they see this as a means of repressing terrorism. Think, dear friends, of the "farewells" we have heard to Buback, Ponto, and Schleyer. Consider what all this means! Does none of this concern groups in the German Christian Student Movement?

Micah at least felt that God's people were involved when people were being roasted or chopped up for the frying pan. And one can hardly speak more coarsely than he does here. This is biblical language. It is also the position which biblical witnesses take toward public responsibility. The confusion in the matter of good and evil is colossal. None of us can avoid its influence. Can we really live with Jesus and not be concerned with what Micah calls "justice"? I wish we would let what is said in 3:1 be inscribed on our consciences, "Is it not your responsibility to be concerned with justice?" It will take work, discipline, love, and above all the obedience of faith if we, after thorough preparation in our own community, are to help distinguish between justice and injustice in our departments and divisions of higher education, if we are to get at the root of these things in a much more conscientious manner than heretofore. The hour is apparently long past when we could speak of violence brought to bear on things and people in a theoretical, playful, or even cynical manner and imagine that we had nothing more important to do than to pal around with our brothers in the Communist Federation of West Germany or similar extremists. Each of us at his or her own place must zealously search for the path that holds out promise.

In this connection vv. 2–3 in chapter 3 make us aware that certainty of faith does not exclude blunt language. Micah becomes rough, his language corresponding to the roughness of the crime he is pillorying, when he states that the wielders of power eat the flesh of his people, break their bones, skin them alive, chop them up like steaks for the frying pan. These words are born of burning sympathy for the sufferers. Jesus also was not prudent in his choice of words when he addressed his hearers as serpents, a brood of vipers (Matt. 23:33), or when he accused the scribes and Pharisees of consuming widow's houses and of being blind leaders of the blind.

We should, therefore, in no way avoid or cut off the conversation because its tone appears to us to be too coarse. The voice of truth and love can certainly have that sound. But we ought to examine ourselves—that must be added—as to whether we are permitting ourselves to be carried along on the path to cynicism or toward despising any of our fellow human beings. If we involve ourselves in conversations with fellow students, either those of the Communist Federation of West Germany or any other declared opponents of Christianity, then in addition to clarity, a winning compassion should be our dominating mood. In Matt. 12:36 Jesus reminds us that we must give account of every careless word. Indeed there has been enough of wounding, yes, of destroying people with words. That is always the first step toward violence. If we wish to further love for what is good, we should exercise ourselves in compassionate speech. If we hate what is evil, we should love the person who is evil all the more unambiguously. Micah's main concern when he chose these rough, realistic words was, of course, to make himself understandable, seeking neither fear nor favor, but speaking in such a way that no one could forget what he said. This is also something we need to practice. It is part of a Christian's responsibility for the world. So speak then brusquely and unequivocally but without harming or destroying.

Verse 4 needs special attention. Here Micah speaks to those who are flaying and roasting others,

> If they then cry unto Yahweh,
>   he is not going to give them an answer;
>   he is going to hide his face from them.

They find out what it means to have the sacrifices they have offered cry out to God without there being any response! Receiving an answer to prayer and caring for those who cry out in trouble—these two things belong inseparably together. When we pray, we can only join those who are oppressed in coming together with them into God's presence. If we fail to listen to the anguished cries that come from outside our community (also here at our universities), then we do not have to wonder why God also turns his ear away from us. Mic. 3:4 urges us to consider this. Thus public responsibility and God's response to prayer belong together; the first person plural of the Lord's Prayer should have taught us long ago that we can enter God's presence only together with those who are oppressed.

3:5–7, MICAH AND HIS FELLOW PROPHETS

In 3:5–7 Micah addressed the same group whose opposition to himself we heard in 2:6f. (and 3:11b).

> [5]Thus says the Lord concerning the prophets who lead my people astray,
> If they have something to bite with their teeth, they cry, "Salvation!"
>> but if a person refuses to give them what they
>> demand, they declare a holy war upon him.
> [6]Therefore it shall be night for you—without vision;
>> darkness for you—without revelation.
> The sun is going down upon the prophets
>> and dark shall the day be over them.
> [7]Then the seers will be disgraced;
>> the diviners shall have nothing to say.
> They shall all veil their mouths
>> because they receive no response from God.

According to this passage, the group of prophets is also losing its contact with God. As the reason for this, a particular phenomenon is mentioned: they are concerned in their proclamation solely with their own advantage. Whether they see prospects of peace or war does not depend on the word and will of the Lord but on the sympathy they receive from their hearers. Such manipulation of the prophetic word results in prophets themselves becoming deaf to God's word. Whoever refuses to take direction from God's word will soon find that it has really nothing more to say to him. Blaise Pascal says (*Pensées* 557), "Both things are true: God conceals himself from those who tempt him, but reveals himself to those who seek him." How could we be urged to spiritual honesty and independence from human opinion more intensively than by this saying directed to the prophets who must leave the public stage completely at a loss, perplexed, disgraced, having nothing to say?

Micah, however, takes quite a different stand. Please join me in my amazement at what he says in v. 8,

> But as for me, I, by contrast, am full of
> authority, justice, and courage.

(The juxtaposition of these concepts is a hendiatreis; all three of them refer to one total concept. We may paraphrase: Micah is gifted with courageous readiness to get involved in the cause of justice.) That is a personal statement which is entirely uncustomary, even in the circle of the great classical prophets of the Old Testament. By contrast, how despondent is Jeremiah! Even Amos, in a similar situation, only refers to the Lord who took hold of him and, against his will, compelled him to speak God's prophetic word. But here for once the certainty of faith expresses itself in the form of self-confident, superior, almost boastful self-glorification. Note that in this ancient saying God is not mentioned at all, "But, as for me, I, by contrast, am filled with authority, justice, and courage." ("The Spirit of the Lord" is a theological gloss, as is indicated by several clues in the original, which need not be detailed here;[78] the tradition found it necessary to refer to the Spirit of the Lord at this point. Of course, Micah's authority comes from the Lord. But he himself did not express that at this point.) Micah wants to emphasize that, in contrast to the prophets against whom he had brought accusations, he is independent of his hearers. He has been given the courage to stand up for his own position against opposition. Alongside power and a sense of superiority there is only room within him for "justice," in contrast to the leaders in Jerusalem who themselves ought to be concerned about it but instead either commandeer people or abandon them to their sad fates.

Who in the world is Micah that he should boast that he, with full authority and surpassing courage, concerns himself with justice for his afflicted compatriots? An English commentator answers the question about who he was by saying that he was perhaps a small-town artisan, a worker, a proletarian, but, be that as it may, in any case a man with great sympathy for the poor, a man who in today's world would have felt much more at home in a factory than in a cathedral. But it seems that Micah was also an elder of Moresheth; if so, it is understandable how, in taking a stand for justice, he was entering into competition with his corresponding counterparts in Jerusalem, the Jerusalem elders. It is also then understandable that he speaks again and again of his fellow countrymen as "my people". Finally, the power and artistry of his language are also understandable. But be that as it may, what he here says about himself is verified by his extant sayings. Paul is able similarly to boast of the full authority which the Lord had given him for building up the church (2 Cor. 10:8).

What a benefit people like Micah are in a world that is uncertain about justice! Because our problems are indeed difficult, we prefer crawling into some pious ghetto to asking Micah, or the Lord, or his representatives what justice is. What a benefit it is that, in a world that is uncertain about justice and in which finding and preserving justice is an enterprise fraught with so much weakness, we have been given not only norms and categorical imperatives but also living messengers of justice, and not merely despondent dejected, uncommunicative messengers at that. In another respect it is very important that reticent and despondent persons are deemed good enough to be witnesses. But at the same time we have received powerful men endowed with full authority. As such Micah is also a precursor of Jesus. In Jesus justice has come to its maturity, not only in the authority of his words but in the fact that he suffered injustice and overcame it. By suffering injustice in the place of the unjust, he put justice in force with final authority. That is something we dare never forget. Therefore we are called to justice; by overcoming injustice he encourages us to give our all on behalf of justice.

In this connection a number of things about the relation of justice and power need to be considered, especially in view of our topic, "certainty of faith and public responsibility." I would like to refer once more to Pascal (*Pensées* 298) who puts it thus,

"Justice without power is powerless. Power without justice is tyrannical. . . . Justice and power must therefore be connected so that what is just is also powerful and what is powerful is also just." And that is why Christendom should pray again and again for members who are surpassingly endowed with authority, with justice, and with courage for public service.

One would wish that in every group of Christian students at every university a sort of Micah would arise spontaneously. Every group of Christian students ought to pray to God for members who are gifted to an outstanding degree with readiness to get involved, with ability to form sensible judgments, and with knowledge of justice. This is what you, dear friends, should look for and pray for! You need such persons if you wish to take a stand for Jesus in your tasks in the German Christian Student Movement (SMD) instead of just holding enjoyable Christian celebrations with one another and taking care of one another. Take time to consult with such persons concerning the difficult questions for which you have no ready solution! We need the full authority of individuals who are capable as members of the local student government committee or as representatives of their respective departments, to help justice achieve power and to keep power just. Two concrete suggestions still seem to me to be necessary.

First, it is not only at schools of higher learning that justice and order have been abandoned to ridiculousness to such a degree that the result presents a serious danger to society, to work, and to inner peace. I want to say clearly that "education for dissent" still remains a necessity. Israel exists today only because once there were persons who obeyed the call of faith, viz., the Hebrew midwives who did not implement Pharaoh's command to kill every male Hebrew child. Exodus 1 repeats the expression, "they did not obey Pharaoh." God's people would not have come into existence if it had not been for the disobedience of these midwives. The principle remains, as Acts 5:29 expresses it, "We must obey God rather than men." "Education for disobedience" remains an important Christian task, but precisely with the biblical understanding that God ought to be obeyed rather than men.

In the present situation I find the reference by the Council of the Evangelical Churches in Germany this September to the fifth statement of the Barmen Theological Declaration of 1934 extraordinarily important and worth attention by all student groups. That fifth statement is, "Scripture tells us that in a world not yet redeemed, the world in which the church also still lives, the state has by divine ordinance the task of taking care of justice and peace according to the measure of human insight and human ability it possesses—through threats and through the exercise of power. The church recognizes with thanks and respect to God the wholesome benefit of this his ordinance. It recalls God's kingdom, God's command and righteousness and therewith the responsibility of both those ruling and those ruled. It trusts and obeys the power of the word through which God sustains all things." The Council then speaks of the Evangelical Church as also being in prison during the weeks of terror insofar as "we did not oppose strongly enough the stance in our midst that is oriented one-sidedly toward conflict nor did we proclaim God's command and promise clearly enough."

If then we are dealing with ordinances of the state like the Code for Schools of Higher Learning or the Code for Public Order, we should study the fifth Barmen statement anew and in any case take a critical look at one-sidedly belligerent behavior. As Christians we should always be concerned in our surroundings with justice and peace, without which we cannot live or work. Above all, in view of the weaker members of society, we should take a stand on their behalf. We should also increase our appreciation of the police more than has been customary among students. I see no better means of working against the growth of a police state than by taking a positive stance toward the police.

Second, if the German Christian Student Movement (SMD) does not wish to succumb to the danger of a false, inbred certainty of faith, then it will have to consider, as a whole and in its individual groups, a new relation to the politics of student government. Marion Graefin Dönhoff recently wrote, after the murder of Jürgen Ponto, (*Zeit* 33, 1977) of the inferno which exploded when Susanne Albrecht "bade farewell" with the bouquet and the words, "Uncle, I wanted to show myself once again" and which then ended in murder. There are in our immediate neighborhood at the schools of higher learning fellow students who know how to justify such a crime; and they do not comprise some few isolated individuals, but rather are official representatives of the students in the student government (ASTA) and in university divisions and departments. Marion Dönhoff rightly says, "The reason for this is that only 25–30 percent of the students vote. Of this minority then, a thin majority undertakes to represent all the students. The students who are indifferent are guilty. We all are responsible." I add, we teachers at the schools of higher learning are also guilty of speaking out on public questions all too rarely. On days when significant events happen or decisions are to be made, we should use at least the first five minutes of the session to come clean on what, in our opinion, is correct. Teachers in higher education in general have done that all too rarely, too equivocally, and in a manner much less than helpful.

But I now also wish to admonish all Christian Student Movement (SMD) groups no longer to look upon voting at schools of higher education as an individual's private activity or as a secondary matter for the group. Do not, dear friends, forget the sharp question in Mic. 3:1, "Is it not your responsibility to be concerned with justice?" You are responsible when you do not vote, also when you do not discuss with one another how one is to vote and for whom one is to vote. Please consider with one another, dear friends, the question of whether or not some of you should stand as candidates, to represent our schools, divisions, and departments or to serve in student government (ASTA). Do you wish to leave everything up to those who indoctrinate with a radical political bias at, to cite instances, the open discussions of the first semester, at the choosing of guest lecturers and their topics or at the construction of official announcements and tracts? When there is an official announcement of injustice, do we then pass by with a shrug of the shoulders? Or give our commentary only privately, or even refuse to look at such an announcement? If so, we are abandoning the institution as a whole to injustice. Remember, there are both active and passive elections! In the name of Jesus please take these questions, dear friends, into your discussion groups. We continue with Micah.

3:9–12, EXPOSING GUILT AND PROCLAIMING DOOM

> Listen to this, you leaders of Jacob
>   and you rulers of the house of Israel,
> who abhor justice
>   and twist what is straight.
>
>   (3:9)

Whenever student speakers violate principles of justice, of honesty, and of their neighbor's freedom, make that violation the subject of your conversation about the Bible; discuss what is to be done! Include this in your prayers! Expose it when what is straight is twisted! Note that such subversion is a biblical topic. If you have been at the university a few semesters, you have had more than enough experience with experts at misrepresentation who with utmost cynicism present the extortioners as the true liberators and earnest protectors of justice as criminals, and who present the security police as the real murderer of Buback. On the other hand, you also know those who accuse as guilty of criminal activity anyone who contributes to taking care of Gudrun Ensslin's teeth. In all these cases precisely that is happening which Isaiah explains at greater length than Micah when he accuses those "who twist what is straight." Isaiah says (5:20), "Woe to those who call evil good and good evil, who make darkness light and light darkness, who make what is sour sweet and what is sweet sour." Friends, does not that apply to us, when something similar happens in our circles at the universities? The prophets unequivocally say, That does apply to us! Many a Christian does not consider himself equal to the task of opposing the art of political misrepresentation. But just for that reason it is necessary that groups discuss these matters and wrestle with one another before God and man for "authority, justice, and courage" as they pray, as they discuss, as they make plans.

Micah speaks further (3:10) about those "who build Zion with blood and Jerusalem with injustice." He may be thinking of construction accidents, or bloody chastisements or brutal exploitation of human labor, or other unbearable working conditions. We will have to think of those who today are effectively stripped of their rights and of those truly endangered and suffering. These include certain foreign students, the sick, unemployed youth, fellow students who have failed their examinations, but also politicians and critics of our society. Think also, dear friends, of your university teachers! Pray for them in their weaknesses; join together with all who are grieved with the fact that "Jerusalem must be built with injustice" and that an allegedly better future must be striven for by crass transgression of God's commandments and of Jesus' instruction.

> Her leaders give judgment for a bribe,
> Her priests interpret the law for pay;
> Her prophets give their revelations for money.
> (3:11)

Nothing is said here against the principle that every laborer deserves pay; instead protest is raised against the fact that the officials bend their decisions according to the extra compensation they receive and not according to justice. Do we wish to be mindful of justice with renewed enthusiasm? Then let us keep in mind that justice is endangered first of all by the devastating power of money. Please become especially sensitive to this fact.

In the Old Testament's ancient legal code for judges, those who decide matters of jurisprudence are warned thus: "Thou shalt take no bribe, for a bribe blinds the official and subverts the cause of those who are in the right" (Exod. 23:8). In addition, pressure from the majority endangers justice according to this same code for judges: "Thou shalt not follow the majority on the path to what is evil; nor shalt thou bear witness in a suit so as to give in to a multitude and deviate from justice" (Exod. 23:2). Read Exod. 23:1–10 at the beginning of the new semester as you begin your deliberations about the strike and elections with Scripture and prayer! Finally, a third thing that endangers justice is mentioned: false pity. "Thou shalt not be partial to a poor man in his suit" (Exod. 23:3). Just because he belongs to the poor does not mean that he is not guilty; there is such a thing as unjustified pity.

These three admonitions of the code for judges deserve careful consideration. Friends, do not be afraid of going to the Bible's school. You will profit thereby. Your life will be made much richer. Specific dangers to justice must be considered if, following the biblical word, we wish to perceive our public responsibility for justice.

Micah sees the rule of justice endangered especially by those who at the same time (v. 11b) "lean on the Lord" and say,

> "Is not the Lord in our midst?
> No evil shall come upon us."

Among Christians this stance can lead to excusing one's own failures and faults by saying, "Man is a sinner and remains one; everyone is therefore dependent on forgiveness. More than that, only the dear Lord can decide. God still rules the world; therefore one may withdraw from public responsibility."

It is true that as persons who have become guilty of transgressions we need to be absolved in the name of Jesus. It is also true that we experience forgiveness only for Jesus' sake and thereby become free and happy. But precisely because of that, justice dare never become a matter of indifference for us. The cross dealt with justice, our justice. Justice therefore dare never become a matter of indifference for us. I give three reasons. First, our injustice cost Christ his life, (our injustice in the profane world itself). Second, in his love we came to know justice, especially our neighbor's justice, in a new and more sharply defined manner. Third, his Spirit helps us recognize the next step that is open to us. Micah already says it so very sharply (v. 11): when we bypass injustice, we lose our genuine certainty of faith (also when we are indifferent to questions of justice). Micah chides in v. 12,

> Therefore because of you
> Zion will be plowed as a field,
> Jerusalem shall be a heap of ruins
> and the temple mount will be given over to the beasts of the forest.

What does this mean? The fate of the city of God depends without question on the behavior of those who are responsible. So does the fate of the Christian church in this provisional world.

"Because of you!" Every student is a privileged member of society, and is therefore called to special responsibility. Every one necessarily grows up into public responsibility. Micah knew that it is up to each individual. He knew that it is possible to take a stand for justice without fearing men. We too are interrogated as individuals. But we also have been given the gift of community. We need it, in order to be upheld and led by the word and Spirit of Jesus in the midst of the tempestuous battle. Our work in the name of Jesus must receive a new dimension, the biblical dimension. Jerusalem's future would be in sad shape, as would that of the Christian church and of our fellow human beings, if Jesus and his predecessor Micah were not still speaking to our consciences, urging us to take a public stand for justice and to take a stand with those who suffer injustice.

In conclusion I repeat: our experience with Jesus can only become richer if we not only live with him privately but also follow him in the surroundings into which he sends us. Very important in this public involvement for justice is our continuous return to the Bible, to prayer, and to the fraternal strengthening of faith and mutual consultation that takes place in community. If, however, we do not push out toward community involvement for justice in our surroundings, our faith will languish and our community will fall sick.

In sum, we cannot take the path that was taken in the years before the last five when evangelical student groups wandered far from Jesus and his word and got lost in their social and political involvements. But we cannot take the path either that has often been taken in the last five years of curtailing the task open to us in the Bible, the path of fostering an inbred congregational life, which has been the danger of Christian Student Movement (SMD) groups up to the present.

What Will Become of the Church?[79]
Micah 3-5

"What will become of the church?" How are we supposed to know that? After all, predictions are all too often wrong, as we realize from our experience with predicting weather and horoscopes. Nevertheless there is a saying of Jesus which aroused a great deal of excitement when it was quoted during the Nazi days: "It is from the Jews that salvation will come" (John 4:22). Today perhaps it arouses less excitement than shoulder shrugging. Yet Christianity has been, and still is, completely convinced of its incontrovertible truth in this respect that Jesus is himself salvation, deliverance from all woe—and he comes out of the midst of the Jews. We can, therefore, understand him aright only if we take into consideration the history of the Jews, the history of Israel out of which he comes to us, especially the history of Israel's prophetic movement. That is what the first Christians did. It was with the help of the Old Testament that they learned to know Jesus ever better and better as the incarnate will of God. At the same time they discovered in the Old Testament the compass they needed for finding their path into the future. The path traveled by God's ancient people became the prototype for the path of God's new people. The Old Testament therefore offers us not so much prediction of the future as opportunity to examine the path on which God's people are traveling into the future, an examination which focuses as much on the successful breakthroughs God's people make as on their mistakes.

The reformers reemphasized the ancient admonition, "Search the Scriptures!" And rightly so, since the path traveled by God's ancient people is a preparatory school for God's new people. Faith lives from experiences. An amazing school for learning from such experiences is to be found in the Book of Micah, especially in chapters 3-5. The sayings there refer mostly to the fate of

Israel and of its capital Jerusalem. But over the gateway leading into Micah's book stands the summons (1:2),

> Hear, you nations, all of you,
>> hearken, O earth, and all that is in it.

According to this, Israel's experiences with the prophet Micah should be instructive for the nations as well as for the church on its long journey through the international world of nations and the upheavals of history. What Israel experienced should help us to achieve the proper orientation for our own situation. Here we will learn to know the most variant and difficult stretches of the road we are traveling on, five portions of which we wish to consider today. At each section we will ask, "Are we having similar experiences?" We will also examine what chances today's church has for a viable future and under what terms such chances are to be viewed. At the same time (and this is crucial) we will be able to practice adjusting to various phases of the future as we pass through them on this survey.

Let me begin by simply listing the titles we will use to characterize each section:

1. Foxes amid Ruins;
2. A Remnant That Limps;
3. Out of the Weakest Battalion;
4. Dew and a Lion;
5. The Final Journey through the Stars to Our Ultimate Destiny.

FOXES AMID RUINS

That is what is foreseen in the most frightening of Micah's threats of doom (3:12). It is aimed at Jerusalem, the very heart of God's ancient people.

> Because of you
>> Zion shall be a heap of ruins
>>> and the temple mount will be given over to the beasts of the forest.
>
> (3:12)

One hundred and fifty years later the prediction came true. Then we hear the lament rising up from out of Jerusalem's ruins,

> Zion lies in ruins,
>> foxes prowl around on it.
>> (Lam. 5:18)

*That is the first of our journey's bitter experiences: God himself
ruins his own beloved city.* He himself delivers up unto total destruction the beautiful sanctuary where he had repeatedly approached his people. Judgment begins at God's own house (1
Pet. 4:17). Foxes amid ruins! Nothing else survives but devastated ruins!

Why are these expectations of the future so completely negative? Micah answers succinctly, "Because of you!" He is addressing the responsible leaders and officials in Jerusalem, including its
priests and prophets. God is calling to account first of all his own
people. Micah had, in fact, in the preceding words just been indicting them for "building Zion with blood," for mercilessly mis-
handling and exploiting the labor conscripts. According to Mic.
3:2–3 they had been chopping Micah's compatriots "like steaks
for a frying pan." Micah had also been accusing the judges of
accepting bribes and the priests and prophets of conniving with
the wealthy, all the while assiduously quoting from their hymnbook, "Is not the Lord in our midst?" (continuing injustices and
unchecked covetousness revealing such pious statement as hypocrisy). In actual fact they had driven God and his goodness
out of his city. That is why the accusation "because of you" precedes the announcement of doom (foxes amid ruins!).

Do we have similar experiences? Have not church buildings
begun to deteriorate also in Oberhausen?[80] Recently I heard of a
new residential suburb in the Upper Rhine Valley in which more
than 200 of the 1800 inhabitants no longer belong to any church.
New residents leave the church simply by not indicating any religious affiliation on their tax forms. Similarly, a church superintendent in the German Democratic Republic told me that over
there (in East Germany) confirmation is for the most part a thing
of the past, dedication of the youth to the state having taken its
place almost everywhere. The membership of the Territorial
Church of the Rhineland sank last year from 3.7 to 3.5 million.
Perhaps a decline of 5–6 percent does not seem great. Yet "continuous dripping wears away a stone," the proverb says. Too
many people consider our territorial churches more stable than
they actually are. Micah's pronouncement against Jerusalem and
its sanctuary gives us a fundamental principle to ponder: it is not
ill-minded people, nor the enemies of the church, nor general his-

torical developments, nor general rules of life that decide the fate of Christian institutions. No, in the end it is God the Lord, the Lord of the church who is able to lay the church to ruins and give it over to foxes. That is why we should deliberately adjust our vision of the future to include the end of our state church.

Why will such sad events come to pass? To answer that we should consider first of all the reasons Micah gives. We recall that Jerusalem's leaders had been mercilessly oppressing the laborers, their eyes focused solely on big money. Next, when we examine the reasons for our contemporary situation, we ought not be superficial, reacting merely in panic. Did not our German churches in the last century at the beginning of the industrial age pay far too little attention to the difficulties of the hard-pressed laboring class while they entrusted their future all too willingly to the "care" of big contributors? Didn't the churches thereby lose a tremendous amount of credibility? Wasn't the church far too self-satisfied, convinced that the Lord was on its side, even though it could have discovered where the Lord is to be sought much more clearly from Jesus and from living under his cross than from Micah? We, as responsible co-workers, ought to ask ourselves, first of all, as we hear Micah's "because of you," "Isn't Micah talking about us, our self-centeredness, our joylessness when we could be working with Jesus in freedom, unity, and joyous hope?" *Let us learn this then as our first lesson: the historic home of God's presence can collapse in total ruin.* Precisely those who wish to make themselves secure ruin themselves and the city of God. Let me remind you of the reformers' experience with God's grace. Grace, they said, is like a passing rainstorm that scatters its bounty in patches here and there. Do we have any chances for a future? Do we not similarly reckon that such judgment is God's own deed?

In any case, Micah's verdict of death for Jerusalem had salutary results twice in ancient times. First, it saved the life of the prophet Jeremiah after he had been condemned to death (Jeremiah 26) because he had threatened Jerusalem. At that point the elders recalled what had happened to Micah; the result was that Jeremiah was freed. They recalled (and they were then referring to the other time Micah's threat had had a salutary effect) that already in his own days Micah's word had led to life rather than to death. King Hezekiah had permitted himself to be inwardly crushed by this word of doom; he had come to fear God. Thus Micah's word of doom saved him; and the temple remained intact for another hundred years. "Foxes amid ruins"—that threat can lead to life. God's word maintains a lively interaction between God and his people. Even while he is threatening, his purpose is to save.

A REMNANT THAT LIMPS

In the year 587 B.C. Jerusalem was conquered by the Babylonian Nebuchadnezzar II. The temple was burned and the upper classes (the royal court, the military, the artisans) were exiled; only a miserable remnant (a proletariat consisting largely of rural laborers) remained in the homeland. Into the midst of that catastrophic situation a new prophetic pronouncement sounded (4:6–7),

> ⁶In that day, says the Lord,
> I will assemble those who are limping;
>   I will gather those who have been dispersed
>   and those whom I have brought into disaster.
> ⁷And those who are lame I will make a remnant,
>   those who are wounded I will make a strong nation.
> And the Lord will be king on Mount Zion.

Any chances for a future here? Only one is visible: the Lord himself is continuing to act. Even though the earthly king has been taken far away, the Lord is still king over the heap of ruins. And his promises now apply to a limping remnant when he says, "I am going to assemble; I am going to bring; I am going to effect; I am going to strengthen." The Lord will be king. He will be active, the promise says, not in a Jerusalem still intact, not in a financially powerful temple hierarchy, not in a flourishing life of worship, but in a "remnant that limps," among those who have been dispersed and who are bleeding from grievous wounds. He remains at work in his forlorn flock. My generation experienced something similar in our own lives. I can still see myself in 1942 (thirty-five years ago!) at the end of an airstrip in Russia sitting in our small tent, reading the Bible with a Catholic from Bavaria. The churches at home had been bombed to pieces. The congregations had been dispersed far and wide. The preachers had been scattered in various widely separated theaters of war. And whatever little group managed to gather was in fact "a remnant that limped." But—wherever two or three met in any place under the biblical word, they experienced the reality that God was at work again.[81] In the midst of ruins a new beginning was being made. *That is the second experience on our journey: he continues to work precisely in the remnant that limps.* Amid the evident signs of dissolution in our state church there are in many places resolute groups of active Christians who gather for personal enlightenment and for active mission. He is making a new beginning. People who resolutely reckon with him alone, who gather around his word in prayer experience the fact that the Lord becomes the king who reigns over a lame remnant. That is what we should keep in mind for the dark stretches of the road on which we are traveling.

OUT OF THE WEAKEST BATTALION

Why is the prophet concerned with military units? A battalion in ancient Israel was called "a thousand." In an emergency every town in Judah had to provide a thousand men for the tribal militia. The tiny rural town of Bethlehem provides the weakest battalion. (Hence the prophet addresses it in 5:2 "Bethlehem, thou smallest among the thousands of Judah.") What can be expected of the wretched companies from a backward country region? "Yet," the prophet continues concerning Bethlehem, "from you shall come forth for me he who is to be ruler in Israel!" It is not Bethlehem that has lost out, but Jerusalem, the state capital where the king resides! A mocking question had been addressed to Jerusalem earlier, perhaps at the time of the siege (4:9),

> Why do you cry aloud?
> Is there no king in you?
> Have your counselors all perished?

And immediately before the oracle addressed to Bethlehem, Jerusalem is told,

> Now scratch yourself to pieces in lamentation, . . .
> Siege has been laid against us.
> With a rod they have smitten the ruler of Israel on the cheek.
> (5:1)

The earthly king in Jerusalem was being scornfully humiliated. And the question was now being raised, "Has God's people also come to its end, if the end has come to its capital, its royal palace, its political institutions, its representatives and their ability to defend themselves?" To be sure, the Lord's representative (the king) is being hit in the face with a cudgel. "But," the prophet continues, "you, Bethlehem, you tiny country town, out of you the Lord is going to come to me," out of the weakest battalion. The promise is itself already a programmatic prototype for us. How much more so is not its fulfillment a precedent for us!

We know that earliest Christianity recognized the promised Lord of Micah 5 in Jesus. He was not born at the royal court, but far apart as a carpenter's son. He did not grow up in official circles at the capital city but in the remote Galilean hill country. (The question, "Can anything good come out of Nazareth?" was intended to make him appear ridiculous.) There was nothing impressive, nothing militarily imposing about his origin. But he is precisely the one whom God established as the Lord for his people; yes, for his people in all the world.

Christendom dare never forget its origin. It must also always keep in mind where it should expect him, where he is beginning his work anew—amid shatterings of official organizations, in the weakest battalion, in remote Christian communities, in the simplest groups of workers or of young people, perhaps in a free church, perhaps in messengers from the younger churches, or in the sermon of a black African. Finally we are getting to know that missionary activity does not take place today on a one-way street which goes from Europe to overseas or from West to East, but that Europe and the West are experiencing missionary activity which is moving in the opposite direction: they are coming to us! All we have to do is to keep our eyes open and expect Christ's new activity to emerge from the direction of the weakest battalion.

What is he going to do? The prophet says, "He will step forth and as a shepherd shall feed his flock in the strength of God." In the ancient Near East a king functioned as a shepherd. His royal responsibility was a pastoral responsibility. "He feeds"—that signifies three things: he protects; he nurtures; he leads. When we hear reports of how he is defending, how he is fostering, how he is leading, we ought to prick up our ears. Whenever I look back to what has been to date the most difficult decade of my life (1937–1947), the words of Jesus to his disciples often come to mind, "As often as I sent you out, . . . did you lack anything?" (Luke 22:35). And I must answer, with the first disciples, "Nothing! Never!" He was always present in the weakest battalions, in the places that were of no account by public standards. "Fear not, little flock!" *That is what we learn from our experiences on the third stretch of our journey: do not despise the weakest and most remote groups! His power has always been made perfect in weakness,* in the case of individuals and of the church; and it will be so in their and our future.

DEW AND A LION

These two comprise an unlikely team! Nevertheless they are the pair that appear in parallel verses and characterize the fourth stretch of the path we are traveling. The first verse is 5:7,

> And then the remnant of Jacob shall be
> in the midst of many peoples
> like dew from the Lord
> like showers upon growing plants.

The second is 5:8,

> And then the remnant of Jacob shall be
> in the midst of many peoples
> like a lion among the beasts of the forest,
> like a young lion among the flocks of sheep.

Both sayings begin, "And then." When? After the catastrophe, "the remnant that limps" experiences the new activity of the royal shepherd as he brings to its diminished life liberation, unification, and joy. Then is when that new life will work itself out (as both verses put it) "in the midst of many peoples." The small group will be equipped by the royal shepherd not for enterprises of its own but for shining forth far and wide among the peoples like dew and like a lion! What does that mean?

Dew sparkles in the morning sun with millions of pearl-like droplets. For six months no rain falls in Palestine. But the heavy dew permits vines and melons to flourish and reach a full, juicy and delightfully sweet maturity. Dew can be as effective as a shower for making the dry land fruitful. To such a successful future the church is called as it lives amid many nations. Hence the church should put an end to sterile and self-destructive activity in the international world of nations and instead develop fruitful cooperation with the nations. It should be "like dew from the Lord." But is not the church much too weak for that?

No, responds the second verse. In fact, what survives the catastrophe will live "like a lion among the beasts of the forest, like a young lion among the flocks of sheep." In the Old Testament this way of picturing self-assured superiority may, to be sure, still be connected with the conception of a rapacious animal. But from the perspective of the New Testament the picture of a royal lion should remind us of total superiority and therewith of fearlessness and invincibility. The fruitfulness of dew and the fearlessness of a lion will characterize the effect that the future little flock will have on the masses in many nations. The younger generation ought not let itself be shocked by the compressed and cramped situation of the Christian community. After all, that community has been set in a worldwide horizon. We experience a foretaste of its future when we sing in worship.[82]

> O God, O Lord of heav'n and earth,
>> Your living finger never wrote
> That life should be an aimless mote,
>> A deathward drift from futile birth. . . .
> We walled us in this house of doom,
>> Where death had royal scope and room,
> Until your servant, Prince of Peace,
>> Broke down its walls for our release.
> How beautiful the feet that trod
>> The road to bring good news from God!
> How beautiful the feet that bring
>> Good tidings of our saving king!

Self-assured, confident joy is what we experience on the fourth stretch of our journey. At the very beginning the tiny group of Jesus' disciples (one can almost tick them off on the fingers of two hands!) experienced that, in the midst of the nations of the Mediterranean world of that day, they were equipped to function as dew and as a lion (fruitfully and fearlessly). From the judgments which are now going on throughout the world and which are beginning at the house of God we ought to experience anew the truth of the ancient promises that God is at work among the international world of many nations through a remnant that is like dew and like a lion.

THE FINAL JOURNEY THROUGH THE STARS TO OUR ULTIMATE DESTINY

Let us finally hear what the Book of Micah has to say about the final stretch of our journey to the goal God has established for us. One of the most breathtaking parts of this prophetic book is the abrupt transition from chapter 3 to chapter 4. The third chapter closes grimly with a description of what we have called in this address the first section of our journey,

> Jerusalem shall become a heap of ruins,
>> and the temple mountain shall be given over to the beasts of the forest.
>
> (3:12)

In sharp contrast (introduced by the word "but," a sort of ruffles and flourishes to get everyone's attention) chapter 4 begins,

> But in the latter days it shall come to pass that the mountain of the Lord's house shall be established as the highest mountain . . .
> Peoples shall flow to it,
>> and many nations shall come and say,
> "Come, let us go up to the mountain of the Lord,
>> that he may teach us his ways!"

Are we hearing correctly? According to this, the heap of ruins is becoming the most attractive pinnacle for all nations! The severely devastated city is becoming the source of definitive peace for the whole world. And that is what makes possible our final journey through the stars to our ultimate destiny. ("For out of Zion shall go forth instruction"; "then they shall beat their swords into plowshares, and their spears into pruning hooks . . . and they shall learn war no more.")

But is not this concluding journey through the stars to our ultimate destiny utopian? Yes, it is, because presently we see very little of it. And yet many of us can, despite everything, report encouraging experiences. I, for instance, am thinking of a sermon which I had to preach during the war on Isaiah 53 in one of the Confessing Church's "emergency churches" (a room in a factory) in Solingen-Wald. I had spoken of Jesus as the one most despised and rejected, the one who meant nothing to most people but for whom God's promise was and still is valid, "I will give the many to him as booty. Even kings will shut their mouths before him." I commented to the tiny congregation, "Some day it will come to pass that everybody hereabout will come rushing to this obscure place into which they have now shoved Jesus' word and us." Only a few months later even the large church in Solingen-Wald could not provide enough places for the many persons who had previously despised God's word, turning up their noses at it, but who now wanted to hear.

> All are alike before the Highest.
> 'Tis easy for our God, we know,
> To raise thee up, though low thou liest,
> To make the rich man poor and low.[83]

We are able to experience this often on a small scale in our personal lives. In that case it is also an experience of what is ultimate. And that is why predictions of our futures that fail to reckon with it omit the chief factor.

But despite such personal experiences of success on a small scale we are still far removed from the goal of peace in our world! To be sure, Chagall's gigantic window about world peace according to Isaiah 11 occupies a significant place in the United Nations Building in New York, as does the sculpture which the Soviet Union has contributed for the courtyard of the same building, portraying a farmer who is beating a gigantic sword into a plowshare. But what good do such symbols do if at the same time the nations' prime energies are devoted to the perfection of neutron bombs and destructive terrorism runs rampant throughout the world, lurking behind every other corner? How does the mere promise of peace help?

Very soberly we hear Micah 4:5 after the promise of a final journey through the stars to our final goal,

> All the peoples still walk, each in the name of its god; but we walk in the name of the Lord our God always and forever.

What is here recognized without any cosmetic cover-up is that the nations are still oriented according to the goals of power politics and ideology, their gods. But we should now undertake the journey toward our ultimate destiny, a journey which they will all have to join after they have recognized that all other paths mislead. "But we"—we see that Zion has become (because of the death on the cross and the resurrection that occurred there) the pinnacle of the world; without a recognition of sin and its forgiveness there will never be peace in the world, neither on a smaller or larger scale. When, however, under the influence of Jesus' word and cross, sin is recognized and forgiveness experienced, then a new world begins.

"But we"—let us now take an unconditional stand on behalf of justice, and in opposition to all twistings and perversion of it. Let us expose sin, without trying to smooth it over, first and foremost in ourselves. Let us continually sharpen our own ears and those of others for the voice of Jesus who forgives sins unto us and unto the entire world and who is calling out to us, "Let him among you who is without sin cast the first stone." Where this call is heard, not even one single stone is thrown, not to mention hand grenades or bombs. Let us, under his leadership, resolutely stand up for peace! God is using also the dark stretches of the road that lie before us to prepare his church to be his messenger: the catastrophes, the limping remnant, the weakest battalion, the fact that already now both dew and a lion are busily at work among the peoples. Let us gather in small groups, groups of co-workers, in Bible classes, in cottage meetings, and in action groups. Let us examine our situation in the light of his word, recognizing the opportunities of the future and *our task of resolutely forming a scouting party to embark on the final portion of our journey, a voyage into the realm of the stars toward our ultimate destiny.* Can we draw better consequences from our consideration of the five sections of our path according to the Book of Micah than the hymnwriter has put into our heart and on to our lips?

> Oh, let me hear you speaking in accents clear and still
>> Above the storms of passion, the murmurs of self-will.
> Now speak to reassure me, to hasten or control;
>> Now speak and make me listen, O Guardian of my soul.
> O Jesus, you have promised to all who follow you
>> that where you are in glory, your servant shall be too
> And Jesus, I have promised to serve you to the end;
>> Oh, give me grace to follow, my master and my friend.[84]

"Neither Shall They Learn
War Any More":[85]
Micah 4:1–5

May God's peace rule in our hearts! Amen.

Hear the word of holy Scripture from the Book of the prophet Micah 4:1–5.

[1]But in the latter days it will come to pass that the mountain of
the Lord's house will be established as the highest mountain,
raised up above the hills.
Peoples shall flow to it;
[2]and many nations shall come and say,
"Come, let us go to the Lord's mountain,
to the house of the God of Jacob,
that he may teach us his ways
and we may walk in his paths."
For out of Zion shall go forth instruction,
the Lord's word from Jerusalem.
[3]He will judge between many peoples,
and shall be the judge for mighty nations.
Then they shall beat their swords into plowshares,
and their spears into pruning hooks.
Nation shall not lift up sword against nation,
neither shall they learn war anymore.
[4]They shall sit every one under his vine
and under his fig tree.
And none shall make them afraid.
Thus the mouth of the Lord has spoken.
[5]To be sure, now each nation is still walking in the
name of its god;
but we walk in the name of the Lord our God
now and forever.

Lord, send out thy light and thy truth, that they may lead us and bring us to thy holy hill and to thy habitation. Amen.

The prophetic promise in today's text plants an unexpected hope into the midst of our lives in defiance of all the experiences we humans have had throughout the millennia with wars, with religions, and finally with ourselves.

It defies also the experiences that we have had with "the mountain of the Lord's house," with Zion, with Jerusalem. In fact, what immediately preceded our text was the prophet's threat (3:12) that

> Zion will be plowed like a field;
> Jerusalem, like a heap of ruins;
>   and the temple mountain will be full of wild bushes.

Down through the ages and into our own days this threat has fulfilled itself, not only in the ancient city of God but also in the spiritual city of God which Christendom should be.

Despite such a past, "in the latter days" this mountain will yet tower over all the heights. Why? We know the answer from the New Testament: because on Mt. Zion the cross was once thrust into the ground and on Mt. Zion an innocent person was nailed to a cross as a guilty criminal because he took the place of those who executed him and because out of sheer love he redeemed those who in sheer hate had abandoned him to raw power; because on Mt. Zion the law of retribution was put out of operation once and for all and love took on the form of unconditional forgiveness. That is why this mount will in the end tower over all the heights in the world.

"In the latter days!" What does that mean? Bright pictures of hope are impressed on us by the prophet. All people of the earth will stream to this mount. Why? I don't know. But I think, it is simply because they lack any other counsel. After all attempts at peaceful survival have ended up again and again in hostilities, after all peoples recognize their inability to live in peace, then finally in their sin, need, and longing for peace they will encourage one another to make the long trek to Mt. Zion. This great about-face is what we expect for all nations. "Things are not all staying the way they were."

What do the nations come for? To open their ears to the *one* voice of the *one* Lord. This voice does not teach them theories, but "his paths," "that we may (finally sick and tired of all programs) walk in his paths." His voice directs them to the path of following the crucified Lord, to the narrow path which leads away from the treadmill of recrimination. Marc Chagall erected in memory of Dag Hammerskjöld a tremendously large church window in the United Nations building in New York. In it he portrays the dominion of the Messiah as Isaiah 11 pictures it, where wolves live together with lambs, panthers with goats, where cows and bears feed together and a suckling child plays over a viper's hole. This vision is what now stands before the nations as their ultimate destiny. The voice of the Messiah will silence those who employ violence. Hunters and their quarry will come to live at peace. The United Nations (as yet so disunited) have merely a transitory significance. Before them there now stands the portrayal of their final end. That is why hope is still active. "Things are not all staying the way they were."

That voice of the Messiah is still powerful; it is still driving the prophetic word home. It is growing in effectiveness. Many quarrels will begin to be settled, many angry disputants will be reconciled, and above all, a great deal of reforging is going to take place. They will make their swords into plowshares and their spears into pruning knives. It will not be eternally true that nations will confront one another in hostility. A century ago lasting peace between hereditary foes like Germany and France seemed unthinkable. Now, however, war between them has become inconceivable. Similarly peace for all peoples (now still inconceivable) will become reality. All weapons will be worked into implements of peace. I imagine it occurring somewhat in this way: the tremendous human ingenuity employed to fabricate bombs will be used for constructing glorious playgrounds; the gigantic amounts of energy now devoted to armaments will be spent for health parks; the fabulous expenditures for rockets will be used for vacation paradises. The war academies will cease to exist and schools for reforging outdated instruments of violence will be established. Such hope is being impressed upon us by the prophetic portrayal set before us.

One feature of the portrayal deserves special note: the idyll of peace for the individual. Every single person will enjoy his or her own peaceful life. "Each will sit under his or her vine and fig tree." Each will have not only a comfortable house but also a garden where vine branches will embrace fig trees; every person will have the choicest fruit for the taking: grapes and sweet juicy figs. And noble wine will be available.

Is it not precious to see how individuals are taken into consideration in addition to the international world of nations? The prophet's God does not take thought only of the organization of the masses in the international world, but also of each individual's fate. Each will be completely satisfied. Therefore there is hope for all in their totality and for each person individually. "Thing are not all staying the way they were."

But when is this utopian portrait—as yet unrealized—to become reality? "In the latter days." That is to say: Not yet! With sober realism the prophetic voice observes, "Now each nation is still walking in the name of its god." The portrait of hope has been placed into a tattered present where Moslems attack Christians and vice versa, where in Ireland Protestants fight against Catholics and vice versa. "Each nation is still walking in the name of its god." The prophet is not speaking theoretically (as when moderns speak in terms of some sort of theological pluralism), but with pertinent realism. The gods fabricated by ideologies are still inflaming peoples one against the other; the ideology of growth is still causing mighty conflicts. Violence is currently an item that still gets past the inspectors without being challenged; the politics of strength is still expected to provide security (though it is only increasing fearful forebodings). People are still giving free rein to sensual passions, indulging them, satisfying them, and permitting their own dissatisfactions to delight in aggression. That is the way things still are even now. Each people is still walking in the name of its god.

"But we walk in the name of the Lord our God." Everything depends now on this expression, "But we"! Only let us not use it pharisaically! Rather, it should be a fresh, spontaneous declaration of a clear-cut move on our part to depose all false gods. A new people, a new community desires to take shape; it deliberately desires to take the path that Jesus took, the narrow way of him who, when he was reviled, reviled not again. Why? Because already this community sees the picture of hope, now (in the midst of the transition) it is conscious of what is ultimate, and its members exercise themselves in a new style of life in relationship to one another and to others.

Already God's new people are listening to what the nations will one day say to one another as they travel toward the ultimate summit, though they have previously heard it spoken of in such Christian admonitions as, "It is better to suffer wrong than to commit it," or "Strive to live at peace with all men."

Already now God's new people are permitting his atoning work to become effective in their lives. We are perceiving his mediation between ourselves and those with whom we have difficulties; he is removing hostility in our midst.

"But we walk in the name of the Lord our God." That means, for example, in the case of the younger generation in Christendom, that young Christians are perceiving the possibility of discharging their responsibility of service to society in the pursuits of peace rather than in those of war; already they are resolving not to learn war any more. Instead, they are exercising themselves in helping the defenseless, the helpless, and the dislocated. Walking in the name of the Lord means resolutely dispensing with the long-standing practices of political baiting and demagoguery, or smearing and abusing opponents. It pleased me greatly last week when a high official, during a heated discussion on television, declared that he had made a solemn vow to give up polemics in party strife and to dispense with attempting to damage political opponents.

As a Christian community we ought purposely to construct in our midst a workshop where reforging may take place. The iron rigidity we all have must be melted down and become fluid. Then we will seek to influence public opinion in the direction of reducing the budget for military expenditures while increasing contributions for peace, health, education and social welfare. Then we will also renovate our own personal budgets; we will give small and large contributions for whatever removes discord and discontent. Giving instead of "making a fast buck," generosity instead of poison and avarice—that should be the principle that guides our expenditures.

What needs to be reforged above all else are those sources of all sorts of evil: our barbed tongues, our sharp pens, and our cutting words.

The best fire for such reforging work burns in the Scriptures in Jesus' word and in an exemplary way, in the biblical Proverbs,

Thoughtless words can wound as deeply as any sword, but wisely
   spoken words can heal. (12:18 TEV)
Deceit is in the heart of those who devise evil,
   but they who plan good have joy. (12:20)
With patience a ruler may be persuaded,
   and a soft tongue will break a bone. (25:15 RSV)

The spirit of such words blows on the coals of the smith's fire. Here we learn how to invite people rather than exclude them, how to greet them rather than cut them down, how to renounce all defamation, and how to put the best construction on everything. To that end it is worthwhile contemplating Luther's explanation of the eighth commandment, "We should so fear and love God that we do not deceitfully belie, betray, slander nor defame our neighbor, but defend him, speak well of him, and put the best construction on everything."

"But we walk in the name of the Lord our God." These words encourage us to separate ourselves daily from the Old Adam. In that way we travel already now the path to the ultimate goal. Our long trek to the ultimate summit began when Jesus entered our history. Let us continue it today and tomorrow, heading out directly toward that lofty goal.

And the peace of God which passes all understanding keep your hearts and minds in Christ Jesus. Amen!

During the Weeks of Terror:[86]
Three Evenings of Bible Study

WOE TO WISHFUL DREAMS
(THE ROOTS OF TERRORISM):
MICAH 2

Micah accuses,

> ¹Woe to those who plan injustice, deeds of wickedness while they
>   disturb themselves on their beds at night, hatching out evil
>   schemes
> so that when the morning dawns they may perform them,
>   because they have the power to do it!
> ²They covet fields, and lay hold of them by force;
>   and houses, and seize them.
> They oppress a man and his family,
>   a man and his inheritance.

Micah warns,

> ³Therefore thus says the Lord,
>   Behold, I too am planning evil (against this entire brood),
>   so that you will not be able to extricate your necks from it.
>   You shall no longer walk erectly (for it is an evil day).
> ⁴In that day they shall take up a taunt song against you,
>   and wail with (this) lament,
> "We're totally ruined—
>   (my people's land is divided into allotments for aliens.
>   "See, they are taking away the ground out from under my
>   feet!")
> our fields are being redistributed."
> ⁵Therefore you will have no one to allot you a share of land in
>   the Lord's community.

The people he was threatening respond,

> ⁶"Do not preach at us" is what they preach.
>   "Such topics are not proper for preaching."
>   "Such insults do not apply to us."

⁷ᵃ"Is the house of Jacob really under a curse?"
  "Has the Lord become impatient?"
  "Is that the way he acts?"

Micah replies in the name of his God,

⁷ᵇIt is true, my words are compassionate to the upright.
⁸But you are rising up against my people like an enemy.
  You are stripping peaceable citizens of their robes;
    carefree wanderers who are disinclined to fight.
⁹The women of my people you are driving out from their cherished homes;
    and from their children you are taking my honor forever.
¹⁰"Therefore arise and go!
  There is no safety here any more!"
  For the sake of a trifle
    you are taking possession of a painful pledge.
¹¹If some one came to deceive you with false lies, saying
    "I will preach to you of wine and whisky"—
    that would be the preacher for this people.

We highlight seven points.

A Prophetic Voice amid a Tumult of Voices

Let us survey the contours of this unit. It is not one coherent speech. Rather it is the documentation of a public confrontation. Only in vv. 1–5 do we have connected speech by the prophet, clearly articulated in an accusation (vv. 1–2) and a threat (vv. 3–5). In vv. 6–7 we hear fragments of passionate objection (imperatives which seek to prohibit free speech and rhetorical questions which contest the prophet's accusation and threaten him by appealing to sacred tradition). Then the prophet attacks with new specific charges (vv. 8–10). He concludes (v. 11) with a portrait of the celebrity preacher whom his opponents really want: one who would pander to their covetous desires, solicitous lest the atmosphere of comfortable fraternalism be disturbed.

Public altercation appears unavoidable. The prophets know that the violence perpetrated by the wielders of power, constituting a transgression of God's commandments, dare not remain unopposed, whereas the wielders of power do not want to have their plans disturbed in any way.

The question for us is: Can a Christian community withdraw from public altercation these days when we read in gigantic letters on the wall along the Neckar River the Red Army Fraction's threat, "If our three comrades are murdered, so will 300 others be murdered"? People who have decided to think, to write, and perhaps even to act according to such slogans live tooth by jowl with us, walking the same streets, eating with us at the university commons, sitting with us in the same lecture halls. A Christian community cannot act as if it were possible to live its life in a pious ghetto. Public altercation is unavoidable; indeed, it seems obligatory. Like the prophets of old, Jesus entered the welter of voices and sent forth his disciples with his word as sheep among wolves (Matt. 10:16). This evening as well as on the two subsequent evenings we intend to listen to what voices from the Bible have to say in the midst of the tumults of our age.

The Prophet Experiences Opposition

He had dared to speak about the expropriation of poorer people's ancestral lands, also about the labor conscription practices that were devastating family life. Micah had threatened the powerful with corresponding dispossession and deportation. Now in response people raise objections to his message. Social and economic politics is not, they say, a proper topic for preaching. A preacher ought to proclaim God's blessings (not curses) and his patience with sinners; above all, a preacher ought to recite the deeds by which God revealed himself in sacred history.

Yesterday I received a letter from a pastor who wrote to me (in collaboration with a professor of theology) after having heard the tape of my Marburg address on Micah 2–3 of October 8.[87] "We consider it dangerous, particularly now, for the church to involve itself in social and political matters," he wrote. I certainly see the danger that Christians might possibly stray toward alien gods through their sociopolitical activity. I also see that the church might possibly betray its sole task of bearing witness to Christ, the sole liberator of all people. Yet there is no less danger that we Christians bear our witness without drawing the proper conclusions from it. Micah responds to those who forbid him speech by asking them, "How can you expect patience and blessing from God for yourselves when you take in pawn for a trifling debt the poorest person's robe, when you take away the roof from over the head of defenseless women and rob children of small joys!" In saying this, Micah anticipates Jesus' parable about the unmerciful servant who expected great benefits from God for himself and received them, but did not transmit even a fraction of them to those who needed help. Micah also anticipates Jesus' identification of himself with the hungry, the naked, and the imprisoned at the great judgment (Matthew 18 and 25).

That is why I consider it dangerous for the church to be incapacitated by a mistaken fear of dangers that might ensue on its taking a stand against public injustice, after the prophets repeatedly took such stands with a passion and after Jesus exposed himself on the cross to mortal danger and called his disciples to follow him. Gustav Heinemann said, "Whoever remains silent fosters what is afoot." Let us contemplate this a moment: whoever is silent to public injustice fosters what is afoot; he is living a life without Jesus and against him. Do we see this danger?

A Heart for the Helpless

That is the sort of sympathy that motivates Micah's activity. In v. 2 he has in mind an individual father and his family, an individual person and his inheritance, and then—after the opponents' opposition had been voiced—individual peaceful citizens who are being plundered, defenseless women "of my people," helpless children (vv. 8–9). Having a heart for the helpless! Isn't this what has been all too often missing in Christendom? Our eyes have not been seeing; our ears have not been hearing; but, above all, there are no helping hands, no sympathetic hearts. All during the years when the Federal Republic of Germany has been rising to affluence, many an area in our midst has remained, and still remains, a neglected reservation. Wherever unjust conditions have prevailed, a seedbed exists on which terrorist movements have been able to develop and justify their existence. Let us not forget the things which Ulrike Meinhof, Gudrun Ensslin and their friends cared about ten years ago: things like the pitiful conditions in children's homes and the like. They saw need and injustice where others were blind and intent only on their own advancement. Let us not forget, "they went out from us" with more of a heart for the helpless than others: they went out from evangelical parsonages, from Christian homes, or, like Rudi Dutschke, from the Christian youth movement in the German Democratic

Republic. Dutschke shows that social criticism did not have to lead to terrorism, for he unambiguously kept his distance from the terrorists. But the activity of these social critics could lead to terrorism.

What are the conclusions we should draw from this? I purposely limit myself to mentioning only one: if we do not want the seedbed of terrorism to grow, we will have to help people in our vicinity who suffer under unjust and intolerable living conditions. Micah exhorts us to take a stand on behalf of those who are unable to help themselves, who have no representatives in the parliaments and in the caucuses of the powerful, those who are always sent back to the end of the waiting lines. Many small scouting parties, sent in advance to search out those who are in desperate straits, should grow up within our congregations. Christian social politics is something we cannot dispense with. One thing should be clear to us after these dark weeks: as long as there is time we should meet the terror with friendliness, trust, comfort, and willingness to help—as long as we have time! Those who desire much more than that could well achieve much less.

Psychological Phenomena

"Woe to those who plan injustice on their beds at night." In this escalation of covetous desires lies the sinister origin of all that subsequently has germinated from it. "Covet" is the key word in the ninth and tenth commandments. Communal life and peace are endangered by individuals' coveting. In the ninth and tenth commandments as well as in Micah "coveting" directs itself toward persons and things. A direct path leads from such coveting, past planning to seize what is coveted, to violence perpetrated against persons as well as things (v. 2). Both types of violence are expressly prohibited in Lev. 19:13 with the very same words Micah uses: "Thou shalt not seize . . . thou shalt not oppress!" The prophetic word, however, is directed primarily against the private fabrication of plans "in bed." We cannot read that without seeing ourselves challenged to self-discipline. What sort of pet desires and thoughts do we foster as we fall asleep and as we awake? Do we permit our thoughts to overwhelm the wholesome instructions of God's commandments? When prayerful hearkening to God's word ceases for long stretches of time, the psyche is endangered by growing brutalization. Do we no longer hear the prophet's shrill *hôy*? *Hôy* rumbled through the streets and squares whenever a death occurred in Micah's day. *Hôy* now designates those who have abandoned themselves to flaming covetousness as those who are doomed to death, yes, who have already been buried alive, even though they imagine that they are still growing in strength and power.

The day before yesterday a young man stated in a larger group discussion, "You older people learned abstinence thirty or forty years ago. We younger people have learned only to desire affluence." I must add, "We older people have all too quickly unlearned what we had once learned." Those who see terrorism's worldwide disasters should begin to lay hold of the covetousness in their own hearts and cease to violate the limitations set up by the prophet's warnings. We should listen to Erhart Eppler and not ask how much growth we need but what it is we need to have grow: desire for things or readiness to dispense with them; income for self-aggrandizement or involvement on behalf of others; giving or receiving. Here is where decisions are made whose consequences we cannot even envision.

A *Mushrooming of Covetous Desires*

During the days of terror such desires led to the replacement of what had been a legitimate concern with need and injustice by an irrational quest for power. Micah characterizes those whom he indicts as people who executed at daybreak the plans they had been making at night "because they had the power to do it" (because they had people "in their hands," "at their disposal," because they had the system in hand). In their zeal for reform our young social politicians attacked acknowledged injustice and that included the wielders of power, big money, leading politicians, and the mighty press. But soon what had first been decisive in their movement began to recede more and more (the very thing that is indispensable for genuine improvement of conditions). Their recognition of others' injustices was not counterbalanced by a corresponding control of their own injustices. As they became involved in the discussion and practice of institutional and personal power, and of violence against people and things, gradually self-control and self-discipline began to disappear.

Furthermore, the fact that the personal objectives they pursued mushroomed and blinded them to the actual improvements being made by their opponents in the establishment was equally fatal; they dared not acknowledge such improvements. In actual fact, however, quite a few people are busy, both in the world of post-capitalism and of socialism, with giving these opposing forms of social organization a more humane face, with creating more justice for all, with curtailing the exploitation of the masses, with replacing class hatred with partnership, with establishing care for the weak, and with preserving human dignity in penal as well as regular situations. Precisely now when this process is gaining momentum—with a great deal still to be accomplished—terror rears its head, felling naively innocent people and dishonoring those who have been kidnapped in a manner no present-day employer would dare use to dishonor his employees. Murderers are feted as "executioners"; in a situation where no regular court can impose the death penalty, people take the law into their own hands most brutally, while suicides are presented as "murders."

Why did the initial legitimate recognition of need and injustice make such an about-face and become a mad rush for power and destruction? On the day after the Mogadishu episode and the suicides at Stammheim, the French newspaper agency AFB in Marseille received this explanatory announcement, "Those who executed the prisoners at Stammheim, their accomplices, and the corrupt medical authorities at the prison who support the theory that they committed suicide will be executed. All across Europe 100,000 bombings will destroy the structure of German capitalism. We give individuals and companies a limit of three months to get rid of their German holdings including vehicles of all sorts, industrial material, and medical equipment. On January 20 the first German aircraft will be blown to pieces." We are living under the pressures of such deadlines!

What are the roots of this sort of thinking that is bent on violent destruction? Often it seems as if in this instance the mask of the old evil foes is again visible, the one whom no human can withstand. But after the advent of Christ do we have to capitulate to him without putting up any resistance? After contemplating Micah's indictment we should at the very least consider three possible roots of current terrorism.

1. The fact that, when people turned from the biblical faith, humans became the ultimate authority for humans has in any case led to the situation that now humans appoint themselves as the final authority, to such an extent in fact that they reject also every other human control. Hence murder and robbery are introduced as political measures without there being any check.

2. Since God's fundamental commandments and Jesus' self-sacrifice are no longer normative in our culture, any recognition of personal guilt as well as any acknowledgement of other people's insights disappears. Arbitrarily one's own personal justice is established as the norm—with a resulting rule of terror.

3. Since the biblical promise of God's coming rule is no longer worth consideration and patient waiting for, it is discounted as false comfort. Since even human attempts at gradual improvement are ridiculed, impatient attempts are now made (by way of inhuman measures) to effect a total transformation—or, failing that, to plunge everything (in complete resignation and total rage) into "nothingness." Thus, once inordinate desires mushroomed, the erstwhile salutary recognition of existing injustice has been changed into the present mad rush for monstrous power.

Those Who Wield Power

If we acknowledge that everyone's wishful dreams need new controls, then we must give special attention to controlling the dreams of those who wield power. In chapter 3 Micah makes it even clearer that all depends on justice being combined with power. Pascal expressed that very clearly in one of his thoughts (*Pensées* 298), "Justice without power is powerless. Power without justice is tyrannical. Justice and power must therefore be connected so that what is just is also powerful and what is powerful is also just." Our democracy is an attempt to interlace power and justice. By means of its acknowledgement of human imperfection a system of government in which a number of parties are involved serves mutual correction; and the division of power among legislative, executive and judicial branches serves to inhibit setting justice and power up in opposition to one another.

The Council of the Evangelical Churches in Germany in its discussion of the terrorism of recent weeks calls attention to the Barmen Declaration which affirms that the state "has the task of taking care of justice and peace according to the measure of human insight and human ability it possesses—through threats and through the exercise of power." The Council speaks then of the Evangelical Church as having been also imprisoned during the weeks of terrorism insofar as "we did not oppose strongly enough the stance in our midst that is oriented one-sidedly toward conflict; nor did we proclaim God's command and promise clearly enough." Perhaps too many of us, particularly those of us at universities—and I include myself—have all too often and all too strongly expressed only criticism of the government, or too often remained silent in the face of unjustified criticism of the government. Today we must realize clearly that basically no better possibility exists at the present time for coordinating justice and power than in this government of ours. Participation in a critical consideration of details of government activities is, of course, absolutely necessary. But those who tend toward wholesale condemnation must allow themselves to be asked most seriously and precisely what they think should replace this government of ours. Those who are one-sidedly oriented toward conflict ought to examine themselves to see whether or not they are helping put injustice into prison or whether they are consigning justice to impotence. Those who wield power deserve our intercession, that they may serve justice and therewith the welfare of the weakest members of society.

God's Plan Over against Human Planning

"Woe to those who plan evil . . . , Thus says the Lord, 'Behold, I am planning evil from which you will not be able to extricate your necks.'" In conclusion, we are able to refer to only one point: the evil plans humans make have been integrated into God's plans; from the outset they have been encircled by his plans. That corresponds to Jesus' saying in the Sermon on the Mount (Matt. 7:2 RSV), "With the judgment you pronounce you will be judged; and the measure you give will be the measure you get." Such a saying is one which each of us must always heed. In view of the terror with which we must live, this means primarily that we do not know when or whether this government or the great international alliance of governments will come to terms with terrorism or whether our government and other governments will succumb to the danger of giving injustice power. But we must include in what we do know the fact that even terror cannot act outside God's will.

From that viewpoint we will have to examine (in the next two sessions) the questions of (*a*) how we may *live with* existing terrorism, and (*b*) whether we may expect terrorism to be *overcome* (if it can be overcome, we must ask how).

Before we do that, however, let us keep in mind what we considered to be the roots of terror in the light of the prophetic word, even though this remains inexplicable at its most profound depths. In every person there lurks a potential terrorist; none of the terrorist leaders had the current phase of his life written out in advance in the biography of his youth. We must consider the fact that the unbridled escalation of wishful dreaming is fostering a seedbed for terrorism. When the living God is denied, self-appointed humans are able at any time to appoint themselves as the supreme authority beyond controls. When God's commandments and Christ's self-sacrifice are despised, confession of one's own guilt and recognition of other people's insights are dispensed with, so that a brutal brand of capricious justice can be installed. The inner compass fails to function.

When the expectation of the coming of God's kingdom disappears, patient waiting and attempts to make sensible gradual advances fall victim to an "all-or-nothing" mentality.

Let each one of us also see what the danger is for us personally, for others, and for our government if we should fall victim all too quickly to a reactionary backlash to terrorism, an antiterrorist movement which is not one bit better than terrorism itself. That would also spell the rule of injustice, caprice, and impatience.

If, however, Micah has showed us at least something of the roots of terror, we should let ourselves be moved by the frightful events of the present toward an entirely different direction: toward a dialogue with the God who in Jesus has not remained hidden but who is leading us to liberty. From him we dare ask for the daily rising of the New Man in whose presence the terrified can recover and the vexed be liberated from mistrust to find a way out of wrath and hatred to new goodness for themselves and for others.

WHAT IS GOOD FOR A HUMAN BEING?
(LIVING WITH TERROR):
MICAH 6

¹Hear ye what the Lord is saying:
  "Arise, plead your case before the mountains
    and let the hills hear your voice!
²Hear, ye mountains, how the Lord is going to present his case
    and listen, you foundations of the earth!
For the Lord has a case against his people,
    and he is going to bring an accusation against Israel.
³My people, what have I done to you!
    In what respect have I demanded too much of you?
    Answer me!
⁴Behold, I brought you up from the land of Egypt;
  I redeemed you from the house of bondage.
I sent before you Moses, Aaron, and Miriam.
⁵Remember, O my people, what Balak planned
  and what response Balaam gave him.
Think of your passage from Shittim to Gilgal
  so that you may realize what the Lord did in order to save you."
⁶— — — With what dare I come before the Lord,
  and bow myself before God on high?
Should I appear before him with a whole burnt offering,
  or with a one-year-old calf?
⁷Does he take pleasure in thousands of rams,
  in countless streams of oil?
Should I sacrifice my firstborn to atone for my sin,
  my own son for my trespasses?
⁸It has been told thee, O man, what is good
  and what the Lord is expecting of you:
to practice justice, to love community solidarity
  and to live attentively with your God.

Once again we direct our attention to a chapter from Micah, in order to clarify basic questions of our personal lives and, more specifically, to seek instruction for living with terror. At the same time I shall attempt to take up some of the questions which were raised in connection with Micah 2 and our deliberations about the roots of terror. Other questions, such as the place which the phenomenon of terrorism has in the eschatological scheme of things, we postpone for the next session.[88] Again, my point of departure will be seven central points in the text.

The Individual in a Cosmic Forum

At the conclusion of our text (v. 8) the question about what is good for human beings is given an unambiguous answer that is directed to each individual. The answer is a response to a question which an individual put in vv. 6–7, "With what dare I come before the Lord?" But this obviously highly personal conversation between God and man breaks forth apparently only within the framework of the public lawsuit which Israel's God has been carrying on with his people (v. 3) throughout its entire history ever since the exodus from Egypt (vv. 4–5) and which, at the climax of that history (with the advent of Jesus), has drawn all nations into what is now an all-inclusive lawsuit. Every one of our individual discussions with God is important by virtue of its being part of the altercation which God has with his people, as that occurs within the wider framework that includes also all humans (the same framework in which today's worldwide terrorism is also taking place). The introduction of our chapter leads us even one step beyond that panhuman context, for this lawsuit is conducted in the sight of the mountains and the foundations of the earth (vv. 1–2). Thereby appeal is made, in keeping with antiquity's world view of the cosmos, to the most conspicuous representatives of extrahuman creation.

That it is this extrahuman forum which witnesses the lawsuit that God is carrying on with his people about the question as to what is good for humans is a point which should be clearer to our generation than to any before it. For we are seeing creation groan under humankind's unwholesome exploitations, as humans devastate and poison the face of the ground. We are seeing the "foundations" smitten as the question plagues us as to where in the depths of our world atomic waste should be buried for the next thousand years. As we consider such problems, the context of our text's famous question about what is good for man ought to remain unforgotten, for the individual decisions we make have extensive consequences that ought to be considered. Every one of the personal decisions we make has implications for the totality of creation, be they the decisions of the terrorists and their opponents or the decisions of all who are directly or indirectly affected by them. The question that an individual human being brings before God about what is good for humanity is a question that is posed in a cosmic forum.

The Indictment of Our Forgetfulness

The lawsuit begins with a speech of self-defense made by God. He sees himself accused by his people and asks in turn, "What have I done to you? In what respect have I demanded too much of you?" Obviously the people are living in frightening times. The Assyrians had been brutal. The Babylonians had burned Jerusalem to the ground. The people cry out, "God has forgotten us." "God is not doing the good or the evil; he doesn't do anything at all." "There is no God!" Practical atheism spreads abroad. Even God's challenge here, ("Answer me!") receives no response but defiant silence. Overburdened, exhausted humans have more pressing matters to attend to than carrying on a conversation with a God who has become illusory. But, wonder of wonders, God continues to converse with these silent and uncommunicative humans. That has been the experience of Israel, of the church, and of every Christian many a time in the days when they have been living defiantly and disconsolately. Before taking up the acute trouble itself, God attacks his humans' forgetfulness, "Did I not lead you out of Egypt's slavery and send you outstanding messengers of my will; did I not transform the curses hurled at you into blessings, helping you over the touchiest situations (vv. 4–5)? Recall what has happened. Think about it!" We latter-day Christians must similarly be asked, Have you really forgotten Jesus Christ who has shown you the greatest love a person can have for his friends by giving his life for you (John 15:13)? Have you forgotten the one friend who really encompasses your entire life with his love? Have you crowded out of your lives the Bible's great message and the good experiences you were able to garner by means of it?

When last week we were looking for the sources of terrorism, we called to mind the areas of injustice, the escalation of covetous desires, humanity's enthronement of itself as the ultimate authority, and its despising of God's commandments and promises. The most recent example is the terrorist warning, "After the murder of our comrades in arms at Stammheim, we will attack the fascist-capitalistic administration of Helmut Schmidt where it will hurt the most. For every one of our murdered comrades we will blow up one Lufthansa aircraft in flight. There is no way our activity can be stopped. Therefore every person should know that whoever sets foot on a German aircraft after November 15 is flying with Death."

If we ask how we may live with terror these days, we must list as the basis for such living a clear recognition of God's benefits, especially his all-inclusive gracious deed of sending the true Friend into the arbitrariness of terror (John 15:13–15 "I have told you that you are my friends"). It is not we who have the primary responsibility for our lives; he considers himself responsible for us. "When in my darkest hour I can on him rely, I have from him the power all evil to defy."[89] Micah's indictment of forgetfulness challenges us to come to faith's clear awareness that God in Jesus not only suffered terrors to the ultimate extent of death but that he also will accompany us through all the terrors we experience. The basis then of all individual decisions we must make when we live with terror is a well-laid trust in the Friend of our life, the sole Lord over life and death, the only one who is genuinely superior to all rivals, the one who encompasses all. What is good for us? Not to forget the goodness of God during the crisis periods of our lives.

A Mistaken Reaction

An individual now reacts to the prophet's accusation of forgetfulness. Awakening to a new awareness of the gracious deeds God has done, he shamefacedly ventures to speak. Now that his previous rejection of divine goodness has been overcome, this previously silent person loosens his tongue and asks, "With what dare I come before the Lord?" This question is mankind's specific reaction to God's demonstration of friendship. Once individuals recognize anew that God has been creating a history of salvation within history (one that first moved toward the advent of Christ and is now flowing forth from him), then a tremendous willingness to respond with sacrifice surfaces. We observe in our questioner's suggestions an almost monstrous escalation of religious zeal: "a steer?" (entailing the irredeemable loss of the giver's capital); "a one-year-old calf?" (an extremely expensive gift); "one thousand rams?" (an offering only a king can afford); "streams of oil?" (entailing the loss of the strength, support, and beauty only oil can bestow); and, as a perverse sort of climax, "one's firstborn, only son?" (one's future is thereby entirely surrendered). None of these offers is accepted. For they all remain two-dimensional (limited to the relation between man and God, restricted to the realm of piety) whereas what God has done for his people has not limited itself to the realm of religion. And it is not to be bargained for by such sacrifices! The real foundation for living with terrorism is trust in God's friendship in Jesus, not the sort of life insurance that is supposed to guarantee that life can be lived in the exercise of privatized religion. So the individual's well-meant reaction is mistaken. What should be the appropriate reaction?

What Has Long Since Been Known Must Be Sought Anew!

The prophet's answer, before it gets down to specifics, begins with a statement of principle: "It has been told thee, O man, what is good and what the Lord seeks from you." Again ancient traditions from the past are called upon to illuminate the present and the future. What is thereby underscored is, You don't have to devise something fundamentally new. In God's past dealing with humankind all that is necessary for your journey has already been readied. It is only a matter of your discovering anew in what has long since been proclaimed that which has a real future. Whenever we busy ourselves with the Bible, the paradox recurs again and again: we are prompted to remember the future. Why? Because then we see that he who has been proclaimed as the savior who saved us in the past will be the future savior, the Lord who is coming to save us. If we are to be able to live day by day with terrorism, we will have to have exercised ourselves first of all in a new intensive searching of Scripture. Then our trust in our Friend will take the form of a continuing conversation. "It has been showed you, O man." We are unable to deal (either tonight or at next week's session) with specifics. They are best considered in daily conversation with trusted friends. Persons whom we have known for years need to be sought out anew on a day-to-day basis as friends and liberators whom we may consult and experience.

The beginning of v. 8 with its statement of principle contains, however, something else that is important. It reformulates the question of v. 6, "With what dare I come before the Lord?" as another question, "What is good (for human beings) and what does the Lord require of you?" It is therefore not a matter of what God needs (as an offering from us) but of what we humans need (help from him for us). You do not need to conciliate God (sacrificing your own child for your sin); you have been reconciled and restored by God's love. The question then is, What, as a result of his deed, is good for you, if you wish to remain under God's goodness, trusting and hearing what has been said? What does his goodness seek from you?

Putting Justice into Practice

This sober suggestion is the first of three specific directives pointing to what is good for man. Luther translated it freely as "keeping God's word," therewith taking up once again what is really the presupposition of new life, viz., trusting the well-attested goodness of God (cf. vv. 4–5). But what is really referred to in the original Hebrew is something more specific (and it is an initial consequence of keeping God's word): doing what is commanded, putting justice into practice. The basic commandments for social living are what is referred to here, as they were formulated ever anew in the Pentateuch, always, of course, presupposing and being mindful of the God who had liberated Israel and whose justice therefore intends to protect the freedom of one's fellowman. In v. 6 the voice had asked, "With what dare I appear in God's presence?" Now the answer is, "Not with anything that you bring as a sacrifice, but only with your fellowman." J. L. Mays comments, "It's you, not something, God wants."[90] To put it even more carefully, he seeks you in the company of your contemporary, your partner, your landlord, your tenant, or your competitor.

"Practice justice." Our word "justice" goes back ultimately to the same root as the word "to judge" and its Hebrew equivalent means basically "to decide, to settle." What is implied then is that justice ought to establish new community. It is a very practical matter. The word clearly implies opposition to arbitrariness, self-will, complacency, and lust for power. Today's terrorism begins, if anywhere, in people's covetous desires for unattainable social utopias. Robbery, deceit, inordinate desire, and destruction of human life become necessary measures toward such a goal. Hence terrorism, as a matter of principle, eliminates (liquidates) justice. That is the sort of terrorism with which we must live for the time being. What is called for in this situation, however, is the exercise of justice: putting justice into practice. We now notice what we did not notice in quieter times, but what ancient Israel knew very well: justice is one of God's gifts.

How do we live this out in practice? I refer now only to a most extreme instance of terror. Like many persons, I asked myself in the days when Schleyer was kidnapped, "What would you have done in such a situation?" My answer, after long deliberation, is, "I would ask God for the strength to declare myself ready to die." Only thus could I contribute toward putting justice into practice; for if my wish were to remain alive, many other persons would presumably become sacrifices to injustice. We all must ask ourselves as we live with terror, "What if it comes to you?" Is not this true, "If we die, we die to the Lord; whether we live or die; we are the Lord's"? Let us remember Paul's words, "I have a desire to depart and be with Christ." Dare we not in such a serious case pray for the ability to tell terrorists what Christ means for us and also for them? To live with terrorism means this: to ask for the authentication of our Christianity when in such a difficult situation we do what the directive says, "put justice into practice (as an aid for others)."

A second point: How do we treat our police? Their task is to contribute to the maintenance of public justice. It is possible for the police as well as for every one of us to make mistakes and to engage in unjust practices. But that does not change their indispensable task of protecting justice and our neighbor's freedom. Over the years a friend/foe relationship has developed between students and police in certain sectors and that is reflected in the name students give those fellow human beings ("bulls"). In the light of the difficult tasks currently confronting the police we should seriously work, each in his own way, toward the goal of having policemen learn to know numbers of students as new friends. We can do this by speaking of them and to them with respect, by easing their work, and by supporting them, even when they make mistakes (as we also make mistakes). To put justice into practice is what is needed. Without the police the masses will have a hard time of living with terror.

A third point on the topic of justice today (perhaps the most important point) must deal with preventing an antiterrorist backlash. This is currently perhaps the most pressing issue in this locality. For antiterrorism is prompted by the same fury and desire to destroy as terrorism! It has taken hold of extensive strata in our population and threatens to exercise a dangerous influence on legislation. We have the task therefore, each in his own surroundings and according to his democratic opportunities, of preventing fury and the lust for destruction form becoming the dictators of our society. Power and justice dare not be disengaged (Pascal, *Pensées* 298). Living with terrorism means, therefore, putting justice into practice.

Fostering Sensitivity to Community Solidarity

Luther translated this second ingredient of what is good as "practicing love." In Hebrew it is "loving *ḥesed*". But what is *ḥesed*? It is what the harlot Rahab practices with the spies: making common cause, joining in solidarity of community with someone else. Psalm 118 says of God, "His *ḥesed* endures forever," that is, the overlord's commitment to his relationship with his vassal will prove ultimate. That, then, is the second specific item that is good for man: loving community solidarity. It is a commentary on the first (putting justice into practice). The concept of "community" implies at least two parties. It can easily happen that the one party prefers isolation, separation, or even divorce and that the other has a difficult time living outside a sense of community. Marie von Ebner-Eschenbach says, "Most people need more love than they deserve." For that reason it is necessary to practice this second virtue and foster community spirit. Kolakowski said in

Frankfurt, on receiving the German Publishers' Peace Prize, "Most of us are too weak to free ourselves from hatred. Yet no one has the right to hate." The biblical reason is this: we all live by God's gratuities and acquittals, by his overwhelming compassion. He can be depended on to maintain his solidarity with us who are not dependable.

As we seek to live with terror, none of us should expect from terrorists what we do not practice ourselves. Here also let me refer to concrete examples. Every helpless person whom we overlook is tinder for terrorist activity. We Christians cannot therefore just join the general outcry, when there are already far too many ranters crying out all too loudly. Rather, for us the rule is Prov. 31:8 (RSV), "Open your mouth for the dumb, for the rights of all who are left desolate." Here we all need a community in which we may ask one another what is good for us as humans here and now. At the university in all departments we need many small groups who in a practical manner foster the sense of community, strengthening one another mutually and taking stands on the basis of principles of which those captivated by terror have lost sight.

From this viewpoint we should also take steps toward conversing with those who sympathize with the terrorists or who have settled down in their neighborhood. Many a good word has already been spoken publicly against false suspicion of the sympathizers. I want to add merely this: only in exceptional cases should individuals carry on such conversations; ordinarily a group ought to know itself responsible and prepare itself accordingly for such meetings. Sufficient motivation for making such preparations in a friendly spirit can come from knowledge that each of us could have landed on the road toward terrorism, since as youths we shared the same backgrounds. Sympathizing ought to be understood in a strictly biblical manner: Jesus sympathized not with sin, but with sinners. That is what we ought to clarify when we deal with sympathizers. We say a no to injustices as a path of senseless self-destruction, but a yes to the activists for whom God's goodness is waiting as much as it is for us. An objective discussion of issues will center mostly on what must be changed in society in general and on what cannot be changed for the time being as well as on how we are able in practice to distinguish between the two in order to proceed step-by-step toward improvement. The patient and persistent practice of fellowship with terrorist sympathizers is, in my estimation, a very great service which Christian groups could perform as we live with terror. We could also then discuss with them how we view the roots of terrorism.

A final point on the subject of "living with terror" under the rubric of "fostering community solidarity" has to do with the grief and disgust which will of necessity increase as a result of retaliatory action and the suppression of further acts of terror when we experience long waits, extended delays in air travel, or occasionally unexpected security checks on streets and at new checkpoints, even unexpected house searches. On such occasions Christians should use all their resources to help people overcome frustrating interruptions and delays with cheerfulness, trying to overcome grief and impatience with understanding and insight, thus, in each instance, "fostering a sense of community solidarity." Here we will all need a lot of exercise and training.

The Rule of Life That Is Decisive

Luther translated the last item that is good for humanity as "to be humble in the presence of your God." Investigations of the word *haṣĕnēă‘* indicate that "humility" is indeed an important part of the meaning of the word, but that basically it is not only a matter of an ethical stance or of being willing to take a subordinate position, but of attentiveness, thoughtfulness, wide-awakeness, awareness. This "attentiveness" refers in the original to "traveling," to steps which are to be taken. But these steps are not to be taken, if we translate carefully, "in God's presence." Rather, they are to be taken "with God"; so it is, therefore, precisely a matter of attentiveness in following or traveling with God (more precisely, "with your God"), i.e., with the God who is not against you but for you, who is knocking out openings and breaches at places where you see only solid walls.

Accordingly I translate the last thing that is good for human beings thus: "attentively traveling with your God who is constructing your path for you." Here reference is obviously made to the real driving power which makes possible in the first place the practice of justice and love for the community in the right spirit. Together with the New Testament we will be able to see here an Old Testament advance pointer toward the thoughtful following of Jesus which pays attention to the steps he took, the actions he did, the words he spoke, to his passion, his silence, his suffering and dying. "Alertly traveling with the Lord who is constructing his path for you."[91]

We spoke last week of terror's irrational roots; "unreasonable" is the only way to describe the decisive shift that took place when respectable social criticism was transformed into acts of violence. The sources of terror remain nonunderstandable, unless one reckons with the sinister power of evil with which we cannot cope as humans. It is precisely this deep irrationality which forces us to an entirely new awareness of the final significance of Jesus' mission. As Romans 8 puts it, powers and forces in the heights and in the depths threaten us and wish to separate us from God's love. But Christ was sent so that they might not succeed in creating that separation. If we wish to maintain a rational view of reality, we will therefore have to reckon with the fact that in terrorism forces are at work with which our reason and our political ingenuity cannot cope. I am convinced that, if reason is not to be blinded, it must permit itself to be illuminated by the biblical documents. To be more precise, every single one of us is advised, as we live with terror, to take steps anew for each day along with the Lord who is breaking a path for us. To put it in concrete terms, while we carry on our dialogue with Jesus, we are advised to open ourselves up to the word that directs us to him. The dangers to which each of us is exposed even then are not to be underestimated.

In this connection let me respond to two questions raised last week. One was, "Why are there so many women among the terrorists?" I am uncertain; but, I ask, could it be connected with the fact that women open themselves more quickly than men to the realm of the emotional, the passionate, the nonrational which has gained control? It is not by chance that "women have become hyenas." Certainly it is therefore no less important for women than men to put their reason in captivity to the obedience of Christ.

The second question came in response to Prof. Friedrich Müller's lecture on the topic of what activities are legal and asked, "Was not Christianity in the first centuries largely subversive?" To understand what is involved here, it is worth taking time to consider individual studies that will clarify the difference between terrorism and Christian freedom movements. I can only refer to two points. Christians never were able to go along with worshiping the emperor; every attempt to make human beings or human ideas divine should have been made impossible by the appearance of Christ (even by the appearance of the first commandment). On this point Christians have (how often?) engaged in passive resistance, even to the extent of being willing to suffer martyrdom. The other example is the abolition of slavery as a legal institution (a process which had begun in Old Testament times). Here Paul's Letter to Philemon needs to be appreciated, for he refrains from forcing Philemon to release Onesimus from slavery. Paul would rather get Philemon to manumit Onesimus of his own free will and view him as a brother in the same manner as he views Paul. Clearly the overcoming of slavery is a desirable goal, but the insights of faith and love should precede institutional change. Paul knows that the law by itself produces wrath. But Christianity unfortunately evaded the question of slavery much too long, even as it has evaded many other similar changes that were long overdue but were pressing for attention from those who follow Christ. Thus Christianity has provoked acts of violence by those who were oppressed and has itself become guilty of many an act of terrorism that arose out of genuine need.

So let me conclude by reading Mic. 6:8 once more: "It has been told you, O man, what is good and what the Lord is looking for in you; namely, putting justice into practice, loving a sense of community, and traveling attentively with the God who is constructing your path for you." There we learn what we have to do during the remainder of our lives.

THE PATH OUT OF ISOLATION
(VICTORY OVER TERROR):
MICAH 7

At the beginning of our series we searched for the roots of the current wave of terrorism. Following clues in Micah 2, we found them in the following developments: what began as legitimate social criticism has been torn up from its original roots; others' personal freedoms have been brutally violated; the basic commandments that protect our neighbor's rights, dignity, and life have been eliminated from consideration while arbitrariness has installed itself on the throne as supreme. The shift from legitimate social criticism to the establishment of a reign of terror we found to be something that cannot be rationally explained. It is, in fact, the result of a loss of sanity that threatens everyone and everything in our world. The pharisaism at its center is not well-founded. As we viewed it from a biblical perspective, we found such irrationality based on man's contempt for the Lord of life and death and for his commandments and promises. We found, therefore, none of the roots of terrorism stronger than the self-deception which arises when humans install themselves as the ultimate authority.

This self-deception must be seen very clearly for what it is if we wish to survive the current days of terror. How we may do this is what we asked during our consideration of Micah 6 last week. The adequate basis for living freely in the midst of terror we found in God's revelation of himself in Israel and in Jesus. Here the one and only Lord over life and death shows himself as mankind's liberator and friend. Thereby we are given the basis for trust. In such a relationship of trust three things were said to be good for man: (1) "putting justice into practice," i.e., resolutely fending off all injustice, focusing our sights on the helpless, being more resolute in our support of institutions of justice, and withstanding (effectively and by legal measures) irrational anti-terrorist backlash activity with its senseless rage and desire to destroy; (2) "fostering a sense of community solidarity," e.g., forming groups for meditation and action who will busy themselves with terrorist sympathizers, groups which will say no to injustice but yes to the activists; and (3) "attentively traveling with the God who is breaking a path for you," i.e., in New Testament terms, exercising ourselves in following Jesus, prudently listening (despite the all-pervasive pull toward irrationality) to the word of the Liberator at each stage of the terror and being watchful in prayer. This way of living with terror could by itself lead to a daily overcoming of anxiety, disgust, and hostility. But such short-term victories do not yet spell the conquest of terrorism itself. To achieve that ultimate victory we must today take up a consideration of Micah 7.

All Exits Are Blocked (7:1–6)

¹Woe is me! For I have become like a person who goes out into the field
    after the summer fruit has been gathered,
    after the vintage has been collected
and—there is no cluster to eat,
    none of the early figs I love.
²The godly have perished from the earth.
    There is none upright among men.
They all lie in wait to murder,
    each hunts down his kinsman.
They are expert at doing evil.
³The official makes demands.
    The judge desires a bribe
        The great man makes arbitrary decisions.
They twist matters as they wish.
⁴The best of men is like a brier;
    the most honest like a thorn hedge.
Yet the day is coming which your watchmen have seen
    when you will be punished.
        Then they will not know whether they are coming or going.
⁵Do not believe your neighbor
    or trust your closest friend.
Even from her who lies in your bosom
    guard the door of your mouth.
⁶For sons treat their fathers as fools;
    daughters oppose their mothers;
the daughters-in-law quarrel with their mothers-in-law,
    and a man's enemies are the members of his own household.

What a magnificent metaphor! An alienated person (in actual fact the prophet himself) cries out of total isolation, "Woe is me! for I have become like a person who goes out into the vineyard after the fruit has been collected!" (Some fruit should have been magnanimously left after the ingathering for gleaning by the poorest of the poor. That is what the speaker had been searching for.) But there is not one single grape, not even a small fig, nothing that could give him even a bit of refreshment. What is worse: the last godly person has died; all the upright have disappeared. ("Woe is me!") And those who remain are all expert at only one thing: producing wickedness.

But is not the metaphor here too strained? No, for when the Bible speaks of overcoming evil, it begins, not with friendly idealizations, but with the darkest realities. The isolated loner of our text finds all exits blocked. The godly person finds no caring and sharing community; those who are condemned, guilty or not, find no one willing to listen to them any more. To cite two contemporary examples: Ingrid Schubert is moved from her cell in Stammheim, where she had been able to collect almost 400 grams of explosives, into a maximum security facility in München-Stadelheim. What does she do? With her fingernails she scratches the very plaster from the wall behind her bed. Or, Wackernagel is arrested in Amsterdam. What does he do? He hangs himself! How many people are not killing themselves in perversions of justice which they themselves concoct or which they imagine have been concocted by their opponents. "They twist matters as they wish" (v. 3b). Even the most intimate tenderness is distrustfully scrutinized ("guard the door of your mouth even from her who lies in your bosom!"). The closest bonds of family are rent asunder without any hope of restoration, "Sons treat their fathers as fools; daughters oppose their mothers." The father of Christian Klar pleads during a television interview with his son, "Come back to us. We will accept you. Christian, think of your mother!" But Christian remains underground. For the present all exits from the life of terror seem to be blocked: piety fails; justice is shockingly exhausted; personal relationships are torn apart. Is it possible to live with terror? Yes, if, with the help of God, one lives in obedience to God! But, is it possible to overcome terror? That is the ultimate question, the one we must address this evening. With radical sobriety the person in our text sees a hopelessly chaotic situation, total isolation. Every exit has been blocked. And yet he has more to say.

The Advanced Position of the Prophet (7:7)

> But as for me, I am directing watchful eyes to the Lord,
> I am waiting tenaciously for the God of my salvation.
> My God will hearken to me.

We cannot expect to overcome terrorism through pious activity or new legislation or judges or penal measures, nor yet by way of bonds of blood or friendship. All have failed and will fail; in a mysterious way much has been irrevocably destroyed as terror has grown and mushroomed. That is what Helmut Schmidt expressed in a most sober and sensible manner when he closed his October 20 declaration on the state of the nation with the words, "God help us!" Those who remain sober in the face of terror's senselessness will permit the prophet to point them in this direction: toward God.

"But as for me, I am directing watchful eyes to the Lord; I am waiting tenaciously." In the prophet's expression, "But as for me" we hear defiant opposition to the current lack of exits. We ought to join such defiance of current realities and say, "But as for me!" If, as we saw, terror has arisen from impatient desires to establish utopian conditions, then overcoming terror can only be granted to patient waiting for God's own intervention. That means, first of all, that the current chaotic situation ought not be viewed as the ultimate end of the line! Also, as we travel the road of short-term reaction to terrorism we ought not fall victim to overreaction, but rather we should seek to foster justice, community solidarity, and trust! Thus we will be protected from undisciplined reactionary activity, since we will coolly and collectedly appreciate the provisional character of all penultimate activity.

"But as for me, I am waiting tenaciously for the God of my salvation." The God of the prophets, the Father of Jesus Christ, is not hidden in darkness; his ultimate will is not unknown. He has laid down his life for his friends. He remains the Lord who breaks out of all dead ends. To wait for him means, above all, to refuse to accept the self-deception that humans are the ultimate authority; this opinion is the deadly virus which terrorism has introduced into the bloodstream of its opponents, the antiterrorists. "God help us" is how Helmut Schmidt ended his declaration, displaying a sobriety that is free of the self-deception to which even a statesman can easily succumb.

"My God will hearken unto me" is what the prophet says in the midst of chaotic times, trusting the God who has sealed his love to us. He is engaged, among other things, also in overcoming terror. Faith has the task of establishing itself in our daily living at the advanced position occupied by the prophet. To be directed by the God who is coming (moving on his way to the future) does not mean that we become lazy but that we contemplate how we ought to communicate this to the present and the next generations. The task is not smaller than that of harnessing solar energy; nor is it less urgent. An advanced prophetic position demands utmost exertion. "But as for me, I am directing watchful eyes!"

Next we hear an entirely new voice.

Enduring Wrath (7:8–10)

> ⁸Rejoice not over me, O my rival,
> Though I have fallen, I am now getting on my feet.
> Though I sit in darkness,
>   yet the Lord is my light.
> ⁹The Lord's anger I must bear
>   (for against him I have sinned)
> until he takes up my case
>   and executes justice for me.
> He will lead me to the light;
>   I will see his salvation.
> ¹⁰My enemy will see;
>   shame will cover her
>   who was always saying to me,
>   "Where is the Lord, your God?"
> My eyes will gaze down upon her.
>   There she lies trampled
>   like mud in the street.

The person we now hear is different from the prophet of v. 7. A feminine figure speaks. It is the Daughter of Jerusalem, the personified city of God, the Old Testament predecessor of God's New Testament people as it now exists among the international world of nations. Included in this community is that individual who was looking in hope toward God's future. It is a community of people who are being scornfully asked, "Where is the Lord, your God?" (v. 10). We too are well acquainted with such scoffing. It is also a community of people who have themselves become guilty. "I have fallen. I have sinned against him." We have already had to recall our share of guilt in the rise of terrorism: (1) the weakness of our lives' testimony to the Lord of lords and Friend of all men; (2) our one-sided, all too belligerent attitude toward the government and its authorities whose provisional justice is still a much-needed emergency aid for the time when we ourselves still live under the protection of law (Rom. 7:10);[92] (3) our inattention to voices which remind an all too affluent church of its mission as the community that lives under the cross, the mission to which, for instance, Ernst Käsemann wished to awaken us when he explained what he intended when he officially left the church; and (4) the weakness of our solidarity with those on the fringes of society which is part of our guilt over against the Lord who was crucified outside the city gate and who fostered table fellowship with publicans and sinners.

"The Lord's anger I must bear until he takes up my case" (v. 9). He is traveling with us in our midst; his anger is incorporating us in the great process (in which he too is involved) of learning by suffering. He is arousing our attention toward him ever anew even though we have been imagining that we are really able to handle everything ourselves.

Thus we have come to travel anew on the road toward the goal on which he traveled as he himself and he alone overcame what we most certainly are unable to overcome on our own. As we travel on this path we need both to confess our sin and to hope in God. "Though I sit in darkness, yet the Lord is my light" (v. 8). But if we are traveling on the path toward overcoming all terror, then the Lord's wrath can be borne. These are hard times for the Christian community, times which call for every individual member's insight and commitment.

The Devastated World (vv. 11–13)

A promise is the response given to the congregation which both confesses its guilt and awaits the overcoming of terror from God.

¹¹The day is coming (O Daughter of Jerusalem) for rebuilding
your city walls;
  then your territory will be enlarged—
¹²that day when they will come to you
  from Assyria to Egypt
and from Egypt to the Euphrates,
  from sea to sea, from mountain to mountain.
¹³Then the earth will be devastated
  because of its inhabitants,
    on account of the fruit of their deeds.

In the Bible the ultimate conquest of the terrors of human history is viewed as part of a total transformation of all conditions. Although this expectation assumes very different forms, as a rule it has two sides as it does here. On the one hand, a total renewal and an immense expansion of the city of God is expected. New inhabitants from all parts of the world will stream in; "your territory will be enlarged" (cf. Zech. 2:5 "I will, says the Lord, myself be a fiery wall round about her"). The Liberator himself will be their protective boundary, extending his unrestricted protection far and wide. On the other hand, the old world will be devastated on account of the deeds of its inhabitants. Isa. 1:31 (RSV) says, "The strong [the man of violence] shall be a tow and his work a spark, and both of them shall burn together, with none to quench them."

The fact that our old earth, according to present understandings, not only had a beginning but will also have an end is ever more easily conceived of by our century, now that we know that humans have the ability to bring about such an end. But our expectation of a new heaven and a new earth is less the result of our drawing logical conclusions from scientific evidence than of trusting the Bible's testimony. Such a new universe will no more be established by men than the old one was created by them. It will, however, be part of God's history with humankind.

In this connection we take up the question of the place terror holds in the eschatological scheme of things. In the synoptic apocalypse Jesus speaks not only of wars, earthquakes, and famine but also of insurrections and terrors of all sorts, of vexations and evil expectations (Luke 21:9, 11, 26, 28). But, he says, they should not be viewed by the disciples as the end but rather as signs that "your redemption is drawing near." In all these variations of the biblical proclamation about the end there is general agreement that terror will by no means have the last word; at the most it will be reckoned as penultimate. If the certainty that terrorism will be overcome is thus expressed, this helps us to take the drama out of the current wave of terror and coolly and collectedly to recognize its provisional and truly temporary nature. Faith says about it what we learned to say about Adolf Hitler's "empire that will last a millenium," *"Nubicula est; transibit* (It is a little cloud; it will pass over)." Over against the devastated earth stands the unlimited city of God, yes, a new heaven and a new earth. And more!

The Miracle of an About-Face (7:14–17)

In response to the promise in vv. 11–13 we now hear a remarkable prayer by the community,

> [14]Shepherd thy people, O Lord, with thy staff
> the flock of thine inheritance,
> who dwell alone in the underbrush
> in the midst of a fruit garden.
> May they find pasture in Bashan and in Gilead
> as in the days of old.
> [15]As in the days of thy exodus from Egypt
> let us see wonderful deeds,
> [16]that the peoples may see and be ashamed
> despite all their superiority,
> that they may lay their hands on their mouth
> and their ears become deaf.
> [17]They shall lick the dust like a serpent,
> like those who crawl in the dust,
> they will crawl out of their prisons with trembling,
> to thee, the Lord, our God
>   and become obedient to thee.

Here Israel begs for something highly unlikely: that it may be led out of its misery ("alone in the underbrush") as it was once led out of Egypt and that the nations ("despite all their superiority") may come in adoration into the presence of the God whom they had not expected to worship. In an unexpected way the history of the nations is connected with the history of Israel in the message about Christ. "They will crawl forth from their prisons and become obedient to you" is how this experience is described in a typically Old Testament manner. The New Testament counterpart is heard in Matt. 8:11 where we hear, in connection with the centurion's faith, "Many shall come from the east and the west and sit down with Abraham, Isaac, and Jacob in the kingdom of God."

The specific, real, lasting victory over terrorism must be seen in this context: it comes about with the forthright and definitive about-face of the last terrorists and their sympathizers, who will recognize how they were deceiving themselves by traveling the path of violence and will discover the path to a genuinely new and free humanity by surrendering themselves to Jesus and following him. That will be the miracle of an about-face! Whoever has this final goal of genuine victory over terrorism before his eyes will be attentive to certain preliminary signs and will hope and pray for more to come. I am thinking of the report of the Italian Communist Luciana Castellina about her one and a half hour visit with Horst Mahler in Moabit at the beginning of this month. In her interview for her newspaper *Il Manifesto* she presented Mahler's attempt to disengage his erstwhile comrades from their mad enterprise by self-critical analysis. Mahler allegedly said, "We began with a trial that focused on the American massacre of My Lai in Vietnam; but now the Red Army Fraction has threatened another My Lai, the murder of uninvolved women and children—in order to free persons with whom the people do not identify themselves. This by itself should have demonstrated terrorism's bankruptcy and cut off the sympathy many have had for it."

What does this "bankruptcy" refer to? The interview explains it as terrorism's third phase. The first generation was dominated by a fresh and lively moralism; "we not longer felt ourselves to be Germans, but the Third World's fifth column. But we discovered that moral protest was weak. So in the second phase we read a lot of Lenin and a little of Marx. We didn't realize that rational people do not move out of an old house before they have built a new and better one to take its place. So in the third generation a completely autonomous inner dynamic appeared, strengthened by hatred for the cowardly 'left.'" It, he claims, led to "an even greater ideological bankruptcy. The Red Army Fraction no longer had any social commitment; it represented no one but itself. It produced a drift toward criminality, drugs, and suicide." Mahler calls this process "in a certain way already a sort of fascism." The twisting of suicide into "murder" (and of murder into "execution") is something he realizes needs to be brought under control. In the main, however, he is condemning the moral bankruptcy, the ideological emptiness.

Mahler's return to a rational evaluation is certainly not the final miracle of a genuine about-face; but it is qualitatively different from the call for suicide or the escalation of threats of murder. The Christian community dare not cease praying for the miracle of an about-face and for steps toward the ultimate goal where terror has been overcome in the terrorists and their sympathizers.

A constituent element in the victory over terror is God's new creation (for which we wait), the inner renewal of mankind. Our chapter and therewith the entire Book of Micah closes with the second portion of the prayer which had begun in vv. 14–17 as a prayer for the miracle of an about-face; now we hear expression of awestruck adoration in which the new creation and withdrawal from sin are united in one new reality.

At the End, Compassion Stands Waiting (7:18–20)

> [18]Where is there a God like you,
>   who takes away guilt,
> who passes over transgression
>   for the remnant of his inheritance,
> who does not hold his anger forever,
>   because he delights in steadfast love.
> [19]He will again have compassion upon us,
>   he will tread down our iniquities.
> Thou dost cast into the depths of the sea
>   all our sin.
> [20]Thou wilt show faithfulness to Jacob,
>   thy steadfast love to Abraham,
> as thou hast sworn to our forefathers
>   from the days of old.

Here we hear the proclamation of the victory over all iniquity (a victory now sealed in Christ). It is the source of all Christian living and it is offered also to every human being. From the vantage point of this valid offer of forgiveness we should view not only ourselves but also all terrorists. Justice and law are only provisional emergency aid in this world to protect both criminals and their victims from further crime. Justice and law are both absolutely necessary and also entirely fallible (yes, they can themselves become guilty, as they are applied to specific situations). To gain some idea of how difficult it is to establish even a fragile bit of justice in our injustice-ridden age, we need merely to consider the example of legal counsel Croissant, who is classified as "in danger of suicide." What legal benefit is worth more, we ask, a life that is supposed to be protected but which can be protected only by means of constant illumination and continual surveillance, or a bit of freedom and dignity, something which even prisoners can demand but which disappears under continual surveillance? Criminals as well as their judges, persons who serve to maintain order in the state as well as the Christian community, all need to have sin exposed unsparingly as the poison that threatens all life in community. For the time being we must all live under wrath: both we in the Christian community who must now live with the results of our neglect and mistaken decisions as well as those who have been committing deeds of terror. But at the end of the path we both are traveling, compassion stands waiting for all of us.

The Christian community must let itself be guided in its stance toward terrorists by the stance it takes toward the God who is coming and toward the ultimate offer of his mercy which is valid for everyone as long as there is time for repentance and which has already entirely transformed the time of temporary wrath. Those of us who have understood what is involved will be concerned that we "redeem the time." "Brethren, not so slowly, for while you dally, they are dying," is how Father Bodelschwingh admonished us. Bishop Kurt Scharf shall remain a shining example by his pastoral visit to Ulrike Meinhof in 1974. We will have to make more distinct differentiations than the twenty-eight Tübingen students of theology did in their confusing letter and the "bouquet" they prepared "for Günther Sonnenberg and for the wounded policeman." We will have to distinguish clearly not only between means and end (they had expressly renounced "murderous power in the struggle for a better form of common life"). We must also, in quite a different manner than was done in that letter, distinguish between justice and injustice and above all between the valid task of the state on the one hand (which should help justice to come to power in order to protect life and dignity for all men), and the task of the Christian community on the other hand (which should help people gain insight into guilt and into the valid offer of forgiveness).

Things have changed a great deal in the course of recent months. Now is the time for Bible study groups and worship and action groups to prepare people from the vantage point of this offer of forgiveness to seek out confused contemporaries, even terrorist sympathizers. Only when all sins are removed from evildoers and sunk into the depth of the sea (as were the hostile Egyptians who pursued Israel), will terrorism and all participants in it and in iniquity really be overcome and a new creation begun with the appearance of new human beings.

Notes

1. An address to the *Evangelische Stadtakademie* Düsseldorf, October 26, 1977.

2. The performance of this oratorio concluded a series of events of which this address was one. Elijah laments, "O Lord, I work *in vain* and spend my strength *for naught* and *in futility.*" Cf. 1 Kings 19 and Isa. 49:4.

3. For the translation, cf. p. 71.

4. See n. 2.

5. The received text speaks of "wooded heights," seemingly a copyist's misreading of a similar word meaning "beasts." Micah speaks of the "beasts of the forest" in 5:8. Cf. also Lam. 5:18.

6. See p. 13.

7. See p. 99.

8. Cf. J. L. Mays, *Micah*, Old Testament Library, (Philadelphia: Westminster Press, 1976) p. 15.

9. H. W. Wolff, *Joel and Amos*, Hermeneia, (Philadelphia: Fortress Press, 1977) pp. 108–11.

10. Cf. 2 Chron. 19:5–11 and G. Chr. Macholz, "Zur Geschichte der Justizorganization in Juda," ZAW 84(1972): 314–340 (317ff.).

11. H. J. Boecker, *Recht und Gesetz im Alten Testament und im Alten Orient* (Neukirchen-Vluyn: Neukirchener Verlag, 1976) pp. 39–40.

12. Cf. 2 Chron. 19:8 and Macholz, ZAW 84(1972), 325.

13. Only twice does the messenger formula, "Thus says the Lord," occur (2:3, 3:5), though it is only editorial in 3:5, as is pointed out by Th. Lescow, "Redaktionsgeschichtliche Analyse von Micha 1–5", ZAW 84(1972): 46–84, esp. p. 48.

14. 2:4aβ must be seen as secondary; cf. Jörg Jeremias, "Die Deutung der Gerichtsworte Michas in der Exilszeit," ZAW 83(1971): 330–54, esp. p. 334. 2:8aα is textually uncertain.

15. Thus W. Rudolph, *Micha–Nahum–Habbakuk–Zephanja* (KAT 13/3; Gütersloh: Mohn, 1975) p. 43 and J. L. Mays, *Micah*, p. 55.

16. Thus A. Alt, *Kleine Schriften zur Geschichte des Volkes Israel* 3 vols. (Munich: Beck, 1953) 2:243 and A. S. van der Woude, *Micha: De Prediking van het Oude Testament* (Nijkerk: Callenbach, 1976) pp. 45–46.

17. The town mentioned is *Muhrashti*; see J. A. Knudtzon, ed., *Die El-Amarna-Tafeln*, Vorderasiatische Bibliothek, 2 vols. (Leipzig: Hin-

richs, 1915; reprinted Aalen: Zeller, 1964) 2.1356 (Letter EA 335, lines 16–17).

18. Joachim Jeremias, "Moresheth-Gath, die Heimat des Propheten Micha" *PJB* 29 (1933): 42–53.

19. W. Rudolph, *Micha*, p. 23.

20. Ibid., p. 22.

21. W. Rudolph (ibid., p. 24) is correct in this, as opposed to A. S. Kapelrud, "Eschatology in the Book of Micah," *VT* 11(1961): 392–405, and W. Beyerlin, *Die Kulttraditionen in der Verkündigung des Propheten Micha*, FRLANT 72, (Göttingen: Vandenhoeck & Ruprecht, 1959).

22. This is the thesis of Chr. Hardmeier. *Kritik der Formgeschichte auf texttheoretischer Basis am Beispiel der prophetischen Weheworte* (Diss., Heidelberg, 1975) 382–91. Also id., *Texttheorie und biblische Exegese: Zur rhetorischen Funktion der Travermetaphorik in der Prophetie*, BEvTh 79(1978): 376ff.

23. E. Gerstenberger, "The Woe-Oracles of the Prophets," *JBL* 81(1962): 249–63; W. Schottroff, *Der altisraelitische Fluchspruch*, WMANT 30 (Neukirchen-Vluyn: Neukirchener Verlag, 1969) pp. 110–112, pp. 117–20; H. W. Wolff, *Joel and Amos*, pp. 242–45.

24. K. Koch et al., *Amos—untersucht mit den Methoden einer strukturalen Formgeschichte*, AOAT 30 (Neukirchen-Vluyn: Kevelaer, 1976) p. 286.

25. Cf. Amos 5:16f. and H. W. Wolff, *Joel and Amos*. p. 249.

26. For the standard work on this form, see the dissertation of Chr. Hardmeier referred to in n. 22.

27. Cf. Amos 5:17 "those who are knowledgeable in the mourning lament" as well as "mourning" and "crying woe" and Mic. 1:8b; cf. also Jer. 9:16–19.

28. In the light of Amos 5:16f. the claim made by A. S. van der Woude *Micha* p. 21 that Micah 1:2–16 was pronounced in the sanctuary at Lachish is not cogent. Significant is the fact that *spd* and *mspd* never occur in the psalter; on the exception, Ps. 30:12, see Hardmeier, "Kritik der Formgeschichte," p. 203 n. 107.

29. On the expansion of the text see the article by J. Jeremias referred to in n. 14 above. Note also the similar wording in Jer. 9:18.

30. Cf. H. W. Wolff, *Amos the Prophet* (Philadelphia: Fortress Press, 1973) pp. 6–16, 67–76; J. W. Whedbee, *Isaiah and Wisdom* (New York: Abingdon Press, 1971), p. 104; cf. Isa. 5:20.

31. H. H. Schmid, "Amos. Zur Frage Nach der 'geistigen Heimat' des Propheten," *Wort und Dienst* 10 (1969): 85–103; reprinted in *Altorientalische Welt in der alttestamentlichen Theologie* (Zürich: Theologischer Verlag (1974), pp. 121–44. The elders who give advice (Ezek. 7:26) are called wise men in Jer. 18:18.

32. The decisive stimulation for my study of the prophetic appropriation of sapiential forms is something for which I am indebted to

Samuel Terrien, "Amos and Wisdom" in *Israel's Prophetic Heritage, Essays in Honor of J. Muilenburg* (New York: Harper & Row, 1962), pp. 108–15. The impulses toward research generated by this provocative essay cannot be reversed.

33. See Mic. 2:2; 3:3, 10; see also Amos 2:6–7; 4:1; 8:4–6; Isa. 3:15; 10:2; Prov. 14:31; 22:16, 22; 28:3.

34. See Mic. 3:11; see also Amos 5:7, 12; Isa. 1:23; 5:23; Prov. 17:15; 18:5; 24:23.

35. See Mic. 2:11; see also Amos 4:1; 6:4–6; Isa. 5:11–12, 22; Prov. 20:1; 21:17; 23:20–21, 29–35; 31:4–7.

36. [Translator's note. This essay ends with a reference to Prof. Wolff's article in the *Supplements to Vetus Testament*, Congress Volume Göttingen 1977 (1978). It was printed under the title "Micah the Moreshite—The Prophet and His Background" in *Israelite Wisdom: Theological and Literary Essays in Honor of Samuel Terrien*, edited by J. G. Gammie et al. (Missoula: Scholars Press, 1978), pp. 77–84. The English translation there is by Ch. E. Weber and includes a brief dedicatory note by Prof. Wolff to Samuel Terrien (cf. n. 32) and more precise bibliographical references than the original German notes. I have incorporated much of that very helpful additional bibliographical material in the notes in this (independent) translation of the essay.]

37. Bible-study at the Synod of the Federation of Churches in Wuppertal-Barmen on November 12, 1977.

38. [Translator's note. The German text has "Gemarke and Wuppertal" and the note explains, "As examples, member congregations of the Kriessynode Wuppertal-Barmen are mentioned. It was before representatives of these churches that this exposition was presented. Later at repetitions of the address before the Bishop of Speyer's Continuing Education Seminar For Priests in Homburg and in Speyer on the 12th and 13th of April, 1978 the names used in the address were 'Homburg and Speyer.'" The translation has used local American names in an effort to approximate the effect.]

39. Report to the Synod by the Superintendent H. K. Stephan Preparatory to the Synod of the Barmen Federation of Churches on November 11 and 12, 1977.

40. Here and in what follows Micah's wordplays are exemplified by means of names of congregations in the vicinity of Barmen. [Translator's note: The names of localities in the translator's vicinity give only an approximation of the extremely vernacular and witty examples of Prof. Wolff, e.g., *"Schellenbeck muss zerschellen."* As such they cannot be readily translated.]

41. When the address was repeated, as mentioned in n. 38, places names near Homburg and Speyer were used, e.g., "Landau wird zum Brandau." Again, the English translation brings similar approximations, using place names in the translator's vicinity.

42. See n. 38.

43. Bible study on the occasion of the hundredth anniversary of the Westphalian Diaconate Nazareth Brotherhood at Bethel near Bielefeld. May 14, 1977.

44. [Translator's note. The German original refers to common German language translations (those of Luther and of the "Zürich Bible"). For English readers it seemed wise to refer to comparable translations: The New English Bible (NEB), The Revised Standard Version (RSV), and The Good News Bible (TEV, Today's English Version).]

45. [Translator's note. Since Prof. Wolff is referring to traditional evening hymns (in this case to stanza 3 of Hymn 356 in the standard German Lutheran *Kirchengesangbuch*) it seemed wise to substitute comparable stanzas from English hymnody, in this case stanzas 1 and 4 from hymn 278, and a bit later in this paragraph stanza 3 from hymn 273 and stanza 2 from hymn 277 from the *Lutheran Book of Worship* (Minneapolis and Philadelphia: Augsburg Publishing House and Board of Publication of the Lutheran Church in America, 1978).]

46. Sermon on the Wednesday after the first Sunday in Advent, December 1, 1976 at the 7 A.M. all-student communion service in The Church of the Holy Spirit, Heidelberg.

47. [Translator's note. Since the stanza from Gottfried Arnold's "O Durchbrecher aller Bande" is not available in English language hymnody, a comparable stanza was taken from "O Savior, Rend the Heavens Wide" © 1969 Concordia Publishing House, hymn 38, stanza 3 from *Lutheran Book of Worship*. Used by permission.]

48. Guest lecture at the Kirchliche Hochschule, Wuppertal on November 11, 1976. First printed in *Theologische Beiträge 8* (1977): 97–108.

49. See above pp. 17–28.

50. An alternate translation is "You hate the person who is good and love the person who is evil." Cf. *Q^erē* (What is to be read) *rā<* instead of *K^ethībh* (what is written) rā<h; afterward it is persons who are the victims of the hatred.

51. Cf. 2:9 "the women of my people you drive from their cherished homes."

52. Thus *KB* and W. Rudolph KAT; a contrary opinion by A. S. van der Woude, *Micha* (1976).

53. On the expression "to sanctify war" for mobilization cf. Jer. 6:4; Joel 3:9.

54. K. Barth, 1916 in Safenwil: *Predigt im Gespräch 3* (1967).

55. See below p. 75.

56. Perhaps it was thought of as a quotation, as in Hos. 8:12. But it had been burned into Micah's heart and lips with the script of fire.

57. Cf. G. von Rad, *Old Testament Theology* (New York: Harper and Row, 1965) 2:178 where he speaks of "exaltation of spirit" and of the "charisma which welled up gloriously within him" as "he became

conscious of his difference from other people." The original German edition (München: Chr. Kaiser, 1960) speaks also of Micah's "authority-challenging boasting."

58. For this reading of the text cf. 5:7; Lam. 5:18 and above p. 12, n. 5 and below p. 83.

59. Guest lecture at the Kirchliche Hochschule, Bethel on May 11, 1977.

60. B. Renaud speaks of a masterpiece of composition which he was able to trace, though we cannot share his perspectiveless view of it. *Structure et attaches littéraires de Michée IV–V* (Cahiers de la Revue Biblique, 1964), pp. 81–82.

61. J. L. Mays has convincingly explained the function of these brackets in *Micah*, 1976, pp. 4ff.

62. Israel is mentioned as an instrument of Yahweh's judgment upon the nations again only at Obad. 18; Zech. 9:13ff. and Ezek. 25:14.

63. See above pp. 40–41.

64. Like the preceding verses, these oracles have prompted A. S. van der Woude (*Micha*, 1976, pp. 176ff.) to assume a debate between a true and false prophet.

65. Bible study on the occasion of the hundredth anniversary of the Westphalian Diaconate Nazareth Brotherhood at Bethel near Bielefeld, on May 15, 1977.

66. Cf. above pp. 45–60.

67. Cf. above pp. 48–50.

68. Bible Study on the occasion of the celebration of hundredth anniversary of the Westphalian Diaconate Nazareth Brotherhood at Bethel near Bielefeld on May 16, 1977.

69. This took place in a platform discussion by Dieter Dreisback and Dietrich von Oppen on "The Practice of Social and Institutional Care From the Perspective of God's Kingdom." Cf. "Hundert Jahre Nazareth" in the series *Bethel* 17 (1977): 59–65.

70. Cf. above p. 103.

71. Cf. on 6:4–5 above, pp. 102–3.

72. Address at the fall conference of the German Christian Student Movement (Studentenmission in Deutschland, SMD) on October 8, 1977 in Marburg. Printed in *Porta* 24 (1978): 16–35.

73. See above pp. 47–48.

74. A student group at Göttingen had told about a thousand fellow students gathered because of the controversial *Hochschul-Rahmengesetz* and the actions (strikes) planned by the Association of German Students that they had asked the appropriate educational minister of Lower Saxony to come for a discussion. That minister had, in response, invited the students to a discussion of the conflict at the University of Göttingen.

75. The evening before Pastor U. Parzany had, in a Bible study on Luke 19:1–10 cited the statement of Gustav Heinemann, "He who keeps silent aids what is going on."

76. See above pp. 17–25.

77. U. Parzany in his Bible study (cf. n. 75) had pointed to ecumenical tasks and warned against driving with parking lights, urging that the bright lights be turned on.

78. See above pp. 74–75.

79. Address at the Reformation Commemoration of the Council of Evangelical Churches in the city auditorium of Obenhausen on November 1, 1977.

80. Cf. note 79.

81. [Translator's note. Here Prof. Wolff quotes, without reference to its source, part of a popular ballad not available in English. No attempt has been made to translate it, but its point has been incorporated in the text.]

82. [Translator's note. Here Prof. Wolff quotes a popular song sung to guitar accompaniment by its writer, Manfred Siebald at the Marburg meeting of the German Christian Student Association on October 8, 1977. The song has been published by the Hänssler-Verlag, Neuhausen-Stuttgart. As is our custom in the case of songs unavailable in English, we have substituted here comparable sections, in this instance from M. Franzmann's "O God, O Lord of Heaven and Earth," copyright Lutheran Council in the USA, hymn 396 in *The Lutheran Book of Worship*.]

83. Stanza 6 of "If Thou But Suffer God to Guide Thee," hymn 518 in *The Lutheran Hymnal* (St. Louis: Concordia Publishing House, 1941). The translation is by Catherine Winkworth.

84. [Translator's note. Prof. Wolff quotes a stanza of a Zinzendorf hymn, unavailable in English. We have substituted comparable stanzas from J. Bode's "O Jesus, I Have Promised," hymn 503, stanzas 3 and 4 in *The Lutheran Book of Worship*.]

85. Sermon preached at the divine service of Heidelberg University at St. Peter's Church, Septuagesima (February 6, 1977).

86. The three Bible studies were held at the Carl Rupert University in Heidelberg on the evenings of November 3, 10, and 17, 1977. At the end of the summer semester of 1977 the student members of the Chapter of the Heidelberg University Congregation had requested that I give three evening presentations in the lecture room at the University during the next semester. I could accede to their request only on condition that I use the chapters from Micah which I had expounded at Bethel in May (pp. 45–60; pp. 99–114; pp. 115–31). The events of autumn 1977 led to the wish that the burning question of terrorism be related to the Bible. Because of current interest, detailed discussion

and group dialogue were added to the individual presentations; I took up some of the main questions that arose in the presentation.

87. Cf. pp. 135–58.

88. Cf. n. 86.

89. [Translator's note: Wolff cites stanza four from Phillip Spitta's *Ich steh in meines Herren Hand.* Since this is unavailable in English language hymnody, it seemed wise to substitute a comparable quotation from English hymnody, stanza 3 of "From God Can Nothing Move Me," hymn 468 in *Lutheran Book of Worship.*]

90. *Micah*, 1976.

91. E. Jüngel, *Die Wahrheit zum Recht verhelfen* (1977), p. 46.

92. E. Jüngel, op cit.

Index

Alt, A., 211 n. 16
Arnold, G., 214 n. 47
Atomic waste, 101, 188
Authority, 25, 151f.

Barmen Theological Declaration, 153, 183f.
Barth, K., 214 n. 54
Beyerlin, W., 212 n. 21
Boecker, H. J., 213 n. 11
Bribery, bribes, 77, 156, 161
Brotherhood, brotherly love, 105, 110, 121

Calvin, John, 73, 131
Carter, Jimmy, 16, 99f., 106, 113
Children, attitudes toward, 9, 48ff., 106f.
Church, 43, 82ff., 85ff., 121f., 159–70, 168ff., 203f.
Church leadership (Council of the Evangelical Churches in Germany), 153, 184f.
Communist Federation of West Germany, 147f.
Community, the Christian, 30f., 38, 51, 95, 105, 120ff., 175, 209f.
Compassion, 130, 142, 209
Covet, 8f., 52, 138, 181
Cynicism, 148, 155

Democracy, 184
Dönhoff, Marion, 154
Dutschke, R., 180f.

Ecumenical movement (World Council of Churches), 141, 143, 216 n. 77
Education for dissent, 112, 152
Elders (office of), 4, 17ff., 22ff., 143, 151, 162
Elijah, 5, 9ff., 64
Engagement (social-political), 75, 135, 152, 179
Ensslin, G., 155, 180
Exile, 59ff., 89, 164

Faith, 119, 145, 152, 190
Family, 179, 180
Following Jesus, 163, 173, 180, 196
Forgiveness, 128ff., 157, 170, 172ff., 210
Freedom, 54, 129, 155, 193, 199
Future, 54ff., 85ff., 88, 108, 123ff., 159ff., 182, 191, 205f.

Gammie, J. G., 213 n. 36
Gerstenberger, E., 212 n. 23
God, 72f., 78, 88, 100ff., 118, 128ff., 174f., 184, 186, 199, 202f.
Goodness (Güte), 190
Grace, 88
Guilt (sin), 12, 77, 123, 129f., 170, 186, 204, 209

Hardmeier, Chr., 212 nn. 22, 26, and 28
Heinemann, G., 180, 216 n. 75
Higher education politics, 143ff., 147ff., 152, 153ff., 215 n. 74
Hope, 87, 118, 123, 171f., 204ff.

Humility, 88, 112ff., 196
Hypocrisy, 11, 83

Intercession, 114, 185
International affairs, nations, 33,
    81ff., 85ff., 88ff., 91ff., 97f.,
    125ff., 127, 188
Inwardness (private activities),
    135
Isaiah, 22ff., 118
Isolation, 116f., 118, 126, 200f.

James, 142
Jeremiah, 13, 74, 79, 83, 150,
    162
Jeremias, Joachim, 212 n. 18
Jeremias, Jorg, 211 n. 14, 212
    n. 29
Jerusalem, 3f., 18f., 65f., 78f.,
    84ff., 91ff., 120ff., 124f., 162
Jesus (Jesus Christ, Christ), 8,
    31f., 43, 49f., 57, 61, 75f.,
    78f., 87, 92, 95, 98, 104, 108,
    113, 117, 131, 135f., 141,
    147f., 151f., 155, 158, 159,
    162, 165, 170, 174ff., 179ff.,
    184, 186ff., 190, 195ff., 200,
    204, 206f.
Judging, 110, 156, 193
Judgment, word of, 13, 84, 131,
    139, 161ff.
Jüngel, E., 217 nn. 91 and 92
Justice, sense of, 5, 10f., 20,
    67ff., 75f., 106ff., 109f., 131,
    143, 146ff., 151f., 157f., 184f.,
    192ff., 209

Kapelrud, A. S., 212 n. 21
Käsemann, E., 204
Klar, Chr., 201
Knudtzon, J. A., 211 n. 17
Koch, K., 212 n. 24
Kolakowski, 194
Küng, H., 136

Late capitalism, post-capitalistic,
    German capitalism, 146, 183
Leading astray, 70ff.
Lescow, Th., 211 n. 13
Lying, 108
Love, 109ff.

Macholz, G. Chr., 211 nn. 10
    and 12
Mahler, H., 207
Mays, J. L., 192, 211 nn. 8 and
    15, 215 n. 61, 217 n. 90
Meditation, 135
Meinhof, U., 180, 209
Mendelssohn, F., 5, 9
Mercy, 110
Message, 56, 60, 68, 189
Messenger formula, 36
Messiah, 93f., 173
Micah, 16
    biographical, 3f., 151
    Book of, 15f., 32ff., 36, 45, 65
    language, 14f., 40f., 147f.
    self-understanding, 4, 74ff.,
        150f.
Miracle (marvel), 102f., 126f.,
    129
Moresheth, 4, 21, 48
Müller, F., 198

National church (*Volkskirche*),
    79, 84, 122, 161ff., 164ff.
Nonresidents, 110

Obedience, 112, 127, 147
Oppression, 9f., 13, 102, 156,
    180f.

Parzany, U., 216 nn. 75 and 77
Pascal, B., 149, 151, 184
Paul, 75, 142, 151, 193, 198
Peace, 15, 69f., 87ff., 94, 96–98,
    149, 153, 168ff., 171ff.
Penal action, 183, 202

Planning, 11f., 52, 55, 138, 181f., 185
Ponto, J., 147, 153
Power (*Macht*), 75, 137, 152, 182ff., 184f.
Prayer, praying, 53, 119, 125ff., 148, 151ff., 158, 181, 200, 206ff., 208
Preaching, language of, 41f., 147f.
Preaching, topics unwelcome in, 49f., 140f., 179
Proclamation, 76ff.
Promise, 87ff., 124, 153
Property, ownership problems of, 50
Prophets (true and false), 63ff., 71ff., 75f., 78f., 135f., 149f.
Puns (wordplays), 40f., 92

Rad, G. von, 214 n. 57
Red Army Fraction, 179, 208
Remnant, 89, 94, 163
Renaud, B., 215 n. 60
Resignation, 116f., 125, 146, 184
Righteousness (justice), 153
Rudolph, W., 211 n. 15, 212 nn. 19–21, 214 n. 52

Salvation, 71f., 123
Samaria, 3, 36f.
Sacrifice, 103f., 111
Scharf, K., 209
Schleyer, H. M., 147, 193
Schmid, H. H., 212 n. 31
Schmidt, H., 37, 39, 190, 202f.
Schottroff, W., 212 n. 23
Self-control, 52
Self-defense, speech of, 101

Sensitivity to community solidarity, 109ff., 130, 194ff.
Sin, 108, 121, 128ff.
Social criticism, 13, 77, 137ff., 146ff., 179ff.
Social service (Christian), *Diakonie*, 50f., 55ff., 131
Socialism, 146, 183
Sonnenberg, G., 209
State (the government), 183f.
Strength/Power (*Kraft*), 75
Strike, 144f.
Student Movement, Christian (in Germany), 143ff., 145, 147, 152, 153, 158
Sympathizers (with terrorists), 195, 208

Terrien, S., 212 n. 32, 213 n. 36
Terrorism/Terror, 3, 13f., 37, 139, 144, 146ff., 153, 169, 180ff., 183ff., 186, 187ff., 193ff., 196ff., 201ff., 207ff.
Theft, 107
Trust (confidence), 140

Violence, 9f., 15f., 138ff., 147, 153, 174, 178, 181ff.

War, 88, 149, 172ff.
Whedbee, J. W., 212 n. 30
Woe, cry of, 23f., 47, 137, 181
World peace, 37, 171ff.
Woude, A. S. van der, 211 n. 16, 212 n. 28, 214 n. 52, 215 n. 64
Wrath of God, 98, 122, 130

Zion, community of, 15, 79, 81ff., 85ff., 88ff., 93ff., 121